Dai.   MW01146097

"Jason McLeod guides us through the harrowing continuation of the events that terrorized a Connecticut family in his breakout, best seller *Dark Siege: A Connecticut Family's Nightmare*. This sequel is a terrifying journey – a real account of what can happen when innocent teenagers dabble in the obscure, unseen world of the negative occult. Unlike the first book which had a gradual build that led to an epic battle between good and evil, this story hits you on the head with a two-by-four from the beginning and never lets up. One unique attribute of McLeod's *Dark Siege* books are the final sections which contain the chapter analysis where the author demonstrates that these things *really do happen*. I recommend the book wholeheartedly as it is packed full of real-world experience from one of the most informed and talented of all paranormal investigators."

Serafin Mendez, Ph.D., Professor of Communication,
Central Connecticut State University

"Cinematic story telling from start to finish. The descriptions in this book were outstanding. The prose is dynamic. This book is a roller coaster ride through the dark chasms of hell as the poor McLaughlin family and their friends and pets endure real demoniacal retribution that would send any of the Stars in the scripted tabloid television shows like *Ghost Adventures* running for their lives. After first reading McLeod's astounding debut novel *Dark Siege: A Connecticut Family's Nightmare*, I wondered if his second book could compare. This book was far above and beyond my expectations."

William DeHaviland, Ph.D. in parapsychology

"This book was a mind-bender. The savage, brutal, physical and sexual assaults brought me to my knees with rosary in hand. If you want to understand what *really* goes on in terrible cases like this one, read Jason McLeod's books."

Christina Morrison – Ordained Minister

"This book should serve as a dire warning to those who identify themselves as paranormal investigators, because I would wager that 99% of those people would soil themselves if they encountered what McLeod and the McLaughlin family endured as revealed in this book and in the preceding volume. The *Dark Siege* Series is not for the faint of heart. McLeod unlocks the door to the dark secrets of this world and swings it wide open."

Chris Applegate

"AGAIN, McLeod does not fail to deliver the perfect, bone-chilling terror. His first book scared me to death and I could barely gather the courage to pick it back up and finish it. This book is even more frightening than the first. It's the scariest book I have ever read – because it's true. McLeod's writing makes you feel as if you are present with the people involved and dealing with the horrors as if you're shivering right alongside them. Definitely a must-own, must-read, must pass-along book."

Cat Young – Radio Host for Live Paranormal

"Like a bat out of nowhere sweeps in Jason McLeod with a sequel that is even better and bolder than his original. McLeod is rapidly setting the new standard in supernatural horror novels and is making waves throughout the entire paranormal community. First, of course, through his dynamic writing, but also with the fascinating information he conveys to audiences at Paranormal Conventions around the world. In case they can't catch him in person, much of that information is contained within the Analysis Section of each of his books allowing us a glimpse into his astounding life experiences and setting himself apart from any other writer in the genre."

Chase Snedeker, Ph.D.

"*Dark Siege* is a truly magnificent book. It easily brings the reader into a world where they witness a family struggling with demonic forces. Because the writing and the characters in this book were relatable in so many ways, the reader could easily find themselves attached to this family and rooting for their recovery. And that is where *Dark Siege: The Nightmare Returns* comes in, placing the reader directly in the world of the characters which is filled with havoc, panic, and possession. This book paints a real depiction of what individuals endure when they are faced with the most brutal force that man can face: demonic possession. *Dark Siege: The Nightmare Returns* is not for the faint of heart. It is a very open and honest presentation of demonic attacks, some of them sexual and the author clearly demonstrates that he understands the true nature of those attacks. The reader should be prepared to enter into a world where the characters' lives are turned upside down and where each one holds on to the possibility that help is just around the corner."

Bishop James Long

For Julie

DARK SIEGE:

The Nightmare Returns

by

Jason McLeod

ISBN 978-0-9884451-7-8 (ePub)
ISBN 978-0-9884451-3-0 (Kindle)
ISBN 978-0-9884451-6-1 (paperback)

Edited by
Tom Kimball, Ph.D.
www.knowbiz.biz

Cover design by Todd Hebertson

Print layout and eBook editions by eBooks By Barb
for booknook.biz

Dedication

I dedicate this book to demonologists and exorcists worldwide who risk their health, their safety, and their very lives to help complete strangers who are desperate for assistance dealing with realms far beyond their understanding, especially the greatest demonologist and the greatest psychic whom I have had the pleasure of calling my friends, my mentors, and in my later years, my colleagues – the late Ed Warren and his gifted wife, Lorraine Warren. Lorraine continues her profound work to this day.

I dedicate this book also to my friends and colleagues who have stood boldly by my side against the darkness. I include the men and women of the cloth who defy the denizens of these realms, specifically, the hierarchy of inhuman, diabolical spirits who seek the ruination of mankind.

What you are about to read is the continuation of the re-creation of the most terrifying case of inhuman, diabolical infestation, oppression, and possession that I have experienced to date, which was described in my debut novel, *Dark Siege: A Connecticut Family's Nightmare.*

To protect their privacy, the identities of everyone involved and certain locations have been altered, but their experiences, both individually and collectively, are completely accurate and authentic.

—the author, Jason McLeod

A storm was coming unlike anything they had experienced before. Desolation and darkness had once again breached the barrier between the world of the living and the realm of the dead.

For they had challenged the darkness, and in doing so, they set the stage where forces beyond their comprehension would wage a terrible war against them in every way conceivable.

Until there was
nothing left
of them
at all.

Contents

ANALYSIS

Prologue

STEAM BEGAN TO RISE FROM THE TINY HOLE in the lid of the stainless steel teakettle that was resting on the glowing, red-hot stove burner. Cloudy white puffs wafted into the exposed wooden beams that supported the white stucco ceiling. The soft, steady sounds of the boiling water churning inside gradually became louder and developed into a faint, high-pitched whistle that grew in intensity until it echoed continually throughout the kitchen.

An orange long-haired Angora cat leaped up onto the counter, licked his lips, and walked gingerly, step by careful step along the outside edge of the sink, and approached the teakettle cautiously. He paused, narrowed his eyes, leaned forward toward the steam vapor, reached out with his pink nose, sniffing several times in rapid succession. As he did so, tiny water droplets began to adhere to his nose and sat on his fine white whiskers, in patterns, spaced on the long lines like notes on a musical scale. He licked the water droplets off his nose and then over and across his whiskers in one continuous swipe.

His ears suddenly perked up and rotated backward. The fine hairs inside, far more sensitive than any human's, could sense that someone was approaching. The cat turned his head in time to regard his human companion, Yvonne Saxon, as she strode into the kitchen. She wore a black shawl draped over her shoulders, with a white blouse unbuttoned low and a long black dress that grazed the floor with each step. The heels of her black boots resounded against the floor as she approached. Yvonne smirked at her cat. Then she patted him on the top of the head, and rubbed his ears between her thumb and forefingers. The cat closed his eyes and immediately began purring. He arched his back and slid his head in against her hand and then along the length of her arm.

The moonlight shone through the window by the sink and splashed softly onto her shoulder, her arm, and her hand. With her free hand, Yvonne reached over and pulled off a brown ceramic coffee mug hanging from a worn wooden peg underneath the cabinet. The faint light caused the polished blue Celestite gemstone fastened in her silver ring to glisten. The cat called out to her. She looked down at him once more and asked, "What is it, Pumpkin?" The cat answered her with a single "meow," and studied her with his deeply penetrating golden eyes. Yvonne smiled as she walked up to the stove, wrapped her delicate fingers around the wooden handle, picked up the kettle off the burner, and turned the stove dial to the 'Off' position. She filled her cup, and she set the kettle on the opposite edge of the stove.

After a few moments, she unwrapped a bag of peach tea and dipped it into and out of the water a dozen times over. Pumpkin approached the kettle and the last short sputtering puffs of steam belching from inside. Then he leaned over and tried to sniff the steam rising from her mug. Yvonne gazed down into the mug and became captivated as she stared at both their reflections in the water. She smiled. Her curly brown hair draped down over her shoulders. She took special notice of her favorite amethyst crystal hanging over her heart. The silver necklace on which it hung glittered in the moonlight peeking in the window. She studied the orange hues cast from both the peach tea leaves that were spreading out into the water, and from the reflection of her cat's orange coat. As the water began to spiral, the images wound their way into obscurity and faded away altogether.

Yvonne sighed. She held the cup under her nose and

enjoyed the feeling of the hot steam rising up as it gently caressed her face, just as her feline companion seemingly loved to do.

"The steam does feel good, doesn't it, Pumpkin?"

She sighed again. Winters were far too long in New England for her liking. A cup of hot tea had a remarkable way of dispelling the cold on even the dreariest of days – when direct sunlight was a rare, welcome pleasure. In the evening, much like this night, it was just about the only instant comforting, healing pleasure available.

Yvonne enjoyed the feeling of the hot mug in her hands. She squeezed gently and the right corner of her mouth turned up in a smile. She decided that she would go sit down and relax in the living room. Just as she began to take a step, however, she felt a familiar tingle on the top of her head. She stopped and set her foot back down.

It began as it always did. First, it felt as if someone had simply brushed against the top of her head. Then it felt as if the vibrations wound their way down each strand of her curly brown hair and down into her scalp. And then, it felt like a thousand tiny electrical pulses traveled down deep into the roots of her hair, and when they had gathered there together, they swirled around inside her mind.

It was altogether different from the times when she would discern a slight tingle on the top of her head, and then visualize someone's face. After something like that happened, she would always receive a phone call from that person, receive a piece of mail or a parcel with their name affixed to it, or bump into that person in relatively short order. Sometimes, immediately afterwards, she would even receive that very visitor at her door. Both were in some ways similar, but were different forms of communication entirely.

Being a clairvoyant and a light trance medium, she was quite accustomed to the phenomena, so she drew a deep breath and instinctively closed her eyes in an attempt to

discern exactly who or *what* was attempting to communicate with her – telepathically. She quieted her mind and
enjoyed the feeling of the silent stillness surrounding her as
she prepared to engage in what she expected to be a two-
way communication.

She pressed her eyelids shut, and she winced and fluttered her thick, black mascara-lined eyelashes. This time,
however, she felt something completely out of the ordinary.
She tilted her head and focused extremely hard. Sounds
called out to her from some distant place, like the call of a
faraway bird. The cat's ears turned toward her. In that turn,
other sounds were muted. The cat could lock his hearing
directionally, this way or that, amplifying regions of sounds
almost to the complete exclusion of others. Then the sounds
filled her mind. Suddenly, all the muscles in Yvonne's face
relaxed. This was not one of her guides, nor one of the
legions of angels sending her a message, as they often did –
nor was it a human spirit seeking assistance – as they regularly do. But what was it that was attempting to commune
with her? She drew a deep breath. She held it. For many
pounding heartbeats, she rolled the question over and over
again in her mind, coming closer to an answer at last. She
felt the blood coursing through her arteries. Yvonne's
breathing became shorter and more labored. Each exhala-
tion became quicker, more powerful and distinct. Yvonne
clutched the edges of the counter on each side of her and
squeezed tightly. She cringed. Then, her eyes opened. This
spirit was...demonic.

She knew Pumpkin could sense it, too. His ears quickly
flattened and his eyes narrowed. He growled deeply and
slowly. Panicked, the cat scanned the room for some hiding
place or some avenue of escape.

Yvonne backed against the cabinets and held her breath.
Then, with her psychic sight, she saw it for what it really
was – the shadowy, translucent specter of the *thing* that
was trying so desperately to breach her mind. She winced in

pain, for what she saw was indescribably foul and wicked. The beast was a behemoth – as large as a great brown bear, with the head and sharp beak of an owl. Even though it was covered with greasy-looking, matted fur, its powerful ursine shoulders appeared to be solid corded muscle. She forced herself to look away, when it turned its head sharply and analyzed her with its overly large, beastly eyes. When Pumpkin regarded them, he scampered away and ducked under the leather sofa in the living room as the garish vision stabbed deep into Yvonne's heart.

As if the vision alone weren't dire enough, the cacophonous sounds of ruffling feathers and the scratching noises of talons scraping the floor filled the room as it moved about the kitchen. Then, it reached out toward her and she felt the chilling cold of a pair of powerful, invisible serpentine fingers slither over her shoulders. She cringed and somehow managed to move to the side, away from their grasp, as they began to wind around her body.

A bead of perspiration rolled down Yvonne's forehead, and for her own defense she reached into her pocket and pulled out a crucifix and rolled it around in her fingers; the silver image of Christ flashed in the light each time it rotated around. She had no intention of challenging or provoking the dark spirit who had come to visit her. But she grimaced and prepared herself for the potential retaliation that often comes when brandishing holy relics in their presence. Instead of an attack, much to her surprise, the black form diminished – first into an insubstantial mist, then to nothing at all.

The whole room seemed to stand still in place and time and Yvonne experienced a sudden, frozen silence as Pumpkin looked on from underneath the edge of the sofa. His glowing eyes stood out in the blackness like distant stars.

She felt an intense tingling sensation all along her arms. She raised her hands before her panic-stricken eyes and turned them over and around. The hair on her forearms stood completely on end. Then the clear image of her friend's face penetrated her mind. Her eyes popped open wide and her jaw hung slack. She gasped and zeroed in on the telephone.

"Oh, no!"

Chapter 1 – Retribution

THE FULL MIDNIGHT MOON SAT HEAVILY in the violet December sky behind scattered gray clouds and the black, scraggly branches of the wide-spread oaks lining the property of Dr. Vincent Decker – parapsychologist, paranormal investigator, and seasoned demonologist. The lights of the main house cast a soft yellow glow upon the snow-covered lawn outside, but the rest of the house, including the outlying office, seemed as cold and dormant as the stale winter air. A sudden gust of wind swept over the lawn, accompanied by a whispering howl that came from both nowhere and everywhere at once. Then a light came to life inside the connecting passageway that led to the home-office.

Inside the long, antiquated hallway, Vincent reached his trembling hand out toward the closed maple door before him and felt for the black wrought-iron latch at its edge. He applied his thumb against the spade-shaped lever and pressed down forcefully until a loud, solid "clack" echoed throughout the candle-lit hallway. He pushed his hand away and the door creaked open slowly before the dark void in front of him.

As he cautiously entered, Vincent held the door open and pressed it against the dark stone wall. He reached out with his foot and maneuvered an iron gargoyle doorstop into position with his shoe in an effort to keep the door ajar and to allow the heat from the main house to cascade inside. When he was satisfied that it was held securely,

Vincent stood there. It took many minutes of scanning the room, his gaze piercing the shadows, before he was able to relax in the confidence that he was indeed alone.

He moved deeper into the room. In doing so, he reached out and slowly approached his desk. When he'd found the corner, he fumbled in the darkness for the edge of a green stained-glass lamp, reached inside and delicately pulled down on the brass chain. Vincent squinted against the sudden bright light and held a hand up to block it out until his eyes had adjusted. He looked all around him, from the grand cabinets, bookshelves and tables lining the walls, to the neat rows of shelving aligned together in the center of the room. Displayed on every shelf and in practically every square inch of the tables were the many arcane objects of varying shapes, sizes, and compositions from the cases he had investigated over the years. Despite the impossible task of examining every single object in the vast expanse of the room, he instinctively felt that everything seemed to be in order.

He clutched the top edge of the burgundy studded-leather desk chair and went to the wall behind it. He admired the neat rows of audio cassettes he had amassed since he first began delving into the strange, mysterious paranormal world he had found himself unable to resist all these many years. There stood before him the records of hundreds of cases he had studied, most of them simply concerning earthbound human spirits who were found to be incapable of crossing over due to varied forms of unfinished business or unresolved conflicts.

Then there were the many cases that involved spirits of a much darker nature – spirits that had never walked the earth in human form. He didn't like to think about those cases, nor of the scars that they left behind, but the dark spirits were from a different reality altogether, bordering on twilight. Its evil and blind terror was capable of becoming a part of the lives of the living in an instant, and lasting forever, despite any attempt to sway its incredible power. This realm was unseen and unheard most of the time, somewhere in-between the sunlit majesty of the physical world that we can see and touch, and the invisible, intangible realm of energy and spirit.

Vincent exhaled forcefully. He paused and then slowly raised one hand and reached behind his head. He scanned the desk before him as he pressed his fingers against his scalp. He moved his fingertips around in his hair and felt for the two rows of indentations left there during the most dangerous final moments of the McLaughlin Case, just two months earlier. He felt the tiny holes in his skull with the pad of his index finger. Once he'd found the divot, he couldn't help that his attention and his eyes were immediately drawn to the small, hexagonal glass jewelry box that was sitting on the outside edge of his desk. Despair took hold of him, because he knew that each time he had left the room, he had placed the jewelry box on one of the many bookcase shelves in the center of the room, and each time he returned, the box was sitting on the right-hand corner of his desk. Each time he noticed that it had moved, it captivated him. He could do nothing to resist looking at and into the box. And once he did so, he could not turn his eyes away from it, no matter how hard he tried. This pattern was becoming all too routine and far too disturbing for his liking. Something had a hold of him and he knew, of course, what that something was.

Without warning, the hair on Vincent's forearms stood on end. At the same time, he felt the familiar tingles on the top of his head. He knew he was being watched. There was no question in his mind. He drew a deep breath, gathered his courage, and held out his palm before him. He fell back a step and assumed a more defensive posture. "In the name of Jesus Christ, I command any negative spirits in this house to return to wherever it is you have come from!" Vincent gasped. He pressed his temples and stumbled back against the wall behind his chair. Cassette tapes became dislodged by the heavy collision. They began to rattle violently behind him. Vincent groaned. He exhaled forcefully from his nostrils to expel a rancid odor that had taken hold there. The odor quickly became overpowering. He doubled over, sucked in his breath and held his stomach. Then, unable to stave off the horrid stench, he pursed his lips and exhaled from his mouth forcefully. "Archangel Michael, defend..."

Without warning, a great force collided with his chest and blasted him back against the wall. Vincent moaned. Cassette tapes shot out of their slots and rained down all around him. He gathered his courage and shouted, "Defend me from this evil and send it away, in the name of all that is holy, in the name of Jesus Christ!" A baleful moan resonated throughout the room and a sooty black form darted away from him and flitted into the deeper recesses of the darkest part of the room.

Vincent gritted his teeth and opened the top desk drawer. He reached inside under a piece of purple velvet and wrapped his pudgy fingers around an old wooden crucifix. He pulled it out of the drawer, kissed its face and held it before him with authority. "I command you to leave this house in the name of Jesus Christ!" He walked boldly toward the shadows. When he took one step further, he felt something come up from behind him and tug his arm back to his side. Then from before him, in one powerful swipe, the crucifix was suddenly and violently batted out of his hand. Vincent felt his stomach turn in knots. He heaved, and brought his arm back toward him – and upon doing so, knocked the jewelry box off the desk. As it fell into the air, the contents clattered inside the glass; the sound became louder and louder as if a hundred wind chimes were clanging inside his head. The jewelry box bounced onto the leather chair and turned upside down, as Vincent wrapped his arms around his midsection and groaned. He fell back and tried to catch himself on the arms of the chair, but it eluded his feeble attempt to grasp it and spun around instead, the twisting motion flinging the jewelry box off the chair. As he fell downward, the nauseating stench of a thousand rotting corpses encapsulated him and permeated his nostrils. Vincent collapsed onto the floor and landed on the plush red Persian carpet. The jewelry box struck the carpet before him on its edge, rolled directly in front of his eyes, fell over, landed upside down, and came to rest there – just as Vincent slowly faded out of consciousness.

Chapter 2 – Sounding the Alarm

DEEP WITHIN THE CONFINES OF THE CHANCERY, in the late evening hours, Bishop Marcus Phelan sat at a large round mahogany table in the center of a massive library. Sputtering candles in an ornate silver candelabra in the center of the table bathed the room in a soft yellow glow. He faced an immense crackling hearth that was a primeval source of both warmth and comfort. Immense mahogany bookshelves held an untold wealth of tomes, scrolls, parchments, and clay tablets for only the most earnest and privileged seekers of ancient wisdom and hidden knowledge. He was privy to them, of course, due to both his status and his station, but also because most of the contents of the library came from his private, personal collection, and there was nothing he'd rather do than expand his awareness and his understanding of their many arcane secrets in every spare moment he was afforded the luxury of doing so.

Bishop Phelan tilted his head and listened carefully. He heard rapidly approaching footsteps in the hallway. Aware of the imminent intrusion, he turned over and thus concealed the crinkled piece of parchment with frayed, yellowed edges that he had been studying in his brief, but quiet respite. Then he braced himself on the edge of the table and pushed himself up from his chair.

On the opposite side of the door, a priest reached out with his right hand and wiggled his fingers before the shiny brass doorknob. He straightened his cassock and arched his wrist back in preparation to knock. Just as his knuckles were about to strike the door, it opened from within.

Bishop Phelan gave a curt nod and asked, "What it is, Tom?"

"Forgive the intrusion, Your Excellency! An urgent call has come in..." The priest shot his hand forward and held out a stark white piece of paper between his first two fingers. Bishop Phelan gently slid the paper out of the priest's hand and unfolded it before him. The priest could not help but study him. The bishop's eyes grew wide as he read the message and wider still as he continued reading it. He understood immediately that there was something sinister and powerful behind the threat revealed in the message. The bishop cleared his throat, nodded at the priest and said, "Walk with me, Tom." He extended his arm back toward the direction from which the priest had come.

Bishop Phelan hooked his hand across the doorknob and took care to softly close the door behind him. He then placed his hand on the priest's upper back. They moved through the winding stone hallways like a whispering breeze. They stepped up to an expansive counter fashioned of white Italian marble. In the office behind the counter, a diminutive nun whirled around in her chair and stood, not so much at attention, but with a great deal of respect and reverence.

"Good evening, Your Excellency," she said with a smile.

Bishop Phelan frowned, cocked his elbow and examined his watch. "Evening already, is it, Sister Margaret?"

The nun covered her mouth to conceal a smile. She knew how much the bishop loved to study, and how often he would become so totally absorbed in doing so, that he would lose track of time entirely, to the extent of even forgoing his meals.

"Sister, has Dr. Vincent Decker returned any of my phone calls over the past several days?" He turned to face the priest and then focused his attention back upon the nun.

He studied her with his penetrating eyes. "You've placed the calls, as I've requested?"

"Yes, of course!" She turned a page in her log book and looked back up at him. "I've placed three calls now, Your Excellency."

Bishop Phelan paused and shook his head. "And there have been no responses?"

She shook her head from side to side. "None at all, I'm afraid."

Bishop Phelan waved his fingers toward himself. "Hand me the telephone, would you?" Sister Margaret reached under the edge of the counter and set the rotary telephone onto the counter before him. The bell inside clanged as she did so. She waited silently behind the counter, always eager to be of service. Bishop Phelan drew a small spiral-bound notepad out of his jacket and set it on the desk before him. He opened the cover, licked his finger and flipped through several pages, turning them by the corners.

The priest studied the wrinkles around the bishop's eyes as he squinted at the notepad. The man wasn't as old as he appeared, but his thinning gray hair and gaunt features suggested that life, not age, had taken the luster of his youth, for he was probably but a few years past fifty. When he had found the entry he was looking for, the bishop traced his finger along its length. He reached out with the other hand, looked at the phone, stuck his finger into the rotary dial and worked the numbers around until he had completed them all. He held the receiver against his ear in the crook of his neck. The priest and the nun watched him intently. He folded his notepad over, tapped its edge against the counter, and waited as the ring tones began. Sister Margaret repeatedly looked up and away from the bishop in an effort to give him some semblance of privacy, but she couldn't help wondering what the matter was that had concerned him so.

The phone rang a total of twelve times until Bishop

Phelan finally grumbled and hung up the receiver. He stared at the countertop for a moment and finally regarded the nun. "Something's wrong," he uttered. He offered a quick smile before turning and walking away. He fished the keys to his office out of his pocket. "And I intend to find out...just exactly what that is."

The priest and the nun exchanged uneasy glances.

The bishop spun around on his heels and walked away briskly down the hallway toward his office. As he unlocked his door, he knew instinctively that the battle he had waged, and that he believed he had won two months earlier, was not over after all. He opened his door and scanned his desk quickly. He snatched his bible and secured it under his arm. Then he collected the rest of his things and grabbed his jacket and fedora from the hat stand in the corner.

It was wickedly cold outside, and a strong wind swept across Boston Harbor from the east. He paused as a bitter gust of wind lashed out like spectral fingers against his face. He hurriedly approached his powder-blue Buick LeSabre sedan, opened the trunk, and quickly retrieved an ice scraper. With his bible still tucked away under one arm, he walked along the side of the car and started to chip the ice off the windshield. He reached around to hoist the windshield wiper blade so he could clear the window beneath it. He pulled on the metal support arm and found that the blade was frozen against the glass. He grunted, pressed his finger around the tip of the windshield wiper blade and tugged. The rubber split along the seam and he tore a deep even line down his finger, slicing it clean open along the inside edge, well past the middle of his second knuckle.

"Lord have mercy!" He groaned and pulled his hand back. Blood collected in pools on the snow-covered windshield in each of the several places it had seeped through the severed flaps of skin on his finger. He squeezed the wound tight and hurried back toward the Archdiocesan Offices.

When he pulled open the door and stepped inside, Sister Margaret peeked over the counter. He called out, "Sister, I've cut my hand." She shrieked and ducked back away. He pushed open the door to the restroom, propped it open with his shoe and washed the wound under cold running water. He watched as a continuous stream of blood washed away from his finger and mixed with the water that swirled its way down the drain. It was a deep cut. Sister Margaret hurried down the hallway and stepped inside. She gasped when she saw the wound. She held it up to examine it closely in the light. "Any deeper and you'd require stitches!" She widened her eyes and looked up at him, embarrassed she'd addressed him in such a manner. She added, "Your Excellency..." Bishop Phelan snorted. "It's quite all right, Sister!" Sister Margaret pressed the wound closed. The bishop handed her two paper towels from the dispenser, which she quickly used to wrap his finger. She looked around frantically. Then she gasped and said, "Come with me, please. I know where we can find some medical tape! Hold that tight!"

When she'd finished tending to his wound, Bishop Phelan was nodding off. "You can't be driving this late at night after you've lost so much blood." The bishop grimaced and finally nodded. He thought of his friend. "Please get some rest and leave in the morning. I'll call Dr. Decker again at first light. If he doesn't answer then, you'll be fully rested and you can go see him after breakfast."

Morning came and, as expected, the calls made to Vincent Decker went unanswered. After breakfast, Bishop Phelan once again thanked Sister Margaret for her assistance and started for the front doors. When he exited, he noticed one of the young priests chipping away at the ice on the windows of the car. He smiled. He was thankful for the help.

He looked at his wound, now secured in three band-aids, and he was grateful he didn't have to put any extra strain on it clearing the ice. The young priest smiled at him and said, "Good morning, Your Excellency!"

"Good morning, Francis. Thank you for your help." He examined the wiper blade and winced when he saw the thin piece of metal bent up in precisely the right position to cause the injury he'd sustained the previous evening.

He inserted the key and the door creaked with age when he opened it. He leaned inside and placed his bible down on the front passenger seat. Then he got in and closed the door. Once inside, he laid both hands on the steering wheel, closed his eyes and prayed silently. He then made the sign of the cross before him. When he had finished his blessing, he opened his eyes, nodded at the attentive priest, headed for the parking lot exit and started on his way. Time, he knew, was of the essence.

Chapter 3 – The Devil in the Dark

WHEN VINCENT AWOKE, he found himself lying on his side in dazed confusion. He felt a dull ache throughout his body as if he'd been through several rounds of a heavy-weight boxing match. All he heard was his own heartbeat, and he felt his own pulse pounding in his head. He didn't know how long he had been lying there, whether it had been a minute or several hours. His clouded vision became slightly clearer after a few deep breaths. The first thing he saw, coming in and out of focus, was the bottom edge of his desk. His eyes traced the fine line of dust that had collected on the carpet against the desk's edge. And then he saw it – the jewelry box, still lying there on his side. He felt his heart as he studied it for a few long seconds.

Then the objects inside became astonishingly clear – the impossibly sharp teeth from what his Yale scientist friend had identified as an eight-hundred-thousand-year-old boar. Vincent wanted to close his eyes to shut the teeth out of his mind but he couldn't move. He was paralyzed. He knew from experience that this was Psychic Paralysis. Then the room began to spin around him, and like viewing a series of twisting, hypnotic, multicolored kaleidoscope images, he became lost again as he recalled the absolutely horrific encounter with the demon in the McLaughlins' basement during the last suffumigation he had performed with the help of his friend and colleague, Jason McLeod. He could do nothing to force the images out of his mind, and he was condemned to relive the encounter that nearly cost him his life – less than two months earlier:

Saliva-muted growls echoed throughout the basement, and invisible claws dug into Vincent's shoulders and hips, fighting to control him, to overpower him, and to ultimately drive him into submission.

For some strange reason, Tyler McLaughlin knew that if Vincent gave in, he would be the next to become possessed. "Get off me!" Vincent demanded. The invisible beast stank of old, wet fur. Vincent had collapsed onto his hands and knees and gagged. He held his breath, trying to avoid the noisome stench that sat over him like a noxious cloud. An ear-splitting screech came from thin air, long and potent, like the combined calls of a lion, a pig, and a crow. Tyler thought Vincent was going to die. Vincent moaned. Deep gouges appeared down his back as if he were being raked by impossibly sharp, invisible claws. "Jesus help me!"

Vincent found the strength to stand. He spun around, trying to shake the thing from his back. Then he gagged and grabbed his throat. The life was being squeezed from him. "Vincent!" Jason screamed. He reached for a shape on Vincent's back. He grabbed hold of something gelatinous, hot and bumpy. Its four limbs ended in clawed hooks that dug into Vincent's sides like pincers.

"Jesus Christ," Vincent roared, gagging and vomiting. "In the name..."

Jason caught on and they continued in unison. "...of Jesus Christ, we command you to leave!" Savage licking sounds came from thin air as if the demon was fighting for control of him. Jason patted his pocket, pulled out his vial of holy water and uncorked it. He saw Vincent collapse, drained and in terrible pain.

"The power of Christ compels you," Jason said. He shook the bottle and held it before his face. It was empty. He panicked. Jason made the sign of the cross over Vincent's back and over the beast riding it. High-pitched whines followed and

then Vincent's face lost all its color. He gasped for breath and reached out.

Jason said, "In the name of Jesus Christ, I command you to leave!"

"Jason," Vincent gagged. Jason looked down on him. "The incense," Vincent continued. "Light the incense and candles." Vincent's body was thrown forward over the workbench. Jason nodded, tore open the bag and dumped it into the bowl. He searched around for a light, then lunged for a pack of matches lying on the edge of the steps. The matches slid away on the cement floor, as if by some invisible wind. Tyler dove after them and snatched them in his hand. He fumbled with the pack, tore off a match, and went to strike it when it was batted out of his hand. He tore off a second match and swiped it across the package. Time seemed to slow to a standstill. He noticed the first minuscule plume of smoke rise off the match. Then a tiny spark came to life and ignited into a bright flame. He held it against the charcoal. The incense crackled and sizzled. He fanned the smoke so that it would rise and spread faster than it normally would. Then he blew it onto Vincent and onto the beast riding him.

A great wail had erupted, shaking the foundation of the house. Dreadful sounds like those of some wild beast savagely devouring its prey boomed throughout the basement. Vincent fell to his knees screaming, grabbing at his head. Horrible, vicious snarls and growls filled the basement. Vincent recovered his breath. He reached up to touch his head and recoiled from the pain he felt when he touched the dozens of small sharp points embedded into his skull in two even arches from close to his forehead all the way to the base of his neck.

The beast had been forced to flee, but not without one last display of power, one dire, vile, desperate strike, so that it would never be forgotten. Jason fished through Vincent's hair. He wiggled one of the objects and tried to pry it loose as Vincent cried out in pain. When he finally pulled it out, he saw that it was a yellowed, half-inch-long bloody, flesh-tipped fang.

Vincent winced and stood up. He shook the dust off his sweater and pants. "We've done it. We've won." He raised his hand and reached to the back of his injured head again. "What in the name of God is stuck into my head, Jason?"

"Vincent, so help me...they...they look like...teeth!"

The dramatic replay of the recent events echoed in Vincent's mind as he stared into the small glass box and the convex angles of its edges. Then he saw an image begin to form, at first tiny and indistinct. It pulsed and vibrated and expanded slowly forward from within the jewelry box as if something had broken through into this reality from some far distant, foreign place. He strained to identify what it was that he was seeing. Then, as had happened so many times since Matthew McLaughlin's exorcism, a presence communed with him and penetrated his mind like a frozen, razor-sharp shard of glass. He cringed, when in his mind he heard the familiar voices taunting him. They spoke as if they were one: "You will all *suffer* for what you've done!"

A tear welled up in Vincent's eye as he lay there helplessly, staring hopelessly at the glass jewelry box, the remnants of diabolical evil within, and the opaque, shadowy image overlaying them both.

He felt as though he were falling backward into a great chasm, falling deeper with each breath.

Finally, he felt that he could control the muscles around his eyes, so he blinked.

As his eyelids closed ever so briefly, a single tear oozed out, rolled down the bridge of his nose, collected and hung there at the tip for several heartbeats, and finally fell onto the carpet below.

Chapter 4 – Divine Intervention

BISHOP PLELAN PULLED UP IN FRONT OF VINCENT'S HOUSE and parked his car on the street. He studied the house for several long minutes. When he was done, he clutched his bible in his hands and prayed aloud, "Heavenly Father, thank You for Your divine protection. Thank You for blessing this house before me and for blessing Vincent Decker. Thank You, Jesus, for standing beside me this day and for all the remaining days of my life." He opened his door and got out. With the door still ajar, he placed his arms on the roof of the car and set his bible down upon it. A strong breeze swept up from behind him, whipped around his ear and caused the cover of his bible to fly open. The pages rustled in the wind. He reached his right hand up and made the sign of the cross before the house in front of him. "I wash this house in the blood of Jesus of Nazareth, removing all darkness, repelling all unclean spirits. I evoke the protection of the Archangels Michael, Gabriel, Uriel, and Raphael and I invoke the august power of my Lord and Savior – Lord Jesus Christ. Amen."

He closed and retrieved his bible, backed away from the car, closed the door and walked around the car toward the front sidewalk. He elected to bypass the front walkway altogether and instead trudged across the snow-covered lawn and around the side of the house. The thin layer of ice crunched beneath his feet as they broke through into the underlying snow with each step. He felt another sudden chilling wind and he heard the distinct call of a nearby crow. He knew the significance of that, so he stopped dead in his tracks and scanned the horizon for the bird. He spotted it, perched high above him on a telephone wire. The jet black creature stared down at him. Its "caw" sent chills up the back of his neck. The bishop pressed his fingers against his forehead and then touched his breast, his left shoulder and then his right. He opened his bible and flipped through the pages and recited the Twenty-Third Psalm aloud. He shouted, "The Lord is my shepherd...I shall not want." The call echoed throughout the harsh landscape. The crow flinched, spread out its talons, wrapped them over the thick black cables and side-stepped away from him. Satisfied that it backed off, he made his way around to the back of the house and approached the office door as he continued to pray. "...He maketh me to lie down in green pastures. He leadeth me beside the still waters. He restoreth my soul. He leadeth me in the paths of righteousness for His name's sake..."

When he came to the office door, the crow cawed in the distance and he heard the ruffling of feathers overhead. He looked up into the gray overcast sky to try and spot the flying bird. A great shadow loomed over the house and a massive winged form streaked overhead. It was no mere bird. The impossibly large wingspan was something else entirely.

Bishop Phelan peered into the windows. There was nothing but darkness inside the room beyond them. "Yea, though I walk through the valley of the shadow of death, I shall fear no evil, for Thou art with me; Thy rod and Thy staff they comfort me..." He rapped on the door with his knuckles. "...Thou preparest a table before me in the presence of mine enemies. Thou anointest my head with oil; my cup runneth over." Bishop Phelan knocked again and continued, "Surely goodness and mercy shall follow me all the days of my life."

The shadowy form inside came out of the darkness and

rushed up to the door. It was Vincent. His eyes were wide with terror. He looked pale and gray – almost lifeless – as if every last bit of life force had been drained from him. His eyes had lost all their brightness. Bishop Phelan quickly finished his prayer. "I will dwell in the house of the Lord – forever."

The door opened slightly and the bishop reached in and grabbed Vincent's arm. He set his bible down in the snow and wrapped his arms under Vincent's armpits. He was slighter than his friend, and he heaved and dragged his friend over the threshold and out into the snow. Bishop Phelan pulled him farther away from the office and set him down. Vincent rolled over and gasped for breath. Bishop Phelan knelt beside him and pressed his crucifix against Vincent's forehead. "In the name of the Father, the Son, and the Holy Ghost."

Vincent curled up into a ball and coughed heavily. He covered his mouth with his fist as if he'd been shaken from some sort of spell. He turned onto his back and took a deep breath. His eyes fluttered and he locked eyes with Bishop Phelan. A corner of Vincent's mouth turned up in a smile and he said, "You knew!" He coughed as if expelling something deep within him. "You knew that I was in danger."

Bishop Phelan nodded and smiled tenderly. "Indeed I did, my friend. But it was a phone call from our dear psychic friend, Yvonne, that alerted me to it. Now, tell me what happened." Vincent reached his hand out to his friend. They locked their hands together and Bishop Phelan helped Vincent sit up. "But...not here! Let's be free of this place and go get something to eat and discuss it there."

The two men trudged through the snow toward the bishop's car.

As they approached the car, a crow cawed from above and flew right over their heads toward the back of the house. Vincent studied it with suspicion. He gazed at his friend who gave him a knowing nod and they both got into the car.

As they started to drive away, they spotted another crow perched high in the shadows of a wide-spread oak. It cawed feverishly into the stale winter air. The crow was soon joined by another. Vincent studied them through the passenger-side window, then through the one behind it, and finally through the rear window as they drove away.

When they were about to pass the diner, Vincent pointed and Bishop Phelan veered into the parking lot. When they walked inside, they were greeted by the owner, a Greek man who knew them both on a first name basis. He welcomed them and directed them toward the general area that they usually liked to be seated in. They slid into opposite sides of a booth. The red-headed waitress handed them each a menu and smiled brightly. "Working on a case, gentlemen?"

Vincent grunted. "Lucille, trust me, you don't even want to know."

She cocked her head at an odd angle. "Ya know?" she said, poking the corner of her mouth with the eraser end of her pencil, "You're probably right." She nodded.

Bishop Phelan chuckled and said, "Hot tea for me please, Lucy."

She winked at the bishop and looked at Vincent. "Coffee, light and sweet, for you, Honey?"

"You must be psychic, Lucille!"

"Psychic?" She laughed, a wheezing sound that revealed her years of smoking had exacted a toll on her lungs. She shook her head. Her earrings dangled against her cheeks. "I don't have to be psychic when you two always order the same beverages. We have some turkey pot pies fresh out of the oven."

"Now you're talkin'," Vincent said, eagerly.

The bishop fumbled with his menu, folded it over, handed it to Lucille and said, "I'd like the Yankee Pot Roast

Dinner, please, with green beans and cole slaw. Butter for the green beans, please."

"You got it, gents!" Lucille took the bishop's menu and slid the one that Vincent hadn't even bothered to look at into her palm. "I'll be right back with your drinks."

Both men smiled at her. Bishop Phelan looked outside and then back at his friend. "So, tell me what in the world happened, please."

Vincent sighed. "They began about two weeks ago..."

Bishop Phelan interrupted him. "What began about two weeks ago, exactly?"

Vincent nodded and replied, "The migraines."

The bishop cocked an ear. "How bad were they?" He waved his hands before his friend. "Where and how did you first experience them?"

Vincent continued, "I first began to experience unexpected and intense headaches just prior to the McLaughlin case. Since then, they have intensified into debilitating migraines."

Bishop Phelan pursed his lips and gave his friend a sympathetic nod. "I'm sorry, Vincent. Please tell me about the first time..."

"I was in my office, going over some new cases I was looking into, when suddenly I felt a pain in the middle of the right side of my head. It was piercing. I closed my eyes and I suffered through it. I then heard a tone in my ears that I couldn't identify or explain."

Vincent's eyes went out of focus as if he were staring deep into his mind to relive the circumstances of that first fateful evening...

Vincent clicked off his tape recorder and finished jotting notes down on his yellow notepad. That's when he heard the whispering. He narrowed his eyes and set his pen down very slowly. He quietly and deftly slid open his desk drawer and pulled out an amber vial and squeezed it inside his palm. The whispers coming from deeper inside his office suddenly careened around the wall beside him. Vincent followed the pattern precisely as it taunted and circled him, and wound around to his left side. Then, the stabbing, piercing pain in his right temple felt as if a vein had become engorged and that it would rupture inside his skull any moment. The pain was excruciating. It felt to him like a balloon was embedded underneath his skin, sitting flush against his bone, and growing larger and larger and bulging away from his head with every panicked beat of his heart. Suddenly, he heard a solid, low-pitched tone in his left ear, and instantly afterward, a stabbing pain caused him to grimace and shrink back in his chair.

"Well, we know what the tones mean!"

Vincent nodded. "I tried to pay attention to discern what exactly was trying to be conveyed to my conscious mind, but I'm no Yvonne. Try as I may, I can't seem to hone my psychic abilities. It took control of me almost instantly and caused me to black out."

The kitchen doors swung wide in the distance, and Lucille glided over to the table as if she herself were a spirit. "Here you are, gentlemen." She reached over and set down the bishop's cup and saucer and stainless steel pitcher. The bishop smiled. Then she set down a saucer with a lemon wedge, six creamers and a tea bag. She slid Vincent's coffee mug and a saucer filled with creamers in before him.

He acknowledged her and said, "Thank you, Lucy!"

She smiled at them and said, "I'll be back in a little while with your lunches."

They all heard the bell ringing in the distance. "But right now, I have to serve those plates that just came up." She winked at them and walked away.

The bishop opened his tea bag and poured his water. He didn't look at his friend when he began commenting. "There is a reason for everything, Vincent! It is God's will that you are not psychically attuned, and I believe it's a good thing that you're not – a defense mechanism, if you will."

"Maybe so," Vincent agreed. "However, when I woke up, I was instantly inclined to open my eyes and look over toward my shelves in the middle of the room, and my attention was immediately and most seriously fixed upon the glass jewelry box that I stored the boar's teeth in."

"Hmm…"

Vincent cupped his hand over his friend's hand and became quite serious. "Marcus, I couldn't," Vincent pleaded, "…no matter how hard I tried, move my eyes away from that box!" His eyes became narrow slits. "So help me, it had a hold of me, and I swear hours went by until I was finally free of it."

Bishop Phelan stirred his tea. "And then…?"

"And then," Vincent continued, "it stopped as quickly as it started." He peeled the foil lid off one of the coffee creamers and poured out the creamer inside. Then he reached for another and continued with his story. "I got up, walked over to the shelf and studied the jewelry box. All the teeth were accounted for." He stared at his friend. "These were no demonic 'apports', Marcus! They never demateri-alized in a few hours like they usually do. Where did they come from?"

Bishop Phelan narrowed his eyes and replied, "Where indeed!"

Vincent took two packets of sugar, held them as one and tore off the upper edges together. He poured the sugar into his coffee mug. "The next time I went into my office, it happened again." He opened several more creamers, one after the other, and poured the contents into his cup and stirred it. "Though not so severely…"

"Details please, Dr. Decker." The bishop took another sip of his tea. "It's all in the details."

He took a sip of coffee and swallowed hard. "The next

time it happened, I was reaching for a cassette tape, because I wanted to review the Devon Case..."

The bishop interrupted him. "You're referring to the demon in the infant's room?"

"That's the one! When I had that cassette tape in my hands, so help me, I felt that same piercing sting in my head."

Bishop Phelan's mouth was concealed by the coffee mug when he replied. "And were you guided to look back over at that jewelry box, I presume?"

"I literally leaped to my feet and raced right over to that jewelry box!"

The bishop swallowed his tea and set the mug down onto the saucer. "Very interesting! What did you do next?"

"It's as if they were calling my name! I reached out toward the box."

"Who is they?"

"The teeth!"

The bishop's eyes grew wider.

"I walked toward that box and reached out for it. My hand was trembling. I knew not to touch it. I tried my best to fight the impulse, but I grabbed hold of it around its edges." Vincent took a sip of his coffee and closed his eyes. "I saw a flash of black light and a face, a ghastly face, but it happened too quickly for me to remember who or what it was exactly."

"That's not all, I presume," Bishop Phelan added.

"As if it could be any worse." Vincent stared at his friend. "No matter where I leave the box when I leave my office, it's always resting on the right outside edge of my desk when I return."

Bishop Phelan shook his head. "You realize the seriousness of this situation, right?"

Lucille arrived seconds later with their platters and set them down. They thanked her and she wheeled around and headed off toward the host stand.

Bishop Phelan extended his cupped hands and rested them on the table. Vincent reached over and grasped them with his own hands. "Heavenly Father, thank You for this food and bless it to our bodies. Safeguard us all from the clutches of the Devil and protect us from evil. In the name of our Lord and Savior Jesus Christ we pray. Amen."

"Amen," Vincent said.

The bishop noticed Lucille smiling at them in the distance. She was reaching for and holding her gold crucifix. He could read her lips. He was an expert at it, due to many years spent with two revered people within the church – a hearing-impaired priest whose faculties had diminished considerably over time, and a nun named Catalina who lost her hearing as a young child. Lucille had said to the Greek man, "I just love to hear them pray."

They both smiled at him affectionately. When she left to attend to her duties, Bishop Phelan pulled a piece of pot roast off his fork with his teeth and held the fork before his friend. "Eat up, Dr. Decker. We have work to do that will require a nourished body and a sound mind."

Chapter 5 – Defying the Darkness

BY THE TIME THEY HAD AT LAST LEFT THE DINER, the sun was halfway to the horizon. As they walked down the steps, they heard the resounding call of three black crows sitting in a tight formation on a telephone wire just above the car. Their feathers ruffled in the whispering winds. The men studied the birds intently as they cautiously approached the car. Just when they took their eyes off the birds, one landed squarely on the roof of the car. The jet-black feet clattered against the metal and scraped and scratched the paint as the crow shifted its weight. Fortunately, it was an old car with plenty of wear and tear. Bishop Phelan withdrew a silver crucifix from his pocket and held it before him. The crow cawed at them. Then in an instant, it went after them. Vincent put his hands in front of his face to protect himself from its sharp talons.

Bishop Phelan held his crucifix before him and shouted, "Be gone, foul spirits, in the name of Jesus Christ!"

The crows sounded their piercing calls in unison. With a wave of his hand, Bishop Phelan urged his friend to get into the car. Vincent was shaken, afraid and in no state to defend himself from the spiritual attack they both knew was coming.

Bishop Phelan reached into his pocket and pulled out a vial of holy water. The crow on the roof of the car lifted one foot, and then the other, cawing continually. It opened its wings, lunged forward at the bishop and battered him with its wings. He dropped the vial and it shattered into pieces at his feet.

Vincent reached over and opened the door from the inside, startling the bishop. When he came to his senses, he opened it wider, slipped inside and slammed the door tight. The other two crows flew down and landed on the front hood. Vincent looked right, then left, and saw several more crows landing on the wires all along the outside of the diner. The bishop started the car. A bead of sweat rolled down his nose. He shifted the car into reverse and backed out slowly. The crows studied them. Mocking them. Calling to one another in a language only they could understand.

As the blue sedan slowly rolled out of the parking lot, the agents of evil descended, one after the other, each narrowly striking the automobile with either their wingtips or their talons. The sound quickly became deafening.

When they turned onto Route 25, Vincent hit the gas pedal and they screamed down the road. Just when they appeared to have lost them, a crow streaked in from behind and struck the passenger side mirror with its beak, splintering the mirror into pieces that fell out onto the open road behind them. The bird came in again and struck the passenger door window. Bishop Phelan observed the black marble-like eye of the bird and thrust his crucifix up against the window. The crow closed its eye, pushed off with its feet and lunged off the outside edge of the window ledge, furiously beating its wings until it was riding the winds far behind them.

After a few brief moments of silence, the birds had swarmed together into a thick black swirling cloud.

When the two men approached the house, they inched forward at a snail's pace, studying the yard, the house, and the power and telephone lines above. They exited the vehicle in unison. "You know what to do?" Vincent nodded. They parted ways. Vincent inserted a key into the lock of the front door and Bishop Phelan walked around the side of the house toward the back. When he'd reached the office, Bishop Phelan cupped his hand over his eyes and peered into the windows. He turned the doorknob slowly and opened the door ever so slightly – alert to the most subtle signs of any reaction. The bishop opened his bible purely out of reflex, because he had memorized the Psalm he was about to recite decades earlier. He glanced down. The word of God filled him with additional strength and resolve. He reached inside the dark room, turned on the light switch, cleared his throat and held a large wooden crucifix before him. In a commanding tone, he shouted, "The earth is the Lord's and everything within it." He paused and listened. He heard what sounded like shuffling papers in the distance. He scanned the room for an additional reaction to his provocation, but nothing more happened. "...the world and all who live in it; for He founded it on the seas and established it on the waters..." He cast his silver aspergillum forward and sprinkled holy water before him in a great curving arc.

A vicious howl belched forth from the darkest part of the room. He shot his head in its direction and shouted, "Who may ascend the mountain of the Lord?" He went deeper into the room and showered the shelves before him, which contained the incomprehensible assortment of cursed relics and negatively-charged artifacts that Vincent had collected from all the cases he had investigated throughout his lengthy career. "Who may stand in this holy place?" The shelves, both wooden and metal, started to vibrate and then they shook violently. Objects upon them rattled and teetered dangerously close to the edges. Bishop Phelan narrowed his eyes. The evil trembling before the august power of the word of the Almighty increased his resolve. "The one who has clean hands and a pure heart, who does not trust in an idol or swear by a false god." Baleful moans resonated from beside Vincent's desk. He approached the opposite corner of the room. The sound of clattering feet on the ceiling above startled him. Then he ducked wildly as he heard the sound of ruffling feathers pass right beside him. He cast his aspergillum forward again and blotted the area with holy water. He inhaled deeply. "They will receive blessing from the Lord and vindication from God their Savior." A piercing whine filled the room. He shouted, "Such is the generation of those who seek Him, who seek Your face, God of Jacob." Vincent cautiously entered via the connecting hallway. He carried a smoking bowl of frankincense and myrrh that he had assembled and lit while upstairs. He set it down and opened the windows and the side door to the office. Bishop Phelan passed into the darkest corners of the room. "Lift up your heads, you gates; be lifted up, you ancient doors that the King of glory may come in."

A terrible cacophonous whine filled the room and echoed throughout. Vincent covered his ears. It was the same protesting call he had heard before he was viciously bitten in the head by the demon in the McLaughlins' basement. He cowered in pain and shook his head. Then, when he could endure no more, he opened his mouth in a silent scream.

Bishop Phelan showered his friend with holy water. "Who is this King of glory? The Lord strong and mighty, the Lord mighty in battle. Lift up your heads, you gates; lift them up, you ancient doors, that the King of glory may come in." The door swung wildly and slammed shut with a thunderous noise. It shook and vibrated. "Who is He, this King of glory?" Vincent leaned back against the large table behind him and dropped his hands away from his ears. He cautiously approached the door, but wisely backed away from it. Bishop Phelan approached Vincent's desk, ever so slowly, casting holy water before him as he went. He stopped and looked down at his feet. There he saw the inverted hexagonal glass jewelry box. He knelt down slowly and studied the container with suspicion. He cast his aspergillum forward and showered it with holy water.

Vincent spun around wildly as if he were deeply affected by the action the holy water had on the box and on the teeth inside. The strange teeth shifted and moved, seemingly by themselves, but the bishop knew exactly what the dark forces were that were responsible for their movements.

Vincent reached up reflexively to feel the holes in his head as if he were reacting to a burn or a wound. "We are connected – those damned teeth and I!"

Bishop Phelan nodded. "Damned indeed!" He narrowed his eyes. "Such was the demon's intention when it bit you – to make a lasting connection. It knew of your fascination with cursed, haunted objects."

Vincent clutched his heart.

"It knew you'd keep them here in this very room, on your desk!" He shook his head and put his hand up before his friend. In a commanding tone, he shouted, "Vincent, you must...you must be rid of these things."

Vincent shook his head violently. "How? If I don't keep them here..."

"Can't you see the hold these things have on you? You think you're so clever keeping these things here, but it is *they* who are cleverly *keeping you!*"

Vincent folded his arms and stared at his friend. He knew he was right.

"If you can't stave off attacks right here in your own office, despite the number of times this room and its contents have been blessed, then *you* are at risk." The bishop walked over to his friend and held his shoulders. "Considerable risk!" Vincent looked away and down at the floor. "We must bless, burn and bury every object in this entire collection. You must be free of these things. I've warned you about this many times!"

Vincent nodded. He lit another bowl of incense. It filled the room within minutes. Then the shelves began to subtly vibrate. Vincent's eyes grew wider. Bishop Phelan opened his bible. A powerful wind blew inside the room and turned

the pages of the holy book. He fought to control them as
Vincent shut the windows and the doors. Bishop Phelan
shouted, "In the name of Jesus Christ..." A thin, black, ashen
cloud formed right before their eyes. The scent of decaying
flesh caused them to cover their noses and mouths. Several
of the objects on the wall unit shelves began spinning in
circles.

Bishop Phelan lunged forward and shouted, "In the
name and in the power of Jesus Christ, I command you dark
spirits to forever relinquish your hold on the objects within
this room!" Bishop Phelan showered the items on the
shelves and the shelves themselves with holy water. The
objects stopped spinning, but they vibrated ever so slightly.
"Depart from this place and never return! For this is the
House of the Lord. It is He who resides here and it is He
who commands you to leave!" He walked around the room
casting holy water upon every object lining every shelf and
table. "Our Father...who art in Heaven, hallowed be Thy
name..." The blackness remained. The stench of ash and
festering flesh hung in the air. Black forms moved out of the
cloud and began streaking about the room. One came
around a corner and flitted right toward Bishop Phelan. He
flicked holy water at it and it moved away into the opposite
corner. He cast holy water into the corner and the spirit
instantly shot up through the ceiling. "Thy kingdom come.
Thy will be done on earth as it is in heaven." Vincent
carried the smoking bowl of High Church incense in a
counterclockwise circle around the room. A sooty black
cloudy form moved out of his way and went through the
wall and vanished. "Give us this day our daily bread and
forgive us our trespasses – as we forgive those who trespass
against us." Both the bishop and Vincent prayed aloud, in
unison. "Lead us not into temptation...but deliver us from
evil." When they met, they turned and stood back to back.
Bishop Phelan cast holy water toward the four corners of
the room and upon the ceiling and down onto the floor. The

black mist slowly receded until nothing was left of it at all. "For Thine is kingdom and the power and the glory forever and ever! Amen." Both men took a deep breath and stood still, waiting in silence for close to a full minute.

Bishop Phelan studied his friend. "Vincent, I mean it!" Vincent looked at him. "Make preparations to dig a massive hole in the ground in your yard this spring. We will bless these cursed artifacts. We will baptize them in fire, and let the Lord and the earth transmute their remains. We will put an end to this once and for all. You *cannot* continue to take things from haunted locations and keep them here."

Vincent walked around to his desk. Bishop Phelan followed him, studying his every move. "We have a problem, Your Excellency!"

Bishop Phelan was sharp in his response. "What's that?"

Vincent pointed down at the jewelry box.

Bishop Phelan studied it.

Vincent pointed at the box three times.

"What is the problem?"

"The teeth!" He nodded and then shook his head from side to side repeatedly.

"What about them?"

"Teeth don't burn!"

Chapter 6 – Devastation

THE BLACK MERCEDES STATION WAGON turned slowly off Route 59, sliding and shifting in the slick falling snow and on the icy blacktop beneath it. Linda McLaughlin counter-steered and maneuvered the car back safely onto the road and accelerated slowly when the wheels regained their traction. She tousled her shoulder-length blond hair and purposefully avoided the intersection of Stepney Road and the Union Cemetery, which was the origin of all the supernatural terror that had engulfed her family in a maelstrom of malevolence just six weeks earlier – the likes of which she could never have possibly imagined if she hadn't witnessed it with her very own eyes.

Linda peered into the rear view mirror and sighed in relief when it appeared that her blond-haired six-year-old daughter Kelly was apparently oblivious to the fact that they were traveling so close to the infamous cemetery. "Thank you, Jesus." Linda said to herself.

Feeling that they were far enough away from the cemetery and safe from danger, Linda became lost in a daydream of sorts as she maneuvered her car through the meandering back roads toward home. Snow fell lazily from unseen heights and landed gently on the windows of the car as Kelly stared out of her window in awe. Then her eyes became as big around as saucers.

"Look, Mom!" Her gaze peered through the window at the wide world beyond.

Linda gasped and prayed silently that Kelly hadn't spotted yet another spectral visitor.

"What is it, Honey?" she replied with trepidation.

"Mom!"

"Please, dear God in Heaven..."

"Mom, it's a deer!"

Linda sighed in relief. She slowed the car to a crawl, and stopped to afford them both a good view. The innocent creature stood beside the trunk of a large pine tree, beneath the bending, thick snow-covered branches that must have served as its shelter. It turned and stared at them for several long moments with its big black eyes. Pale sunlight cast long shadows through the tree branches and speckled the ground before them. Linda smiled and said, "How beautiful. How very peaceful they are." A sudden chilling wind swept across the lake and caused the powdery snow to fall from the frosted pine needles above the deer. It began to collect on and partially conceal its sand-colored coat. Linda thought about all the precious moments she had spent with Kelly watching Bambi and Rudolf the Red-Nosed Reindeer cartoons. How her daughter adored all animals. She turned around and looked at her. They smiled brightly at each other. They could not help but be drawn back again to the deer, being given a window of opportunity to get a glimpse of nature. Connecting with it in this way brought a joy to Linda's heart, especially seeing little Kelly filled with such happiness.

Kelly examined the deer closely and said, "I hope it stays warm in all this snow and cold."

Linda countered, "Oh, I'm sure it'll be just fine with that winter coat, Honey. Montero loves it when Sarah takes him out in the snow, remember?" Kelly giggled when she thought about the time her big sister's horse galloped off into the snow with Sarah hanging on for dear life.

Linda shifted the car back into gear, and the deer

lurched and leaped out of sight into the woods as the car accelerated and moved away.

They drove down the road beneath snow-laden trees and frosted evergreens. Linda peered into the rear view mirror several times and admired her daughter. "Auntie Julie is bringing over a pot of homemade beef stew and fresh garlic bread for dinner."

Kelly smiled enthusiastically. "Yum!"

Linda grinned. "Doesn't that sound delicious?"

"Yes," Kelly agreed. She looked down into her lap and noticed a wrinkle in her plaid skirt. She huffed silently to herself while doing her best to try and rub it away. Then she looked up and said, "Because I'm hungrier than a hungry-hungry hippo!" Kelly giggled.

They meandered through the back roads on their way home. Linda wasn't expecting her best friend Julie Marsh until after they had arrived, even if they had slowed to a crawl, so she was careful to take her time getting home safe and sound in the inclement weather.

When they finally arrived home, Linda stopped the car just inside the driveway and shifted into park. Kelly tapped her feet against the back of the passenger seat and watched her mother from the warm confines of the car.

"What are you doing, Mom?"

"I'm just getting the mail, Honey." Linda got out, collected the mail, climbed back inside and closed the door. She briefly sorted through the envelopes and held up a green envelope. "Grandma and Grandpa Tanner sent us a Christmas card. Would you like to open it?" Kelly hopped up and down with excitement. Linda reached around and handed it to her and set the rest of the mail beside her. Kelly stuck her tongue out as she dug her finger under the paper flap on the back side of the envelope, while Linda maneuvered the car down the driveway. She touched a button on the remote control affixed to her visor and the garage door opened slowly. The light inside the garage came on, and Linda pulled the car inside just as Kelly flicked open the envelope and pulled out the card. Kelly gasped and said, "Pretty!" She smiled and turned the card around for her mother to see. It was a snowman surrounded by snowflakes and both had a good deal of glitter.

"Oh, isn't that just darling?" Linda turned off the car, got out, went around to the side and opened the door for Kelly. She extended her hand. Kelly took it and hopped out of the car.

"Let's put the red ribbons we bought on the lamp post," Linda suggested.

"Okay, Mom."

Linda closed the door and they walked around to the back of the car and opened up the back latch. The door swung open; inside the cargo compartment sat a bright white box. Kelly pulled it back toward them and opened the lid. Inside was a glittering red oversized bow.

"Take it out and bring it with you. I'll bring the wire to affix it with."

Kelly nodded. She always loved to help out, no matter what needed to be done. She felt very useful.

Linda closed the back door and they walked together down the driveway toward the black painted lamp post. Kelly held up the ribbon and Linda wrapped the wire around it several times and looped it under and around two screws. She gently pried the ribbon from Kelly's hands and affixed it to the lamp post at last. Kelly clapped her hands excitedly and said, "It looks pretty, Mom." Linda held her own chin, stepped back a few paces and scrutinized its positioning. Then she smiled and reached out for her daughter's hand. They heard the sounds of the approaching vehicle. Kelly turned and gazed down the road at the headlights growing closer.

They walked hand in hand down the driveway and then up the walkway toward the front door of their house. A

sharp wind blew their blond hair in their eyes, so they
paused briefly. Kelly moved her hair away from her eyes.
She looked up at her mother and tugged on her fingers. "I
feel really bad for Auntie Julie, Mom!"

Linda rolled that statement around in her mind, trying
to make sense out of what she had just heard. She looked
down at her daughter in confusion, studied her intently, and
begged, "Why would you say that, Honey?"

Kelly lost all expression in her face as if all the muscles
that normally animated her bright and cheery expressions
suddenly went limp. She answered her mother's question
quickly, full of certainty, and said, "Because she's going to
get hurted!"

Linda gasped as the minivan slowed as it approached
the driveway. "Honey, don't say that!"

Kelly slowly turned toward the road and continued,
"Really, really bad!"

Time slowed to a standstill. Linda couldn't believe her
ears. She felt as if she were being pulled into a vacant space
in another plane of existence altogether – where everything
was gray and lifeless. She had a sense of what was going on,
but she felt it was as if she were watching a movie, and she
was in a strange landscape where real things were shadows,
and ominous misty forms hovered in suffocating silence
where none had been visible to her before. She heard the
sounds of her friend's minivan, but she also heard the
sounds of something else, something much larger approaching.

Shrieks filled the stale air of the phantasmal landscape.
They sounded like the cacophonous calls of steam engines
on the railroads of yesteryear. The sounds were the
approaching truck's air brakes vainly attempting to slow it,
and the sounds of the tires fighting the elements for control
on the snow-littered road. Then she heard what she knew
was coming – a thunderous crash. It was all surreal, like the
disjointed, time-distorted images of a fantastical dream that

we try so hard to make sense of when we are prisoners lost inside it. Linda felt a weight in the pit of her stomach. She fought, with all her will, to turn around to see what had happened, but she knew exactly what it was. A scream belched forth from deep inside her. But it, like everything else she tried to think of, or do, was mysteriously delayed by some invisible, indescribable force. Linda's scream slowly echoed throughout the harsh, brittle winter landscape. Julie's minivan was rent, crumpled and pulverized before her eyes – struck from behind by a large white, unmarked delivery truck. Linda watched in horror as Julie's driver's side door collided with the large boulders lining the property. She watched in slow motion as the glass from the rear windows cracked and splintered and shot out into the air in all directions. Suddenly, without warning, the invisible force that had a hold of Linda diminished ever so slightly. She was then able to force an outcry. "No!" Linda screeched.

Linda touched the side of her daughter's face and said, "Wait right here!" She dropped Kelly's hand and scampered off toward the wall, toward her dear friend, probably gravely injured and most assuredly in great pain. Linda approached the driver's side door but the van was flush against the stone wall. She could not reach it. She climbed on top of the wall to get close to the door. It was slippery and wet. Her hands stung on the icy-cold, smooth contours of the boulders. It did not matter. She could endure the pain long enough to peer inside. There was blood on the dashboard and Julie lay motionless, hunched over the steering wheel. Linda banged on the window frame with her palm. "Julie! Julie, are you all right?" She heard a hissing sound. Steam was rising from the damaged radiator as she maneuvered over the wall and walked around the front of the van. She looked toward the back and saw the delivery truck just sitting there in the road. Its radiator also belched steam; its emergency flashers were blinking, and its left headlight and grill were smashed in.

The delivery truck driver leaned out of his door with his CB Radio in his hand. He was obviously calling for help. He got out, leaped down into the road and hobbled over to Linda and said, "I...I can't believe it! I swear, I saw the van turn down the driveway, and one second later, it was right back in the middle of the road – as if it had never turned down the driveway at all." He wiped his bleeding nose with his hand and wiped the blood on his blue long-sleeved work jacket. "I can't explain it. Jeez, I'm so sorry."

Linda cursed their misfortune. Of all people in the cruel world, why Julie? Why did this have to happen to such a wonderful, kind, caring, loving woman? She wept for her friend. She turned her bloodshot eyes toward the driver and asked, "Did you call an ambulance?"

"Of course," the delivery man said. He examined his sleeve and the blood stain. "It's on the way!"

Linda then remembered her daughter whom she had left alone in the front yard. She looked over the wall and saw Kelly standing in the exact spot where Linda had left her. Kelly stared at her blankly. She looked away, and then back at her again. Something was off. Kelly hadn't moved at all. She remembered Kelly warning her about the accident – before it had even happened. Linda could feel pressure growing in intensity against the sides of her head, as if it were stuck within a vise. Then she sensed something. She wondered if it were Kelly staring at her at all – but something else that had control of her or that was influencing her.

Linda closed her eyes. She felt as if she were being pulled backward through a dark, empty tunnel. She felt as if her soul was drifting away from the world. In danger of blacking out, she leaned herself against the ice-cold stone wall. She drew a deep breath.

Moments later, she heard a car door slam and the

familiar sound of her husband's voice call out into the silent stillness. "What's happened? Who's hurt?" Matthew reached out and gently cupped her shoulder. Linda still felt dazed. "Honey, are you okay?" The last syllable echoed within her, as if it were a familiar part of a song, stuck on repeat, playing over and over in her mind. Linda was gone. Fading in and out of consciousness, she secretly begged for her husband to shake her out of her spell. In a haze, she saw him rush up to Julie's van. He pressed his hands against the twisted frame, bowed his head and closed his eyes in prayer. "Heavenly Father, please help us!"

Matthew hugged Linda, who leaned into the tender embrace. She nuzzled inside the soft fabrics of his coat. The distant call of the sirens forced Matthew to look in the direction of the delivery truck. His blue eyes looked like sapphires in the white, wintry landscape. His black hair shifted and moved in a sudden wind gust.

Less than a minute later, the fire trucks, police, and paramedics arrived. As soon as they got out of their vehicles, one of the paramedics came up and immediately wrapped Linda in a blanket and sat her back on the stone wall. Matthew waved another off, signaling that he was unharmed, and he instead pointed at the mauled caravan next to him. He made fists with his hands, gritted his teeth and walked over toward the delivery truck driver to question him along with the police officers.

A chilling wind swept up the back of Linda's neck and tousled her hair. Linda shuddered. It woke her from her spell. She turned and looked behind her. She saw Kelly still standing in the spot where she was left. She was staring right at her. Linda shook her head, still feeling foggy. All she could do was pull the edges of the blanket close around her neck.

A sudden crashing sound startled her. She looked in time to see that the firemen had broken open Julie's passenger door. Linda looked back again at her daughter.

She hadn't moved. She noticed that the paramedics had pulled her friend out of the van and laid her down on a gurney. They wrapped her neck in a brace and began calling out her vitals. Linda walked up and touched Julie's hand. Julie smiled. "Is everyone okay?" Julie asked. "Did I hit, or hurt someone? Oh, heavens!"

Linda shed a tear that rolled down her cheek. She bent over her friend and kissed her. "Julie Marsh!" She shook her head. "It's just like you to worry about everyone else, even when *you're* the one who has been hit...and hurt in a car accident." Linda rubbed Julie's hand and arm. "Are you in pain? Are you okay?" Julie nodded.

The sounds of the tow truck passing by and then stopping before the smashed minivan forced them all to look away momentarily. When the driver got out, a paramedic came over and began to wheel Julie away from the minivan. "Ma'am, we need to check her out thoroughly, and we need to get the damaged vehicle off the road and out of the way." Linda nodded.

The paramedics lifted the gurney into the back of the ambulance. A crisp breeze swept in and cut against Linda's face. She recoiled and pulled up the edge of her jacket to block out the wind. The flashing lights at the back of the ambulance forced her into a daze.

Moments later, the sounds of the back doors of the ambulance slamming shut startled her so badly, she jerked herself forward off the boulder she had been leaning against. Her hip was numb from the cold temperature of the stone. The driver walked around her and opened his door. Linda peeked inside the rear window at her best friend and waved. The heavy lurching sounds echoed throughout the immediate area as Julie's minivan was hoisted up on the metal tow bar. The sounds of rattling chains followed. It was all too much for her senses.

"I..." Linda exclaimed, as she grabbed hold of the ambulance driver's sleeve. He stopped and looked at her. "I have to go with her..." She nodded. She looked around her, at the scene of the accident and tried to make sense of it all. "...to the hospital, I mean. She has no one."

The ambulance driver nodded briefly, waved her over, opened the rear door, and called inside, "Plus one."

Linda rounded the corner and stared at the paramedics inside who were going about their usual protocol. One stared at her blankly and then held out his open hand toward her. Linda grabbed hold, and with the aid of the driver, she hopped up into the ambulance. Matthew raised his hand and made the "call me" gesture against the side of his face.

Once the doors were closed, Matthew looked through the glass and blew her a kiss. The tow truck pulled out and wrenched the crumpled minivan away from the boulders. The shrieking sounds of metal scraping against the stone caused him to cover his ears and duck away. Within moments, the ambulance and the police that followed it were gone and all the turmoil and commotion involved with the accident had finally come to an end.

Matthew felt relieved. He gathered his senses and looked all around him. The road was bare in both directions. A light snow had started to fall. When he looked up over the stone wall toward the front yard, his heart nearly burst through his chest.

Chapter 7 – Caught in the Web

KELLY WAS LYING MOTIONLESS ON HER SIDE IN THE SNOW. "Kelly," Matthew shrieked. He clawed at the boulders before him, choosing the more direct route over them, rather than around them to get to his daughter as quickly as possible. He withdrew his hands and held nothing but snow, ice, and the last brittle remains of several fallen leaves. He shouted out to her again, "Kelly!" He ran around the wall into the driveway, slipped at the edge of the driveway, but maintained his balance enough to continue sloshing through the snow and making his way across the lawn. When he reached her, he drove his knees into the snow and reached out for her. Kelly wasn't moving. He touched her gently and retracted his wrist. "What if she's hurt? She shouldn't be moved." He looked up and wished that the ambulance had turned around and was going to be passing by, but he knew that it had driven away. Panic set in.

Matthew looked down at his daughter tenderly and asked, "Honey, are you okay?" He gazed up at the sky and at the falling snow. He caressed her face, and stared at his precious daughter with tear-soaked eyes. "Kelly!" Kelly was wide-eyed and unresponsive as if her consciousness were in some faraway place.

As he knelt there in the snow, a blue car turned quickly into the driveway. Matthew ran toward the car as it pulled up close, beside the walkway. The look of concern on the occupants' faces spoke volumes, but Matthew knew they were unaware of what had transpired on the street just a few minutes earlier. Matthew rushed up to the car. Bishop Phelan shifted into park, turned off the ignition and got out quickly. Matthew moved away from the door, as Vincent climbed out of his seat.

"What's happened?" Vincent pleaded.

"It's Kelly!" Matthew started to explain. Vincent gasped and regarded the bishop. The look of concern grew ever more evident on the faces of both Vincent and Bishop Phelan.

Kelly shot her eyes open and sat up.

"Details please, Mr. McLaughlin," the bishop demanded.

"Julie's minivan was struck from behind and after the paramedics left, I found Kelly lying in the snow!" When he turned around he saw Kelly making her way to her feet.

Bishop Phelan looked over at Kelly and acknowledged that because she was moving, she seemed to be unharmed. He looked up the driveway. "A collision here, in front of your property?"

Matthew called out to him. "Yes!" Vincent and Bishop Phelan looked at each other. "My wife said that Kelly knew Julie was going to get hurt just seconds before the accident took place!"

Vincent squinted and walked right up the walkway toward her. She saw him and moved back several steps.

"Stay away from me," Kelly demanded. She snarled. Vincent gasped and froze in place.

Matthew recalled the story Linda had told them about what little Kelly, or whatever *that thing* was that was influencing her, did to Julie that one dark afternoon at the Friendly's restaurant. 'Would she, *could she* turn on and attack me, the same way she attacked her Auntie Julie?' he wondered. Matthew hurried over to her.

Rather than attack him, Kelly maneuvered herself to hide behind his legs. "Leave!"

"The demons are trying to use her to gain entry to the

house," he warned. "They're controlling her now!" Vincent knelt down and reached around Matthew's legs as Kelly shifted behind them to elude his grasp. He finally snatched her hand, tugged on her and dragged her out kicking and screaming before him. Matthew grimaced. Kelly snarled at him and growled. "Get away from me!" Then she thrust her palm forward and blasted Vincent back away from her as though he were a rag doll.

Vincent collapsed into the snow, flat on his back, a good five feet away. He groaned. Matthew couldn't believe his eyes. There was no way that his daughter was capable of such a feat.

"Keep him away from me, Daddy! I don't want to see them. I want to go up to my room and go to sleep." She looked up to her father and then, as though a switch had been turned off, her demeanor changed entirely until she appeared to be just as sweet as she had ever been. She smiled lovingly at him. "I feel better now, Daddy. Really." Kelly tugged at her father's coat. "I'm all better." She fixed her gaze upon Vincent and put her hand before her gaping mouth. "Oh! I didn't mean to hurt the nice man."

Vincent lay in the snow. He stared at the pale sky in an effort to regain his senses. He finally sat up and looked at her. His pants were getting soaking wet, more so every second he remained there, so he twisted around, wedged his knee into the snow and pivoted to a crouching position. He shook the snow off his reddened palm and wiped it clean on his jacket. He stared at Kelly, or more accurately, what he knew to be a demonic spirit oppressing Kelly and her thoughts and actions. His eyes became narrowed slits. The instant he thought about reaching into his collar for his crucifix, Kelly wailed and leaped upon him, clawing and hacking at him and digging her nails into his face.

"Kelly!" Matthew pleaded.

Her blond hair shook violently as she tore and pulled at

Vincent's flesh. Vicious growls belched from deep within her.

Then a hand came from nowhere, wielding a small silver crucifix. The hand pressed the holy symbol against Kelly's forehead. Her face tightened and twisted and the burning flesh sounded like bacon sizzling in a breakfast skillet.

"Release this girl in the name of Jesus of Nazareth!" Bishop Phelan wedged the crucifix in the center of his palm and pressed it firmly against Kelly's forehead, wrapping his large fingers around her face and skull and holding it there.

She...it...wailed in agony. "Release her now!" Bishop Phelan secured his other hand around his first and pressed against her forehead with all his might. Vincent ignored the pain from the stinging wounds and came from behind to help steady the bishop in the slippery snow and ice. The spirit affecting Kelly shook and rocked her body one moment and wailed and screamed the next. "Archangel Michael, Lord Jesus Christ, thank You for standing with us here and now..." Even with Vincent's help, his shoes slipped in the snow.

The demonic spirit wailed in opposition, "No!"

"Thank You..." Bishop Phelan continued, regaining his footing. "Thank You for coming to the aid of this precious child and for protecting her now in her most desperate hour."

Matthew grabbed his head. It was all happening again, but this time it was Kelly instead of him who was being seized. This was his precious, beautiful daughter. His stomach turned in knots. He could barely force himself to look at her. When he did, all he could see was Kelly's mouth hanging wide open, but that was not the worst of it. He saw her throat bulging like some mutant frog. And then the terrible voices bellowed from somewhere deep inside her, but they were not coming from her, they couldn't be, because her lips never moved, yet the words that came from the air all around his daughter seemed to split the sky with each terrible syllable, "Azhneagho Fianneshhta Kora Mon Gialestapha..."

"Silence! Silence, Satan! We rebuke you in the name of Jesus Christ!" the bishop countered. "Leave this family in peace, in the name of the One True Son of God, our Lord Jesus Christ!" Bishop Phelan strained to maintain his grasp on Kelly's forehead. He knew the crucifix was biting into the demon's soul, as surely as lightning would cut a tree in half with its blinding, brilliant light. Kelly's arms flailed about as the demon fighting to control her wailed in agony.

Vincent shouted, "Our Father, who art in Heaven, hallowed be Thy name..." Matthew joined in and they spoke the words in unison, "Thy kingdom come, Thy will be done on earth..."

Kelly's body bucked and kicked and squirmed, but try as she could, she could not break away from the crucifix that was sapping the demon's power and its resolve.

Bishop Phelan added his commanding tone to the multitude of voices, "As it is...in...Heaven!" He nodded, staring up into the cloud-covered sky. He found new strength in his extended arms that were struggling against the evil spirit. "Give us...this day our daily bread, and for-give us our trespasses, as we forgive those who trespass against us."

Kelly kicked out, flailing against anything she could connect with. Her hands dug into the frozen earth. She crushed snow and ice in her palms and flung it in random directions with each wild swipe of her arms.

"Lead us not into temptation, but...deliver us...from evil!"

Every muscle in Kelly's body shook violently as if she were going into a full seizure as they finished the prayer for her benefit.

"For Thine is the kingdom..." The bishop shouted to the

sky in a commanding tone, "and the power...and the glory forever...and ever!"

Kelly finally collapsed and went limp, surrendering her body down into the snow. Matthew looked on, terrified, wondering if the demonic spirit was playing tricks or if it had truly released its hold upon her. Bishop Phelan wiped away the sweat on his forehead with the sleeve of his jacket. He pulled the crucifix away from Kelly's forehead. There were no temporary burn marks, as he feared there might be, only subtle indentations in her flesh from the blunt edges of the holy symbol. She had not been fully possessed, but she had been dangerously close. Her eyes fluttered. The bishop turned around to Matthew and nodded at him, so he knew he could safely approach. He came rushing to Kelly's side, patting her face, her head and her body tenderly, trying to ascertain whether she was all right or not.

"The demon that was affecting her...is gone!"

Then she thrust open her eyes.

Bishop Phelan made the sign of the cross before Kelly and said, "Glory be to God!"

She appeared to be utterly dazed and confused. She sat right up and said, "I don't feel good." She pouted and started to cry.

"It's a natural reaction. When one is oppressed by the demonic, one has a considerably difficult time readjusting. The body can be severely traumatized," Bishop Phelan warned.

Kelly looked toward the front door and asked, "Where's Mommy?" Tears welled up in her eyes. Vincent pressed against the small of his back through his brown leather jacket. He had been battered too many times for his liking, all too recently. His muscles ached and burned, but he was far from any breaking point.

They all shifted their attention toward the road when

they heard the high performance engine screaming up the road, drawing nearer.

Chapter 8 – A Rainbow in the Dark

THEY ALL TURNED IN TIME TO SEE a turquoise Pontiac Trans Am fly into the driveway. It rolled down past the bishop's car and came to a screeching halt out of sight behind the garage. Vincent sighed, but Matthew hadn't a clue who had just driven in. A moment later, they heard the heavy, solid car door slam shut and then listened carefully to the clapping heels on the pavement as the unlikely visitor made its way around the back of the car and came into view.

Vincent smiled from ear to ear. "Yvonne," he called out.

"Yvonne?" Matthew added.

The sensitive, or "psychic" woman, who had been so instrumental in solving their plight a few short months earlier, hurriedly walked up the snow-frosted walkway, panting, "I got here as soon as I could!" She approached Vincent, pulled his arms away from his sides and gazed into his eyes. "You're okay?" She hugged him tight. "Oh, thank God! I had a terrible vision about you!" She wiped a tear from her eye.

Vincent nodded. "Your vision was spot on." She pressed her open palm against his cheek.

Yvonne shook her hands. "My mascara is going to run." She knelt before Kelly as her father held her and she studied her with her big brown eyes. She felt the sides of her face and raised a hand a few inches above the top of her head and held it there. She closed her eyes briefly and mouthed a few words. Matthew studied them both. Then she pulled her hand back and looked both to the right of Kelly and to her left as if she were examining the child, though not by looking directly at her. She held her hands out before her and, without touching her, traced the contours of her body, past her neck, her shoulders, arms and torso, down her legs, to her knees and ankles and finally to her feet. She held her open palms beneath Kelly's feet.

Matthew began, "Yvonne..."

Yvonne whipped her head around and gave him a wild, crazed look. "There's been a car accident!" She stood and looked over at the stone wall. She exhaled forcefully several times as if trying quickly to be rid of something within that caused her considerable discomfort. "Julie," she said. She lifted the edges of her dress with both hands and walked across the lawn toward the edge of the driveway. Her tall boots protected her from the snow and the cold. Matthew sat Kelly down on the porch and touched the top of her head, then followed Yvonne.

Bishop Phelan drew out his aspergillum. Without revealing his true intentions, he said, "I'm going to bless the house!" He raised it over the porch and cast it downward before the front door, splattering Kelly in the process as she sat on the porch. She flinched and moved her head away. Then he swung his arm from left to right, swiping it across her body. She winced and held her hands up, purely out of instinct, with no more severity than she would have if she had been hit by a passing fan of water from a lawn sprinkler. The bishop proceeded to walk around the house, swiping it with holy water every few feet. Vincent looked up at the second story windows and followed the bishop around the house.

When Yvonne arrived at the edge of the driveway, she turned around in circles. She then held her hands out and walked away down the middle of the road.

"Yvonne, that's dangerous," Matthew called out after her.

Her heels clapped along the pavement as her deter-mined footsteps carried her where her psychic senses told her that she needed to be. She turned around and shuffled her feet as fast as they could carry her without breaking into a run. Matthew stood there in the road with his hands inside his trench coat pockets.

Then she saw the pitch-black wolf stepping closer toward her from within the thicket of trees. Its padded feet had allowed it to creep silently toward her, unnoticed until now. Its red eyes glared at her with a hatred she hadn't felt since the demonic attack on Linda McLaughlin in her bedroom. She narrowed her eyes and stood defiantly before the wolf and shouted to it, "Away from me, dark spirit! You have no power here. I know who you are!" She started toward it. "I know *what* you are! Be gone!" The wolf growled, turned around and plodded away deeper into the thick treeline.

Yvonne rushed up to Matthew, grasped him by the biceps on each arm and stared into his eyes. "I saw the accident," she exclaimed. Matthew cocked his head slightly. She looked frightened. "I saw this collision in a vision that I had last night." She paused. "And I saw Vincent...and Kelly..."

"What? You saw something happening to Kelly?" he insisted.

She dropped her hands away from him and hurried off toward the house, stopping before the gigantic boulders where Julie's minivan had been pulverized. She gasped and covered her mouth. Matthew followed silently behind her. He didn't have Yvonne's senses or her gifts, so he was curious to learn what she was discerning.

Yvonne looked back toward the direction from which the delivery truck had come, before it struck Julie's van. She walked six steps just inside the driveway, turned around to face the street, reached inside her shirt and pulled out her amethyst pendant. She let it hang there against her chest.

Then she positioned her legs so they were shoulder-width apart. She reached inside her jacket pocket and pulled out a large chunk of black tourmaline, held it up before her, raised it above her head at arm's length and held it there. Then she lowered it slowly and set it down on the blacktop by the edge of the lawn. Matthew leaned in to examine the strange black stone. Its deep black, prismatic crystals were thick and columnar.

Yvonne backed away from the stone and studied it and the edge of the driveway beyond. Matthew backed away and stood beside her. He looked at Kelly, who was rocking back and forth on the edge of the porch.

"Yvonne," Matthew pleaded.

Yvonne held up her palm to silence him. She closed her eyes and moved her hand to meet her other hand so that her fingers and thumbs created the shape of a pyramid. She stood there in silence for several seconds and then sighed and dropped her hands.

She smiled at Matthew. "I'll explain in a few minutes, Matthew." She looked up at him and touched her palm against his cheek. "How are you feeling, Honey?" Her look was one of genuine compassion and concern.

"Fine!" He started toward the walkway and Yvonne followed. "It's Kelly that I'm concerned about."

"As you should be," Yvonne nodded. "As am I."

Matthew stopped dead in his tracks. She walked past him up the walkway and knelt before Kelly. Matthew followed and stood behind her and watched silently.

"Kelly?" she called out. Kelly's eyes fluttered. "Honey? Can you hear me?"

Vincent was following the bishop's footprints in the snow and walked around to the side of the house.

"Kelly?" Yvonne asked. "Honey?"

Kelly watched Vincent until she could no longer see him. Then she turned toward Yvonne. In a sweet voice, she finally answered, "Yes."

Yvonne batted her eyelashes. "How do you feel?"

She yawned and said, "I felt funny before, but now I'm just really, really sleepy."

"Oh, sweet girl. Everything's going to be all right."

Kelly smiled again, brightly.

As Yvonne shifted her weight, the amethyst necklace hanging from the silver chain rocked forward toward Kelly. Kelly smiled and reached out for it.

Yvonne knew she was admiring it and asked, "Do you like it?"

"Yes," Kelly said with a nod. "It's a pretty purple."

"It's a very special stone," Yvonne said, looking at her tenderly. "For very special people." She studied Kelly's eyes as she took hold of the stone and rubbed her thumb along its smooth facets. "Would you like one of your own?" Kelly's eyes lit up like sparkling sapphires as the day's last rays of sunlight beamed down upon her. She nodded and her hair shifted. "I brought one just for you," Yvonne smiled.

"You did?" she grinned. "For me?"

Bishop Phelan completed his circuit around the house and proceeded to shower Yvonne's car with holy water from his aspergillum. He then showered his own car. When Vincent had finished walking the perimeter, he joined the bishop in the driveway and conversed with him in private.

On the porch, Kelly looked up at her father who smiled warmly and asked, "What do we say when someone does something nice for us?"

Kelly began to mouth the words, but then waited until she was facing Yvonne directly, so that she could look her in the eyes. "I would like one very much. Thank you."

Yvonne reached into her pocket and pulled out a glittering, child-sized silver necklace. Kelly's jaw dropped when she saw the vibrant purple, single-terminated ame-thyst stone, wrapped in silver, slide down the chain and come to rest in the center as Yvonne held its ends in her fingers. Yvonne reached around Kelly's neck so that she could fasten it there. Kelly batted her eyelashes as Yvonne finally clasped it into place. When she leaned back, Yvonne studied her.

The sun was already passing its zenith, and was moving lower in the western sky. Yvonne turned her head so that she could regard Matthew. "Matthew, if you don't mind, I'd like to lay Kelly down in the living room so we can keep a watchful eye on her." Matthew nodded. "Then, after a little while, I'd like to walk through your house just so I can make sure everything is all right." He took Kelly by the hand, opened the front door and led her inside.

Yvonne put her hands inside the pockets of her loose-fitting black sweater and proceeded down the walkway toward her friends. She called out to them, "You have no idea how pleased I am that you're both all right."

Vincent called out loudly and proudly, "You saved my neck, Yvonne! There's no doubt about it. If you hadn't had the wherewithal to call the bishop, and if he hadn't come when he did, I'd have been in real trouble, or worse!"

Yvonne felt a slight bit of satisfaction, but Vincent was her friend, and she was rightly concerned for his safety. She knew how badly the first part of the McLaughlin case had affected him. She now identified it as the "first part," because they had all believed that the case had been permanently resolved back in October through their combined efforts. But as with every case, the underlying festering fear in the back of their minds was that somehow the demons would find a way to return. And now it seemed they had found just such a way to return – with a vengeance. She focused again on her stalwart friends waiting patiently by the bishop's car for what she was going to say next. She finally said, "I sense that the house is secure. I need to take a thorough walk through to make certain."

"We need to go see Julie," Vincent added. "If I'm right, this could be only the beginning and we need to act quickly." Vincent got in and closed his door. Bishop Phelan said, "You did a fine job calling me last night, Yvonne. Please continue trusting those instincts of yours. They are quite valuable." Bishop Phelan climbed into the car and closed the door.

Yvonne grimaced and waved them on. She never liked flattery.

The car backed out of the driveway and turned cautiously onto the main road. When they were safely on their way, Yvonne turned and walked back toward the front door.

Chapter 9 – Picking Up the Pieces

IN THE HOSPITAL EMERGENCY ROOM, the heartbeat monitors beeped with mechanical precision. Linda sat next to Julie's bed, staring tenderly at her friend. Then an elderly man with a cheerful smile rapped on the door with his knuckles and poked his head inside. He then walked into the room and checked the monitors. He leaned over Julie and examined her carefully. "Ms. Marsh? Can you hear me?" Julie's eyes fluttered. The doctor placed both hands on the sides of her neck brace. "Ms. Marsh, please don't move your neck. You've been in an automobile accident. You're in the hospital."

"Oh, heavens! Yes, I remember."

"I'm Doctor Phillips. Your friend, Linda, is here."

Julie smiled slightly and opened her eyes. She scanned the room as well as she could and a tear welled up in her eye.

"Are you in pain?"

"Yes, doctor. I hurt."

"Can you tell me how severe the pain is on a scale of one to ten, with ten being the most severe pain?"

"My forehead is pounding right now, so I would say that the pain is a ten." The doctor nodded and listened, concerned. "My neck is about an eight." She moaned. She looked at Linda and reached her left arm out for her hand. "I guess I'm not very tough – or at least my pain tolerance isn't very high."

The doctor nodded and said, "Well, you're aware and

present, so those are two good signs." A nurse came into the room and handed the doctor a clipboard. He said, "Let's increase her pain medication." He signed the clipboard and handed it back to the nurse. He looked back at Julie and said, "We're going to take you down for some X-rays and an MRI to make sure that you're okay." Linda looked worried. The doctor raised his hand and said, "It's just routine protocol. In my estimation, there is nothing to be concerned about."

Two orderlies came into the room and prepared to move Julie's gurney.

Linda kissed Julie on the forehead and said, "I'm right here with you, Julie!"

Julie smiled. "Thank you, Linda. You don't know how much that means to me."

Linda smiled lovingly at her friend and the orderlies rolled her away out the door. Linda sat back down in the chair, wrapped her hands together and lowered her head until her forehead was touching her fingers. She prayed hard and she prayed silently that the doctors would find nothing seriously wrong with Julie.

Thirty minutes later, Bishop Phelan and Vincent Decker walked into the hospital room and surprised Linda completely. She gasped and began to cry. She had no idea these two men had become aware of her friend's plight, or how they knew where to find her, and when she thought about it, she realized that the matter might be much more serious – spiritually – than she had realized. "Oh, Your Excellency!" She smiled affectionately at him. "Vincent!" They exchanged welcoming smiles. "How did you know to come?"

"Our dear psychic friend, Yvonne, is responsible for that. It's a long story, one we can discuss over a cup of hot tea or coffee." Linda sighed. Coffee sounded like the best thing in the world at the moment. She suddenly remembered how hungry and thirsty she was.

They walked together down to the cafeteria to discuss the particulars of the case, specifically about Kelly's precognition of the imminent accident and about Linda's time-warping experience she'd had on the lawn before, during, and after the collision.

They sat in the cafeteria for nearly an hour, discussing what had happened. When they finished their conversation, Bishop Phelan laid his hand on Linda's and told her, "I have a hunch why this is happening and I need to speak with Julie when she returns to the room." Linda nodded and collected her purse.

Inside the McLaughlin home, Yvonne laid Kelly down on the sofa and propped a pillow under her head. She took off her shawl, covered Kelly's upper body with it and tucked in the edges. She then knelt beside her and gently ran her fingers through the girl's hair. Kelly's eyes fluttered. She whispered to her, "Go to sleep, precious girl." She turned to regard Matthew as he sat down next to Kelly in the open space beside her and began massaging her feet over her white socks. Yvonne continued, "She's had quite a shock. She can use a good nap." Yvonne whispered to him, "I'd like to walk through your house to make sure everything's as it should be."

Matthew nodded. "Yes, of course. Please do, Yvonne." Matthew waited patiently with Kelly for several minutes until she finally drifted into a sound, restful sleep. Matthew leaned his head back against the wall. Then he lurched forward, realizing that he hadn't the time to nap himself. He said aloud, "I should start some dinner." He struggled to his feet and crept silently into the kitchen.

Yvonne reached inside her shirt and held her amethyst pendant. She stood first before Kelly, then she turned around slowly and walked up to the sliding glass door. Sensing nothing there, she walked a few steps and stood in the exact spot where she felt the inter-dimensional doorway used to be, the exact spot in which the three teenage boys had used the Ouija board. She knew that they never meant to summon demonic spirits into the house, but that is precisely what they did when they inadvertently opened the vortex allowing them entry. She closed her eyes and reached out with her feelings. Her eyes fluttered as she rubbed her thumb on her amethyst pendant. She felt nothing out of the ordinary. "Well...that's a relief." The doorway had been properly sealed. She opened her eyes and walked up the three small steps into the kitchen where Matthew was searching through the cupboards and cabinets for something to make for dinner.

Yvonne then looked behind Matthew, into Linda's art studio. She decided to walk through it, and continue through the formal dining room and back through the foyer before going upstairs, just to make absolutely certain. She passed wordlessly through the kitchen, opened the French glass doors into the art studio and stepped inside. She held out her hands and waited for a full minute. She felt no subtle temperature changes, or shifts in energy at all. She nodded. The house seemed to be sealed. She closed the French doors and walked through the dining room and back out into the foyer. She examined the doorway, and traced the outline with her eyes from the lowest corner of the left side against the floor, up to the top, over and across and down the right side all the way to the slate beneath her feet.

She found nothing out of the ordinary.

When they walked into the emergency room, Julie was resting soundly in the bed. The look of sheer joy radiated from her when she saw the bishop stride into the room and approach her with a wide grin. "Oh, Your Excellency, what a wonderful surprise!" He gazed down at her lovingly and made the sign of the cross before her. "In the name of the Father, the Son and the Holy Spirit, bless Thy servant Julie

Marsh and keep her safe." Julie closed her eyes and basked in the energy and sanctity of the bishop's prayers. "Julie, while you're resting and recovering, I'd like you to grant me access to your home and allow me to personally bless it, so as to make absolutely certain that the demonic spirits who caused so much trouble for us all a few months ago do not have any chance of entering your home. I want..." he smiled. "I *need* to make sure I've done everything in my power to protect you."

"Oh, my! I don't know what to say," Julie replied. "I'm honored." She intended to turn her head in an effort to find her purse, but then she reconsidered and asked her friend for help. "Linda, would you find my key chain inside my purse and hand it to His Excellency?" Linda nodded and quickly found it. She handed it to the bishop, who took it in his fist and smiled. He opened a glass vial of holy water, dabbed it on his right thumb and pressed it against Julie's forehead. She enjoyed the feeling and fluttered her eyelids. Then he made the sign of the cross. He reached over to Linda and did the same to her.

Linda hugged both men, one after the other. "Thank you, both of you!"

Back in the McLaughlin house, Yvonne stepped up onto the landing, wrapped her hand around the black wrought-iron railing and climbed the stairs to the second story. As she peered down the hallway, she was relieved to see all the doors open because she knew and understood that it allowed for the free flow of energy throughout. There was nothing that felt stagnating or suffocating to her at all, which is a common feeling that she gets in "haunted houses." But this house was no longer haunted. Her cohorts had made sure of that by performing two suffumigations in the house – Roman Catholic house-cleansing rituals which make the dwelling, any dwelling, inhospitable and incompatible with negative energy and negative spirits.

Yvonne walked first into Tyler's room on the left side of the hallway. She smiled. It was surprisingly neat and orderly compared to the rooms of most teenage boys that she knew. She felt a warmth inside and detected the subtle traces of Tyler's favorite cologne rather than any of the foul smells normally associated with demonic spirits.

She turned softly and entered Kelly's bedroom up and across the hallway. It was soft and pink and bright and cheery, just as any sweet girl's bedroom should be. Coloring books lay on the floor, one half open, the other closed and turned upside down. Several crayons were tucked into the creases of the open book and several others were lying beside the books on the carpet. She sat on the bed and looked around. Then she set her hands down into her lap, opened her palms and held them up. She closed her eyes.

Yvonne's eyes darted back and forth within her closed eyelids. She inhaled deeply and held her breath, reaching out for even the subtlest vibrations or sensations. She smiled and opened her eyes and looked up at the four corners of the ceiling. There were no black shapes, not even dark gray or even light gray. She exhaled in relief. There were no forms at all, despite her belief that we are immersed in a vast sea of oscillating vibrations and densities within dimensions and the fact that spirits are all around us for most every waking moment of our lives. She smiled to herself. She had always known this to be true, even as a little girl. She had always been gifted. She had always been able to see the essences or spirits of the people who once animated but who had shed their physical, three-dimensional bodies. She had to constantly remind herself, no matter how many times she tried to remember, that most other people did not have the second-sight as she did.

Yvonne looked at the corner of Kelly's bed by the pillow and studied the strange one-eared stuffed bunny lying flush against the wall as if it were waiting patiently for Kelly to come play with it. "Why a one-eared bunny?" she thought to herself. The McLaughlins could certainly afford a replacement, or any other toy that Kelly could desire. She reached out and shook the animal's arm. "Hello there!" Then she lovingly picked it up under each of its arms and held it before her. She easily felt Kelly's loving energy all over her stuffed friend. How she loved this bunny so. She plopped it down onto her lap and held its hands. There was nothing negative about this toy whatsoever. She set the bunny down where he had been resting and stood up.

She walked out into the hallway once more, and this time took a quick look into the bathroom. She didn't bother with the light. Sometimes she could see things better without any light at all. She looked into the shower and then studied the mirror which was the first impression she had received the first time she walked into the McLaughlin home back in October. She had known immediately that something terrible had just happened to Linda, something involving a mirror. The four foul words etched into the mirror by some invisible hand, a demonic hand to be sure, flashed in her mind. She dared not dwell on them or give them any more recognition than she had.

She peered into the eldest daughter's room. It was dark inside and Yvonne couldn't find a light switch. When Yvonne walked inside, she saw a looming shadow in the corner of the room. She gasped and stood there in the darkness, reaching out with her senses. It wasn't until the light from a passing car flashed inside, that Yvonne was able to see that the shadow in the corner was a giant six-foot-tall stuffed animal in the form of a giraffe. Yvonne chuckled to herself. The giraffe was so large that it brushed the ceiling with its orange mane.

She walked out and entered Linda and Matthew's bedroom at the end of the hallway. When she went inside, she froze. It was not due to anything she detected at present, but because she recalled the horrific activity she had personally witnessed in the room two months earlier. Chills ran up her spine when she remembered discerning the presence of pure diabolical evil there during her initial investigation. She reached out with her feelings again.

"What'chya doin?" came the shrill voice from behind her.

Yvonne screamed like a banshee and whirled around. Her panic-stricken eyes forced Tyler to cringe and back away.

"I'm sorry!" he pleaded. He placed his hands over his face to conceal his gaping mouth.

"Tyler!" Yvonne panted, trying her best to catch her breath and regain her composure. She steadied her breathing and sat down on the edge of the bed and held her heart. "Are you trying to frighten me to death?"

"I'm so sorry, you have no idea!" Tyler offered. They sat in uncomfortable silence for nearly two minutes as Yvonne's heartbeat returned to her normal rhythm.

Yvonne eventually chuckled to herself. "Sometimes I think I'm just getting too old for this."

Tyler narrowed his eyes. "You don't look *that* old."

Yvonne scoffed, "Thanks a lot."

Tyler smirked. "How old are you, anyway?"

Yvonne patted her curly hair. "How old do I look?"

Tyler eyed her, started to answer and then decided it was wiser to keep quiet.

"What?" she said. "Speak your mind!"

"I know better than to fall into that trap, thank you very much. No matter what I say, it's not going to end well..."

"Try me!" she chuckled.

Tyler huffed. He slapped his hands against the sides of his legs and belted it out, "Seventy-five?"

Yvonne leaped up and tried to slap him across the shoulder, but he laughed and scooted out of the room. He scampered away down the hall. "Seventy-five! Oh, you're gonna get it!" Yvonne snickered. She knew it was a good thing to shed some laughter into the room. Laughter was positive energy and it was good to fill the house with as much of that as possible.

After a few minutes, Tyler walked into the room again in some sweatpants and a loose-fitting T-shirt. "Anyway, you look like my Mom's age and she's forty-something. Does that make you feel better?"

"Yes, it does, thank you very much!" She sat back down and held her arms out toward him. He came up slowly and took her hands. "Tyler, Honey, has anyone experienced anything strange, you know, since October, after the funeral?"

Tyler shook his head. "No, not at all. Everything's been fine, thank God. I remember all the investigators telling us to not give anything any recognition at all, but honestly, there hasn't been anything to give any recognition to."

Yvonne nodded. "Well, that's a big relief."

"Why do you ask?" Tyler inquired. He then squinted and added, "And honestly, why are you here, come to think about it?" He thought that was a bit rude, and he wanted to qualify that last statement as best he could. "I mean...you're welcome of course, any time, but why are you here now in my mom's room?"

Yvonne studied him. He was a smart, brave young man. He liked to get into trouble at times with his friends, but generally speaking, he was a normal, good kid. "I just had... a feeling that I needed to come over here."

"What do you mean?" Tyler begged. "What feeling? When? How?"

"Last night in my kitchen," Yvonne replied. She made a disturbed face and told him, "I don't expect you to understand, and it would take too long to make you understand, but I get visions and when I do, they are always spot on."

"Well," Tyler continued, "what kinds of visions did you have?" He looked concerned.

"I'd best keep that to myself, because, as you already

know, recognition is one of the worst things we can give these sorts of things."

Tyler began to interrupt, but she knew exactly what his reply would be. "I know you're understandably curious, and rightfully so, but I feel it'd be better for everyone involved if I kept this to myself for a while. As I said, I always trust my own feelings."

Tyler huffed and turned away to walk out the door when Yvonne suddenly called out.

"And, Tyler..."

"Yeah?" he replied.

"The next time you think about approaching someone from behind when they're obviously deep in thought..."

Tyler smiled from ear to ear.

"Don't!" Yvonne chuckled.

"I won't. I promise," he offered. "I didn't mean to scare you, honestly I didn't."

He turned to walk away, then looked at her again. "Dad almost has dinner ready, which is the entire reason I came up here, honestly. Come on down when you're ready. It's nice to see you."

Yvonne gave him a smile. "Thank you. I'll be down in a moment."

Tyler walked away and disappeared down the stairs. Yvonne walked beside the nightstands next to the bed and felt the bed itself by holding her open palms over it as close to the center as she could reach. She put her hands on her hips and sighed in satisfaction. Then she checked the bathroom, and finally walked out of the bedroom, down the hallway and down the stairs.

When she entered the kitchen, Matthew was stirring a pot with a wooden spoon, and Kelly was coloring at the kitchen table. Yvonne smiled affectionately and patted Kelly's head. "Feeling better, Sweet Pea?" Kelly nodded and smiled at her.

"Hey, Dad! Where's Mom?" Tyler inquired.

Yvonne gave him an apologetic look. She had completely forgotten to tell him.

Matthew looked at his son and said, "Your mother is with Auntie Julie at the hospital."

Tyler gulped. "The hospital? Why?"

"Julie's minivan was struck from behind by a delivery truck right in front of our house this afternoon."

"Oh, God!"

"Your mother went with her in the ambulance to the hospital."

"Oh, man, that's terrible! Is she okay?" The look of concern was clearly evident on his face. He was quite fond of "Auntie Julie," as she was called – though she had no blood relation to the family at all.

"She didn't look badly injured," Matthew responded. "I think she'll be fine, but her van is definitely totaled." Deflated, Tyler sat in a chair next to Kelly. Matthew continued, "I'm making tomato soup and garlic grilled cheese for dinner."

"That sounds awesome. I'm starved and all, but honestly, I'm majorly bummed."

Kelly chimed in as she was coloring and said, "Auntie Julie was going to bring over her beef stew for dinner, but then she got hurted – really, really bad." Kelly began to color with more intensity. She studied her drawing and while her eyes were glued to the coloring book, she whispered matter-of-factly, "Just...like I said she would!"

Tyler whipped his head toward his little sister and asked, "Huh?"

Yvonne studied Kelly and then examined her drawing. She leaned over and inched closer to see what it was she was doodling. She narrowed her eyes and tried to make out the images. It appeared to be a group of children and was nothing to be concerned about. Kelly worked her crayon around and around in tight narrow circles.

Matthew took the pot off the stove and poured the

steaming soup into four ceramic bowls. "Tyler, would you help me, please?"

Tyler looked up and said, "Sure, Dad." He got up and walked over to the counter. Matthew handed him a platter of fresh golden grilled cheese sandwiches. "Man, these look great. I think you make better grilled cheese than Mom does."

Matthew chuckled. "I've been known to pull my own weight in the kitchen." He set the platter down onto the Lazy Susan and said, "Yvonne, please, you start."

Tyler placed two sets of two bowls of soup down on the table.

"Thank you, it smells delicious."

Kelly smiled at her brother, reached over for a sandwich and set it down on her plate. "Ouch!" she shouted. She dropped the sandwich. It flopped onto the edge of her plate and slid down onto the table. She stuck her fingers in her mouth and pouted.

Tyler grinned. "You always make the funniest faces, Kelly."

"They're still hot, Honey." Matthew said.

Yvonne retrieved Kelly's sandwich by wedging her fork beneath it, set it onto her plate and reached for Kelly's butter knife. It was then that she noticed the children Kelly had drawn and those circles she'd been coloring because the outside edge of her coloring book was sticking out underneath her dinner plate.

Yvonne held her breath. A twinge of energy shot up the back of her neck. In the place of normal eyes, she had drawn empty black orbits, dark voids absent of any color at all. Alarmed, she immediately looked up at Matthew. He was looking down into his bowl of soup. Then she regarded Tyler taking a bite of his sandwich. His eyes were rolling back into his head as though the sandwich was sheer ecstasy. Both were oblivious to what she had just seen in

Kelly's coloring book. She gulped, picked up the knife and cut Kelly's sandwich into quarters for her.

Before Yvonne had set the knife down, Kelly picked up one sandwich quarter and took a bite. She smiled and said, "Yum! That's good, Daddy!"

Tyler studied his sister, nodded and took another bite himself.

Matthew dipped a piece of his sandwich into his soup and soaked the corner. He pulled it out and held the dripping sandwich over his bowl.

Kelly giggled and called out, "Daddy, you don't dip grilled cheese in soup!"

Tyler regarded his little sister and chuckled. She always came up with the cutest things to say. Matthew cleared his throat and asked, "Oh, yeah? Who says so?"

Kelly shook her head and said, "It'll get soggy." She beamed when she emphasized the word "soggy."

Meanwhile, after Bishop Phelan and Vincent had left, Linda sat patiently in a chair next to the bed. The lights were dimmed low and she was just waiting for Julie to fall asleep. She wanted her friend to know that she was there for her. She knew that the McLaughlins were really the only type of "family" she had. She smiled at her affectionately. Once Julie had finally drifted away into realms of silent stillness, Linda looked at her watch, frowned, collected her things, tip-toed around the bed, opened the door and closed it silently behind her.

The activity in the hallway was minimal, as she'd expected it would be at nine o'clock in the evening. She walked up to the nurses' station and met a pair of young women there. "Excuse me, is there a phone I can use for a local call? I need to check in with my family."

Inside the McLaughlin home, the telephone rang. Tyler got up to answer it while Yvonne and Matthew collected their silverware. "I'll do the dishes, it's the least I can do to help out."

"Certainly not! You're our guest," Matthew countered.

Tyler held the receiver to his ear. "Hello? Oh, hi, Mom! What's up? I've heard about Aunt Julie, what's going on over there? Is she okay?" He paused for a moment, listening intently. "Yeah, Yvonne's here too. We just had dinner. Oh, okay, hang on." He held the phone out to his father. "Mom wants to talk to you, Dad."

Matthew set his plate on the counter and retrieved the phone from his son's hand. "Hello, Honey..." Everyone watched him intently. He looked at his watch and nodded. "Of course, I'll come get you." He listened carefully for another full minute and said, "See you shortly, Honey. Bye, bye."

He hung up the phone and handed it to Tyler who set it into place upon the cradle. He put his hands on his hips and addressed the others, "Julie should make a complete recovery." Yvonne sighed in relief. She smiled. "They're keeping her for observation, and I'm going to pick up your mother. When Julie's ready to come home from the hospital, we'll go get her and bring her home, or here, or wherever it is that we all feel it's best for her to be."

"She can stay in my room," Tyler offered. "I can sleep on the couch. It's no bother."

"That's magnanimous of you, Tyler."

"Well, she took us in when we had to stay at her house. I think it's only right to give her my room...if she needs to stay here, that is."

"Thank you, Son. Well, let's get these dishes washed and the kitchen cleaned up so your mother doesn't have to come home to a mess."

"Are you sure I can't help with the dishes?" Yvonne offered.

Tyler eased the two plates that Yvonne was holding out

of her hands and said gently, "Yvonne, you go relax. Guests don't do dishes. You've helped our family so much."

"That's right, Yvonne. We should be treating you like royalty. Please make yourself at home for as long as you like."

Kelly gasped and looked at Yvonne and asked, "Do you want to play Princess?"

Yvonne grinned and touched her cheek lovingly. "Aren't you the most precious thing?"

Matthew looked at Kelly and said, "It's almost bedtime, Kelly."

"We can play Princess another day, Sweetheart."

Kelly scooted off her chair and collected her coloring book. She sighed and said, "Okay."

Yvonne called out to the guys who were busy doing the dishes, "I really don't mind helping with the clean-up, honestly. I'd like to stay until Linda comes home so we can all have a little talk here together in the living room." Tyler studied her and rolled that last statement over in his mind.

As Linda waited for Matthew in the lobby, she reflected on her day. What began as a peaceful, beautiful morning and early afternoon communing with nature, turned into a tragedy, but she thanked God that her friend wasn't seriously injured. She recalled Kelly's shocking precognition and the disoriented feeling she experienced when the collision was about to take place. Then she recalled the panic she'd felt when she witnessed it all in slow motion. Linda trembled. She suddenly felt cold – chilled to the bone. The last time she had felt that, was when she was sitting alone in her art studio. She wanted no part in recollecting that awful experience. She shook it off and leaned against the wall.

When she saw Matthew's car pull up, Linda walked over to the huge glass doors. They parted with a great whoosh.

When she walked out to the car, Matthew was walking around the back and met her by the passenger door. He reached out for her and she snuggled into the soft leathers of his jacket. They held each other in silence for several moments, until Matthew backed away, opened her door, and motioned for her to climb inside. Linda got situated and Matthew closed the door snugly. Within moments, they were on their way home. Linda leaned back and enjoyed some much needed rest. The heated seats felt so warm against her back and legs. Matthew reached over and squeezed her hand. "Mm, this feels so good."

"Honey, I need to talk to you about Kelly."

Linda sighed. She couldn't even open her eyes, but she said, "Bishop Phelan and Vincent Decker told me all about it." She shook her head ever so slightly. "I just hope and pray that everything will be okay."

"You and me both! Yvonne is waiting for us to return so we can discuss things before she goes home for the evening. You get some rest and we'll talk about it when we get home."

"Just let me sleep for ten minutes, it's all I need."

"Okay, Honey." Matthew dimmed the interior dash and console lights, turned the heated seats knob up a notch and drove in silence until they arrived safely at home.

After they had pulled into the garage, Matthew turned off the car and unwound his seat belt. When he got out, the garage door slid shut and he walked around to Linda's door, opened it carefully, reached in and kissed her on the cheek. "We're home, Honey."

Linda opened her eyes slowly, inhaled deeply, took his hand and climbed out of the car. When he'd closed the door, the door to the kitchen opened and Tyler stood there waiting for them to enter. Walking in, Linda saw Yvonne Saxon sitting at the kitchen table. "Yvonne! Matt told me you'd be here. I'm so happy to see you!"

Yvonne stood and gave her a long, tender hug. "It's very nice to see you again, Linda."

Unblinking, Linda turned and scanned the living room. Tyler stood there with his hands in the pockets of his sweatpants. "How concerned should we be for Kelly?" she asked.

"She's all right now," Yvonne assured her.

"That means she wasn't fine before..."

"She's just fine, Linda. She's sleeping soundly. I just checked in on her. I walked through the house earlier just to make sure everything is as it should be. Aside from Tyler catching me off guard and scaring me half to death, everything went–"

Linda wheeled around and confronted her son. "You've got to be kidding me! You frightened this nice lady?"

Tyler rolled his eyes. "I didn't *intend* to scare her, Mom."

"You are unbelievable!"

Tyler snorted. "I just wanted to see what was going on, and I guess I approached her a little too quietly." He really hadn't meant to scare her.

Yvonne's nod confirmed his feelings. "It was innocent enough, honestly," she agreed. "There was no harm done. It wasn't his intention at all."

Linda swiveled the white plastic chair around and plopped down on it. She folded her coat over in her arms and exclaimed, "What bothers me the most is that Kelly said she knew that Auntie Julie would get hurt!"

"Yes, she admitted that very thing right here at this table," Yvonne continued. "She's gifted and she doesn't even know it."

"Gifted?" Tyler asked. He had always known his sister was special, but didn't quite know how to explain it in layman's terms.

"Yes," Yvonne continued. "She's psychically attuned.

That's why she so easily saw the spirit of Brock Manning in Union Cemetery."

Linda said, "Hmm!"

"Sure, you planted the idea in her head, but she already had the ability to see spirits, even without the suggestion to begin actively looking for a ghost, which of course is exactly what she did. That's also why she was able to see the demonic spirit masquerading as the black cat in her room when no one else did." Yvonne reached out for Linda's hand. "Can you tell me more about what happened this afternoon just before the accident?" Tyler took a seat and listened intently. His father followed suit.

Linda held her face in her palms. She drew a deep breath. "The entire scene as it unfolded there on the front lawn was just – *surreal*." She moved her hands away from her face, then propped her face up with her fingers while resting her elbows on her knees. "Kelly and I had just put up a wreath on the lamp post out in the front yard because we had a few minutes left before we were expecting Julie to arrive with dinner. As we were walking toward the front door, Kelly yanked on my fingers and told me that she was upset, sad – actually – that Auntie Julie was going to get hurt."

Tyler gasped. He sank down in his chair. Matthew shook his head.

"Then," Linda continued, "everything started to stretch out away from me, and I felt like I was sucked into another reality." Tyler shuddered. "It was totally bizarre. It's as if I knew instinctively that the crash was coming, just as Kelly did, but I was locked into slow motion." Yvonne studied her. "I wanted to help her, but it's like I was being prevented from doing so." Yvonne held her hand out for her. Linda took it and smiled briefly. Then she continued. "The crash was incredible. I mean, I heard it, not only in my ears, but in my head and in my very essence, like it reverberated throughout my entire body."

"Man, it just gets weirder and more insane," Tyler interjected.

Matthew batted his eyelids and waved Tyler off so he'd stop interrupting. Tyler took offense but wisely said nothing.

"Then, everything went back to normal, like whatever had a hold on me had decided to let go. I went right over to Julie's van to see if she was all right. Then all the lights and noises started to overwhelm me, and I just backed away into the stone wall. I felt like I was being taken away again to that strange place that I had sensed on the walkway with Kelly." She looked at Matthew and then at her son, neither of whom could do anything but stare at her helplessly. Their wordless shrugs could do nothing to comfort her. She looked at Yvonne, who smiled compassionately at her. Then her expression changed.

"I fear that the demonic spirits we fought off in October...have returned."

An uncomfortable silence descended and hovered in the kitchen like a stagnant fog. Finally, Linda spoke out. "How?" She covered her mouth with her hand. "We've experienced nothing at all out of the ordinary. No one has used a Ouija board or anything of that nature." She looked around at Tyler, and at Matthew. "Right?" she encouraged them. Tyler and Matthew both nodded.

"As I told you, I walked through your entire house, and I have sensed nothing at all out of the ordinary, anywhere."

"Well..." Linda added, "That's a relief."

"Well, what should we do?" Matthew asked.

"Stay on guard. Keep notes," Yvonne replied. "Do not give anything any recognition, but stay vigilant and keep one another informed." She cleared her throat. "I truly believe that your house is secure. It's been properly blessed and cleansed and it is off limits to the spirits. You should be perfectly safe here."

"Thank God," Tyler interjected.

"*Thank God*, indeed!" Yvonne said. "You're all protected. Linda, I gave Kelly an amethyst necklace just like mine to further protect her from negative spirits. Amethysts help deflect negativity. As I have said, she is very sensitive. She can definitely use an added level of protection and it's important that you watch her carefully. She is definitely the weakest link in the family unit because of that sensitivity and the demons always go after the weakest, most vulnerable person possible."

"Cowards!" Matthew exclaimed.

"Matt!" Linda protested. She couldn't believe her ears.

Yvonne pursed her lips and exhaled heavily. "Matthew, you *really* must choose your words more carefully, especially with regard to what happened to you the last time you issued such powerful statements." They all knew that the last time Matthew had challenged the demonic spirits, they viciously attacked him, wore down his defenses and seized control of his body.

"I don't care," Matthew replied. "What kind of cowards go after a little girl?"

"Spirits who don't care about what you think of them at all. Spirits who would take advantage of any opportunity to come after you personally and punish you for your victory over them," Yvonne said. Matthew was looking off into the corner. Then Yvonne shouted, "Do you hear me? That's who!"

Matthew was stunned that she could have lashed out at him as she did. He thought that the time she had spent with the family meant that they had formed a special bond. He was wrong, apparently.

"You cannot – *ever* – say things like that, for your own sake, for the sake of your little girl, and for the safety and well-being of your family and their friends."

Linda grabbed at her husband, fumbling with his hands and fingers. "Matt, please don't go down that path again, please, Honey, you mustn't!" She squeezed his shoulders tightly.

Yvonne stood and put on her coat. "I'd best be going. It's getting late and I've got a thirty-minute drive. She hugged Linda. "Call me if anything happens. I'm just a phone call away."

Tyler's eyes grew wide and he asked, "It's cold out. Would you like me to warm up your car for you?" He loved sports cars and he thought it a great opportunity to slip behind the wheel.

Yvonne handed Tyler the keys. "That would be very nice, young man. Thank you."

Tyler snatched the keys and disappeared down the foyer in a flash. He put on his shoes and went right out the door.

Yvonne reached out and held Matthew's hands. They all heard the high-performance engine revving outside. She squeezed his hands. "I'd like to come back tomorrow to check on Kelly and to talk with Julie if she feels up to it. I just want to make sure she's safe."

Tyler came back and took off his shoes. Then he slid down the foyer into the kitchen smiling victoriously as if he'd accomplished a great feat.

Matthew said, "Sure, whatever you think is best. I apologize for reacting the way I did. It's a father's instinct to protect his children."

Yvonne smiled and said, "It certainly is. Just be more careful." She squeezed Tyler's chin.

Matthew continued, "I know what happened the last time I challenged them and the very last thing I would ever want to do is call that horror we've all experienced back into our lives."

"Jesus spare us!" Linda agreed.

Yvonne smiled. "I'd best be on my way."

Matthew led her down the hallway into the foyer, opened the door and held it for her.

He said, "Thank you for coming. You're welcome any time."

Yvonne nodded. "Good night." She smiled and walked outside. Matthew gently closed the door behind her. Outside on the landing, Yvonne carefully studied the yard before her. After a few moments, she walked down the sidewalk and stopped before her car. The engine vibrated oddly and gray smoke puffed out of the exhaust pipes and slowly billowed into the night sky.

The McLaughlin family went up to their rooms, confident that their house was indeed safe and protected. It was a most satisfying feeling to know that there was nowhere else they needed to escape to for their own safety and security. They all included Julie Marsh in their bedtime prayers and wished for her a complete and speedy recovery. As silvery moonlight shone down upon the house, they each drifted off to a sound restful sleep, prepared to face a new day.

The next morning, the family settled around the kitchen table for breakfast and quickly dived into the mountain of hot waffles Linda had set down in the center. Tyler looked over at his little sister while crunching the last bits of his third waffle. He swallowed and asked, "How are you feeling, Kelly?"

"Good," she replied, softly. She admired her amethyst necklace.

"Even so, Kelly's staying inside today, and I think we all know why!"

Matthew put his newspaper down and agreed whole-heartedly. "That's a good idea. If this house is safe, then there is no reason to go out where it isn't, until they figure out what's going on and how to put a stop to it."

Kelly whipped her head around and smiled. "You mean I don't have to go to school today?"

Tyler nodded. "Good plan!" He got up quickly, set his

plate in the dishwasher, kissed his mother and sister and said, "Well, unlike *some* people, I have to get to school. I wish I could stay home today, but I feel confident that I'm safe. Can I take the Benz?"

"Sure, Honey. I'm not going anywhere today." She reached over and pinched Kelly's cheek. Kelly smiled and pulled away. "I'm going to stay here and watch this cute girl and make sure she's safe."

"Great, thanks!" He walked into the foyer and put on his jacket and shoes. When he grabbed his book bag and started toward the door, he turned and said, "I'd like to go to the mall after school to pick up a few Christmas presents, if that's okay."

"Of course, Tyler. Have a nice day, Honey." She blew him a kiss.

Kelly turned to regard her brother. "Bye, Tyler!"

He stared at her for a moment, wondering if she was going to say anything else. When she looked away, he said, "Bye, everyone. See you tonight."

Chapter 10 – Humiliation

JIMMY AND TYLER SAT AT THEIR SCHOOL DESKS in history class exchanging smirks and giggles as they glanced at each other's notebooks. They both worked busily at makeshift sketches of their teacher – an elderly German man with a gray crew-cut and goatee, delivering his lesson through pursed, chapped lips. Tyler smiled as he admired his friend's sketch of Dr. Schroeder dressed in his black Nazi tank commander uniform perched high and proud in the turret of his King Tiger Heavy Tank. Tyler snickered and said, "Nice, Jim!"

Jimmy grinned and dug his pencil into the notebook. Then his pencil tip snapped off, ricocheted off the paper, flew one desk over, and struck the girl sitting in front of him in the back of the head. She reached back and touched her head out of pure reflex, but had no idea what had actually happened. Jimmy smiled widely at Tyler. He retrieved a second pencil out of his book bag and went busily to work on the sketch. Tyler watched him and then actually started to pay attention to the class. With his big blue eyes and his long chestnut-colored hair flopped down past his eyebrows, he studied Dr. Schroeder and jotted some notes down in his notebook.

Suddenly, Jimmy groaned. Tyler glanced over at his friend. He was wincing in obvious pain. Jimmy dropped his pencil on his desk. It rolled off the edge of the desk and struck the floor. Jimmy reached down, clutched and held his stomach, and moaned deeply. He dropped his forehead onto the desk. His hair spilled onto his notebook as he moaned and gritted his teeth.

Tyler frowned and called out, a little more loudly than he should have.

"You okay, Jim?" He definitely said it louder than he had intended to, because several students turned around and studied them. Jimmy bounced his head up and down on the desk, lightly, several times in succession. Each time, the muscles around his jaw and eyes were clenched tighter and tighter.

Dr. Schroeder stopped in mid-sentence, turned his attention away from the dry-erase board and looked over at the pair. Jimmy moaned and Tyler reached out for him. Tyler asked, "Jim?"

Jimmy didn't move his head as he forced a reply, "My stomach is in knots!"

Dr. Schroeder called out, "Mr. Reading, do you need to go see the nurse?"

He looked up. "Yes, Sir!" He shot a worried glance at Tyler.

The other students looked on.

Tyler didn't know what to do. He looked at his friend, in great pain, and then up at his teacher and asked, "Can I go with him, Dr. Schroeder?"

Dr. Schroeder exhaled heavily and replied, "No, Mr. McLaughlin. You may not."

Several of the other students looked at Tyler and snickered. One girl shook her head from side to side, and another simply rolled her eyes and looked away. A brutish jock wearing a red letterman's jacket with white sleeves scoffed and interjected, "Wanna hold your boyfriend's hand along the way?"

Tyler's eyes lit up like fire. The stupid jocks as a whole were juvenile thugs. He wrinkled his nose at him and hollered, "Shut up!"

A group of three other football players responded to the

challenge by turning slowly around and sizing up both Tyler and Jimmy.

"Morons," Tyler hollered.

One of them, the largest of them all, a blond with a series of gold pins on the front of his jacket, smirked at Tyler and winked at him.

Jimmy huffed, collected his things, stuck them inside his book bag, draped a single strap of his book bag over his shoulder, and walked out the door holding his stomach. He was either too preoccupied, or in too much pain to worry about closing the door properly. In either case, he closed it too softly for the latch to catch. No one seemed to notice.

As the excitement diminished and the class was returning to normal, Tyler turned the page in his notebook, and jotted down the date and time, and the information about the events that just transpired. He was sure it had nothing to do with ghosts or demons, but he recorded the events just as he was instructed to do – just in case.

Dr. Schroeder reached up to the dry-erase board and began to continue his lesson when the door unexpectedly slammed shut forcefully, startling everybody in the room, including him.

One of the jocks shouted, "Jesus!" forcing several of the other students to snicker. Dr. Schroeder walked briskly toward the door as they all looked on. He opened the door and peered out into the hallway. Tyler studied his teacher, who came back inside immediately, closed the door behind him, uncapped his dry-erase pen and walked to the front of the class, as Tyler went to work writing in his journal.

When class was over, Tyler trod silently through the crowded halls, lost in a trance. He didn't even regard the faces of the other students coming toward and passing by him. They were obscured, just as people are when caught inside the shadow of trees swaying in the winds of a turbulent, stormy afternoon. Then he heard some commotion behind him and suddenly felt the dull ache of a series of swinging fists bludgeoning him from behind in the ribs and back. He heard their voices as they beat him. It was the very same group of jocks who had made fun of his genuine concern for his friend, Jimmy.

"Faggot!"

Another knocked Tyler to the cold floor and kicked him. His books shot out of his hands and he turned his head around in disgust. Another confronted him by saying, "Miss your boyfriend?"

Tyler moaned. They beat him again and shoved his head inside his own locker. Then the class bell rang and the jocks ran off, laughing among themselves. Tyler turned around and leaned back against his locker. He held his ribs with one hand and pulled one of his books toward him, sliding it along the floor until he had it secured against his thigh. He hooked another book with one of his shoes and maneuvered it safely between his legs. He placed it on top of the other. He winced in pain when he tried to get up.

Whether he meant to or not as he passed by, another kid kicked the third book away with his foot. Realizing what he had done, he stopped, knelt, retrieved the book, turned and walked back toward Tyler in a gesture of kindness that Tyler did not expect in the least. Most kids, especially freshmen, usually ignored the scene altogether when one kid got into a fight, especially with jocks who had a nasty habit of going after anyone else who tried to intervene or interrupt. The boy looked genuinely concerned for Tyler – even though they had never met. He looked around to make sure no one was watching. Then he smiled quickly and briefly, handed the book to Tyler, waved at him, and ran away down the hall.

Tyler promised himself that if he ever spotted that kid again, he'd do his best to thank him for the rare kindness he'd shown him.

In the nurse's office, Jimmy sat on a chair and hunched

over himself, grimacing in pain. He had always disliked anything to do with medical services, specifically the smells of sanitizers and chemical concoctions that seemed to hang in the air after they were used. The nurse walked out of her office wearing the usual white stockings, shoes, skirt and lab coat. He stared at her white shoes and traced his eyes up her ankles, to her knees, and quickly up until he could see her pudgy face looking down at him suspiciously. That unsettled him.

He had heard the rumors, all of the students had. Apparently, the nurse never believed that *any* of the kids who came to her without obvious, gaping wounds on their bodies, or bloody noses, were really sick at all, but simply feigning it, so they could get a pass to leave school early for one reason or another, and always, of course, so they could go cause trouble someplace else.

Jimmy sometimes wondered if any of the adults in the school system, or in general, remembered that they were once teenagers themselves. Or, on second thought, perhaps they *did* remember, and clearly, so they were even more suspicious of the teens that they used to be. As much as he hurt, he found enough humor in the situation to chuckle to himself. Then, he regretted it, because he immediately winced and held his stomach. The nurse seemed to be a bit taken aback by his sudden painful outburst, so she waved him over toward her as she walked away briskly toward her office. When she saw that he had not moved, she huffed, set a fist against her hip, and beckoned him by saying, "Come with me, please."

Jimmy stood, still in severe pain, and walked into her office, through the door that she held open with her arm. "You have to watch the door. It closes on its own." She pointed toward the adjacent room, which Jimmy hastily walked into.

"Sit down, please," she asked – or more accurately – commanded.

"Yes, Ma'am," Jimmy replied.

Jimmy set his book bag down at his feet and did as he was told to do. The sound of the white sanitary paper crumpling beneath his blue jeans made him cringe. "More sanitation protocol," he said to himself. He groaned.

The nurse reached out with both hands and touched each side of his neck. Jimmy nearly leaped off the table. Her hands were as cold as ice. "Well, Jesus Christ!"

"I'm sorry," the woman replied. "It's winter, don't you know?" She talked as though she had a mouth full of mashed potatoes. Maybe something was wrong with her tongue, or she had a speech impediment, or maybe it had something to do with her ridiculously fat, swollen face.

"Why couldn't anything associated with the medical profession be at all comfortable?" Jimmy thought as he drew a deep breath and let the she-wraith continue to paralyze him with her icy fingers.

"Your glands aren't swollen," she said in a robotic, emotionless tone.

Jimmy licked his lips. He was parched. The nurse backed away. Her jaw hung down to her collar bones. "Stick out your tongue again..." she asked. She leaned in suspiciously and continued, "...fully for me, please."

Jimmy rolled his eyes and complied. Out came a pasty white, slithering, slime-coated skin flap, rather than anything that resembled a normal tongue. Jimmy didn't know it, of course, but that alone signaled a condition that warranted an early dismissal and, much to Jimmy's chagrin, a referral to a specialist.

Minutes later, the main door to the nurse's office opened, and Jimmy stepped out into the hallway with a white slip of paper held in his fist. He stopped and stood in place for a moment contemplating his situation. Then, the door slammed shut behind him. He was deflated, agitated.

"Great!"

Chapter 11 – Into the Fray

TYLER WAS LEAVING HISTORY CLASS that was let out a few minutes early, when out of the blue, one of the football players who regularly loved to taunt him plowed into him from the side and forced Tyler's shoulder into the locker. Students walked around and away from them, not wanting to get involved in any way or invite an attack on themselves.

Tyler sneered at him. "What the hell is wrong with you?"

The jock rushed up, grabbed Tyler's shirt in his fist, leaned in and practically spat all over Tyler's face as he shouted at him. "I'm so sick of you and your butt buddy sniveling in the back of class, giggling like a bunch of little girls."

Tyler tried to knock his hand away, but it wouldn't budge.

"Faggot!"

"Bite me, you stupid jock!"

"Yeah, you'd like that, wouldn't ya?"

Tyler snarled at him and said, "Yeah, I would!"

"I'm gonna beat you!" The jock shoved Tyler again, but Tyler resisted and stopped himself before he struck the locker. Tyler shoved the brute back as best he could to show him that he wasn't just going to take it. He couldn't stand him, or the others. They made school miserable for him and he genuinely loved his classes, when Jimmy wasn't distracting him.

Just then a teacher opened his classroom door to let his students out. He saw the conflict and approached them. The jock saw him, so he backed away, but he moved his finger across his throat implying that he intended to slice Tyler's throat open the first chance he got.

The teacher didn't know his name. Tyler wasn't at all popular in school. "Is everything all right, young man?"

Tyler winced. "Yes, Sir," he said. He looked at the floor and then up at the teacher. "It's nothing I can't deal with." He forced a false smile and walked off.

He saw the jock in the distance. He mouthed the words "You're dead!" to him one last time before he turned around and jogged off.

The chaos created with all of the students rushing to their lockers and then to catch the buses on time was unnerving. Tyler couldn't tell who was coming or going, and if any of the jocks were coming back for him. He parked his mom's car in the parking lot at the front of the school and that's where everyone, including the jocks, were headed. Tyler could do nothing but follow cautiously from a distance.

As they made their way down the hall, and he approached the main school entrance, one of the other students rushed up to him panting and said, "They're waiting for you by the buses. They're talking about kicking your ass to hell and back!" He gave him an apologetic look and said, "I just thought I should tell you is all."

"Thanks, man, seriously," Tyler said. He fidgeted with his books.

"I'd better go out the back by the basketball courts, cut through the woods and circle around to my car later when the coast is clear," he said to himself.

When he walked through the back door, a hulking football player said, "You're fucking dead," and took a lumbering swing, which Tyler easily ducked. A second wild hook missed, badly, and the crowd of teenagers circling around the outside of the gymnasium where the fight was taking place howled with laughter. He was set up. Tyler saw the sniveling kid who had lured him out exactly where the jocks were waiting for them grinning from ear to ear. Before Tyler could react, a third punch caught Tyler on the side of the jaw and he went flying to the pavement while the crowd howled.

"How do you like that, Fag Boy?" said the football player as he bent down and jeered at him.

Tyler grimaced in pain. Why he was convinced that Tyler was gay was really beyond any scope of reason, but the accusation was a staple in middle school and in high school, as an excuse to do just what the jock was doing to him – maul him – simply because he wanted to. It never mattered to the bullies if the accusations were true or not.

Tyler realized his vulnerability and quickly came to his senses. If the jock came in on him again, Tyler knew he was too vulnerable and too badly gouged up from falling onto the blacktop to mount any real defense. And, as anticipated, the brutish jock came in to kick him while he was down. But before he did, he had an opportune time to taunt him.

"You're used to being the submissive little butt-bitch, aren't you?"

Jimmy flew in from behind the jock out of nowhere and shoved him forward with his hands. The jock tripped over Tyler, though not without catching Tyler in the ribs with his foot, landing on his elbow and sliding along the pavement. The jock turned around as Tyler clutched his ribs. The jock seemed to be stunned. The event shocked and wowed the crowd as well, but when the jock shook it off and flexed his muscles, a cacophony of outbursts erupted. The crowd was thirsty for more.

Tyler scrambled to his feet. Jimmy grabbed him by the shoulders and asked, "Are you all right?"

"I thought you went home sick!" Tyler replied.

"Nah, I was waiting by your car and then heard what was going on."

"Good timing, buddy!"

The jock looked down at his red letterman jacket and stared at the gaping hole where the material at the elbow used to be. Then he examined his elbow, now a bloody mess. He turned and sneered at them. It didn't matter if there were two of them now. He obviously wanted a piece of them both.

"You two 'butt buddies' are dead!" He charged at them. Despite the fact that Tyler was faster and more nimble, the jock was about to connect with his chin, but Tyler turned perfectly with the blow so as to avoid any real damage. It glanced harmlessly off his cheek. A left hook, though, cracked Jimmy across the face, whipping his head to the side. Jimmy went reeling back into the crowd.

The jock then came right in after Tyler, who brought his hands up to block, but the football player's tremendous uppercut hit him in the gut with enough force to lift him up off the ground. He wrapped his arm around Tyler's neck, secured it with his other hand by wrapping it around his opposite wrist, and squeezed hard. Tyler gasped and fought to breathe, grabbing at his throat. He was furious. This was "dirty pool" as far he was concerned. The crowd that Jimmy had fallen into caught him and prevented him from crashing down onto the pavement. Jimmy realized the danger his friend was in, so he came in and landed a swift right hook directly on the jock's eye socket. He groaned and let go of Tyler so he could crouch low and protect his eye from further damage. Still angry about the choke hold, Tyler rushed right in against the bigger guy and pounded at his ribs repeatedly with his fists.

Out of nowhere, as in a professional wrestling show that the friends loved to emulate, a second jock, the one who had winked at Tyler in his history class, charged in, took Tyler by the shirt collar and dragged him down to his feet. The kid was solid muscle. He was blond, with brown menacing eyes, and he glared at Tyler with a look of pure disdain. He held him by the collar, clenched a threatening fist and held it above his face. Tyler heard Jimmy's outcries as he was beaten by the other jock. Just as the blond was about to lay into Tyler, he heard the commotion nearby.

"Stop it! Stop!"

It was Kyle. Even in the commotion and even with all the hollering classmates, he was sure of it. He heard his panicked shrieks and saw his black tennis sneakers to confirm that it was him. The blond jock kept looking down at Tyler and then away at Kyle. As far as he knew, the jocks never even had any problem with Kyle. They just had it in for himself and Jimmy, for reasons neither of them ever really understood.

Another teenager protested, or started to, for as he spoke, the jock moved toward him, and by the time he finished the thought, he was crouched over, covering up, and cowering.

The crowd of hooting and hollering teenagers intensified, believing that yet another participant had entered the testosterone-fueled ring of calamity. Jimmy and the first jock wrestled with each other on their feet, causing the other to misjudge his footing and fall into a more vulnerable position. The blond jock threatened to pummel Tyler any second.

Just then, the doors swung wide open and out came the teacher who had seen the incident with Tyler and the football player earlier in the hallway.

A girl that they didn't know called out from the crowd that was now quickly dispersing, "Just leave them alone, you dicks!"

"What did you say?" the jock roared.

"This ends now," the teacher hollered. Those three words forced a suffocating silence to descend over the entire crowd, which went dead silent in an instant. The jock holding Jimmy let him go and shoved him away. Sensing it was time to cease and desist, Jimmy stepped back cautiously, all the while staring at his friends.

The blond jock raised his fist higher, threatening to finally strike Tyler, and as expected, he stopped.

Kyle shouted at the jock, "Unhand my friend, you douche!"

The jock looked at Kyle, who was the skinniest of them all, yet he had the audacity to verbally challenge them. He sneered at him. "What did you say?" he demanded.

Kyle nodded and replied, "Yeah, you heard me. Leave him be!"

The blond jock winced in obvious pain. Kyle's words wounded the dim-witted jock.

"Another one of his boyfriends coming to his aid, huh?" He studied Kyle. "You a fag too?"

"You must really wish we were, because all I see you doing is using a fist fight as a way to touch Tyler and hold him like you're doing now!"

Tyler smirked. Whether he meant to or not, he knew what Kyle had said stunned the stupid jocks so badly that they didn't know what to do or how to react.

He sneered and let go of Tyler, who spun around and backed away out of reach. The jock shook his head, puffed out his chest.

Kyle shook his head up and down slowly. "Yeah, now can you please just leave my friends alone?" He took off his jacket and said, "If you are so hell bent on touching another boy, come on and get some of *me*, then! I know you'll like it."

The blond looked at his buddy. Neither of them knew what to do.

One of the students shouted at them, "Pick on someone your own size."

Another chimed in, shouting, "Yeah, you're so tough to pick on weaker kids!"

The jocks were totally dismayed. Their list of allies grew thin. They looked at Jimmy, who backed away and displayed his open palms before him, signaling that he wasn't interested in continuing the fight any longer. His opponent tugged at the lowest corners of his letterman jacket and then examined his bloody elbow. He pressed his lips together as a sign of rage and spat on the pavement.

Tyler patted Kyle on the shoulder and waved Jimmy over to them. He readily complied. The blond jock stared at the trio, but wisely said nothing, as a good portion of the crowd of students had turned against them and had huddled around the three friends. One girl reached out and laid her hand on Kyle's arm, offering her support and admiration for his bravery. Several others followed suit.

As they walked away down the hill in a group toward the parking lot, Tyler looked back to see what was happening behind them. The two jocks were conversing, and the only other student who stood by them was the one who had betrayed him. He was most likely a freshman, on the junior varsity team, who had stuck by them out of what was in all likelihood only a sheer sense of duty. The blond jock looked at Jimmy and then, defeated, looked away and punched the air before him.

"That was a brilliant save, Kyle," Jimmy offered.

"Yeah, sometimes you have to hit 'em where it hurts."

"Well," Jimmy said, "I like to hit 'em in the nuts, because that's where it really hurts."

"No doubt about that," Tyler grimaced. "Man, just thinking about it makes mine hurt."

Jimmy roared with laughter and wrapped his arms around his friends' shoulders as they stepped down off the grass onto the parking lot.

After they climbed into the car, Tyler said, "Well, I need to do some Christmas shopping. Are either of you warlords interested in accompanying me?" He started the car.

"Sounds fun, but honestly, my stomach still hurts pretty bad. I don't know if it's something I ate, or *someone* I ate..."

"You're such a sicko," Tyler scoffed.

Kyle shook his head. "It's most definitely not anyone you ate." He laughed. "I'd bet the house on that."

Jimmy reached up from the back seat and swatted Kyle in the side of the head.

"Stop it!" Kyle laughed. "Anyway, I have to watch my little sister when she comes home from school. I can't go, sorry."

Tyler drove down the hill and out toward the main road and said, "All right, suit yourselves. I'll have all the girls in the mall to myself..."

"Whatever, Tyler." Jimmy retorted. "Whatever..."

Chapter 12 – Confrontation
with Chaos

AFTER HE DROPPED OFF HIS FRIENDS, Tyler turned into the main entrance of the Trumbull Mall and rolled down the steep ramp. One of the things he had time to do when doodling in his notebook in history class was to compile a short list of Christmas presents he had in mind for his family, and he finally had a chance to go off on his own and get some shopping done.

Tyler loved the entire Christmas season. What kid didn't? He could recall every Christmas his family had spent together since he was six years old. To him, nothing smelled better than a fresh Scotch pine and hot cookies coming out of the oven. He loved the glittering lights, the shiny ornaments, the festive music, and of course – the mountains of presents under the tree. Tyler chuckled to himself, "Yes, it's definitely nice to have mountains of presents under the tree – that is for sure!"

The mall wasn't as packed as it usually was, but it was just shortly after school had let out, so he thought that he had timed his excursion perfectly. He pulled into the first open parking space, double-checked that he had his list, stuck it in his mouth, turned off the ignition and hopped out of the car. He studied the horizon with his deep blue eyes. The sky was clear, but it was windy and growing darker with each passing moment. He locked the doors, stuck the keys into his jeans, clutched the shopping list in his fist and started toward the entrance. He spotted the Salvation Army Santa Claus clanging a big brass bell, shouting the customary "Ho! Ho! Ho!" As Tyler approached him, he thought about what kind of job that was, and wondered how the guy could ring a bell like that for hours on end and still be full of glee in the process.

Tyler called out to him and said, "Merry Christmas." He fished into his pocket and pulled out a quarter. He didn't have much to give, he knew, but he felt better about himself when he felt like he contributed to those who were less fortunate than he was, no matter how small a token his contribution usually turned out to be.

Tyler yanked open the door and stepped into the mall lobby. Once inside, he was immediately immersed in a sea of Christmas cheer. The mall was decorated into a virtual Winter Wonderland. Ornaments hung from practically everywhere. Garland was draped around every railing. A Christmas tree adorned every hallway and festive music floated from every speaker. He smirked. He almost skipped down the long corridor toward the escalators that wound their way down into the food court. His stomach was growling, so he grabbed the black, ribbed handrail, and the instant his white sneakers plopped down upon the metal pad, he was on his way down. He thought about how easily the mall had always made him forget his problems. Then he laughed at himself and thought, "Of course, it does!" It was designed to help people wipe away their worries by spending every last penny. When he saw the people approaching him as they rode up the opposite side of the escalator, he laughed and said, "Shop till ya drop!"

Just as the tips of his sneakers were about to strike, he hopped off onto the main level of the food court and spun around in a circle trying to survey and select which restaurant attracted him the most. He'd always been partial to McDonald's, but the hot dogs and French fries smothered in melted cheddar cheese available at the Nathan's Famous

Restaurant were making his mouth water with just the thought. He went right up to the counter and eagerly placed his order. Then he thought about The Merritt Canteen and slapped his forehead, because he preferred their hot dogs and fries by far. "Oh well, too late!" he said aloud to himself.

When the cashier set Tyler's tray before him, he took it and sat down at one of the many open tables. He went over his shopping list as he chewed his food. Like any other hungry teenager, he had consumed every last morsel within a few short minutes. He chuckled to himself when he recalled the way his parents liked to call him "the bottom-less pit." He stood, dumped his trash into the can and set his tray on the ledge.

He walked down the long hallway past several stores that didn't interest him and went right into the computer store. He browsed through the latest games and video consoles, but realized that the only person in the family who would be interested in presents from this store was him, and quite honestly, he preferred books to video games any day. He loved to immerse himself in a good mystery or whodunnit.

After he exited and decided that he'd better get going, his eyes lit up when he saw the calendar kiosk in the center of the adjacent hallway. His mother always loved a vibrant, cheery calendar. She sometimes found inspiration for her paintings from them. Then he noticed the coloring calendars, too, and The Far Side cube-shaped tear-off black and white calendars as well, so this kiosk was a score for his mother and for both his sisters. He smiled as he sorted through them all until he found the perfect choices.

When he left the kiosk, he had his first Christmas purchases in hand. He looked up and saw a whole bunch of people coming down the escalator with smiling faces; he eagerly leaped on to discover what treasures awaited him up there. As he was ascending, he saw that his shoelace was untied. "Oh, great!" he said to himself. He remembered the macabre stories he had heard about what happened when people got their shoelaces caught in escalators. He didn't know if they were actually true accounts, but he decided it would be better if he didn't have to find out – the hard way. He knelt down and tied his shoelace in a double knot, just to be sure.

When he stood, Tyler's smile disappeared instantly. He dropped his white plastic bag; it landed on the escalator with a thud. His eyes narrowed to tiny slits as the bright glowing red letters came clearly into view. It was the Toy and Hobby Store where he and his friends had purchased the Ouija board. Tyler's jaw hung slack. When the tips of his sneakers struck the edge of the escalator, he nearly fell, but he righted himself, leaped off, moved away to the side and leaned back against the railing, which he clutched tightly with both hands. His knuckles were white, his fingers intertwined in the hand holes of the plastic bag.

Tyler watched two boys, no older than twelve, walk into the store with huge smiles on their faces. He followed them inside, curious to see what they were after or what they were interested in. When he glanced over at the check-out counter, he hoped to see the same red-haired teenage girl he had interacted with the last time he was in the store, when he had inquired about the sudden disappearance of the old woman he and his friends had seen.

The old woman had warned them not to buy the Ouija board and then she vanished without a trace while the guys were staring at each other, laughing. The redhead was not there. Instead, a man of Middle-Eastern descent, wearing a white button-down shirt and jeans, walked out of the back office and stood before the counter. Tyler moved away to avoid making any eye contact at all with the man.

Tyler strolled down the aisle of board games and saw precisely what he had expected to see. The boys were holding a Ouija board and pointing at the words printed on the back. Tyler felt a fire ignite in his core, winding up into his heart and into his throat. His eyes fluttered and for some reason, they began to tear up. He felt his hands begin to shake. The adrenaline was coursing through his veins. Tyler didn't know what had come over him, but before he knew what happened, he lunged over and ripped the box out of the boys' hands. Their faces revealed their astonishment and they seemed to be at a loss for words. Tyler's face was red. He crushed the edges of the box in his hands as he commanded, "Do yourselves and every person you love and care about a big fat fucking favor..." The boys stepped back and stared helplessly at him. "Put this horrible thing out of your mind completely and forever, so you can avoid the God-awful 'shit storm' that me, my friends and family are *still* going through, because we were stupid enough to buy and use one of these, like you two dip-shits are obviously planning to do."

The boys looked at each other, shrugged and said, "Okay." It didn't take much convincing at all. They turned around and walked right out of the store. When they got to the exit, they sprinted away down the hall.

Tyler sighed with relief and said to himself, "Well, that was easy!" He closed his eyes. The feeling of sparing two innocent kids from the horror he'd experienced was immensely fulfilling to him. After several moments, though, he opened his eyes and realized that he was still holding the Ouija board. He gasped and yanked his hands away, letting it fall to the red-carpeted floor below.

The manager peered around the corner and sneered at him. "If you damage my wares, you will have to pay for them, because no one else will!"

Tyler was on the verge of exploding. He felt his heart pounding. "No one should *ever* buy these horrific boards!" The manager was aghast. He disappeared back behind the wall. Seconds later, he came right around the corner and went up to Tyler, who could barely restrain himself from lashing out and striking the man. The look of disdain on his face was apparent, he knew, but he could not contain himself. "Do you know what a Ouija board, sold right here in this store in October, has unleashed into my house and how it has practically destroyed us and cost us everything?"

"Kid, what the hell are you talking about?"

"What the HELL is right!" Tyler held the box up before the astonished store manager and pointed at the image of the board. "You sell these here in your store to unsuspecting customers, kids mostly, who think it's nothing more than a game!"

"It is...just a game," the manager countered. "It's in the catalog."

"It's not just a game! Do some research, for shit's sake!"

The manager looked around him and at two customers who were standing there silently watching them both. Tyler saw the man's greed take hold of him when he saw the edges of his wispy moustache curl up and when he pointed at him threateningly. "You are frightening my customers and affecting my business."

Tyler scoffed at him. "They should be frightened!"

One lady took her child by the shoulders and steered him out the front entrance.

"You get out of here or I'll call the police!"

Tyler handed the man the Ouija board box, shoving it into his chest, and stormed out of the store.

Minutes later, when he had finally cooled off, he realized that he was powerless to stop other ordinary people from traveling the dark treacherous road he and his friends had taken. It was really up to them to gain the wisdom to choose not to play with the Ouija boards at all. Something could be done, he was sure. But at the time, he didn't quite understand how he could effect that change in awareness.

The wind whipped his hair away from his face, and his eyes began to water quickly from the invisible onslaught that he fought all the way to the car. He knew that weather in New England could change in an instant. He hopped into the car and shivered in the cold. After he inserted the key into the ignition, he looked up over the steering wheel. He shrieked. He leaned forward and blinked several times, believing that his eyes were playing tricks on him. For what he saw was the little old lady he had seen in the toy store two months earlier. The same wizened woman who had warned him and his friends against buying the Ouija board. The same woman who had vanished in an instant afterward. He couldn't believe his eyes, or his luck for that matter. She looked to be about fifty yards away, standing in the middle of the bare parking lot. It looked like she was staring right at him. Tyler started to get out of the car. When he pulled on the door handle and looked back up, she was gone again without a trace, as quickly as she had vanished in the store the last time. He grunted, pushed open the door and stood before it. Then he scooted around and ran toward the spot where she had been standing. He walked around in a complete circle and held his hands in the air.

"Where did you go?" he shouted.

Tyler looked around and put his hands on each side of his mouth to help project his voice even further. "I need to talk to you!" He squinted and looked off toward the edge of the vast parking lot. "Please!" All he heard in response was the whistling wind.

When Tyler turned around and started walking back to the car, he spotted a rock, so he whipped his leg back and kicked it with the tip of his shoe. It skipped into the air, struck the windshield of his station wagon, ricocheted off back down onto the pavement and tumbled away. Tyler slapped his hands against his thighs and cursed his luck. He walked up and traced his finger along the three-quarter inch crack in the glass. His heart sank. It'd be easily enough explained away, he was sure. He hated to lie to his own parents, but he knew he'd never hear the end of it if he told them the truth. Tyler shook his head in disbelief. "Just my freaking luck! You've gotta be freaking kidding me!"

He got back into the car, slammed the door and sank down into the seat. When he looked up at the glass again, his eyes narrowed. Was that really the same woman, or was it the demons playing tricks on him? He didn't even want to think of the demons, but he had to remember to trust his gut feelings and not the things registered with his eyes or ears. "Keep your head in the game, Tyler," he said to himself, borrowing one of his father's favorite phrases. He gritted his teeth and turned the key in the ignition.

Nothing happened.

Tyler gasped. "What the..." He turned the key back and then cranked it forward again. When nothing at all happened, he huffed and switched on the radio. He turned the knobs and was frustrated that the radio had no power at all. He whined and tried the headlights by flicking the switch on and off repeatedly. Then he checked the interior dome lights to see if maybe he had left them on by mistake.

He fumbled for the hood release. When he found it, he tugged on the lever and the hood popped open. He climbed out of the car, walked around the front, bent down and reached into the grill and opened the hood. He stared wide-eyed at the engine, his jaw hanging open in awe. Every single wire he saw had been disconnected, stripped and stood straight up in the air, wound up so tight that the copper was frayed and exposed as if they had all exploded. Even wider went his eyes when he saw the bubbling acid burning through the battery case and dripping down onto the engine. It crackled and fizzed wherever it collected.

"Son of a bitch," he shouted.

Out of nowhere, a hand slapped him across his shoulders and back. "What'chya got here, buddy?"

Tyler screeched and ducked away from the strange man.

"Need a jump?"

Tyler regarded the tall, bald man looking at him inquisitively with big smiling eyes. When the man turned his head slowly toward the car, the man leaped back at least two feet in shock. He regarded Tyler for an instant and then lunged under the hood for a closer look. He put his hands on the front of the car and stared slack-jawed at the engine compartment.

The man froze in place.

Tyler's world was collapsing, as was his mood. His hope that somehow he would be spared from the demonic retribution affecting the others seemed suddenly a cruel joke.

"What we have here," he said, emulating the man's initial query, "is a big ol' pile of '*You wouldn't believe me if I told you.*'" He laughed sadly.

The man reached in for one of the wires and Tyler shouted through his clenched teeth, "Don't do that!" He thought about the time in his kitchen when Sarah's boyfriend Bill was reaching out for the black goo spewing from the pipes under the kitchen sink, and how his friend Jimmy saved him from tragedy by protesting, grabbing his finger and yanking it away before he'd succeeded.

The man shot up in shock, smacked his head on the inside of the hood, stumbled back and struggled to maintain his balance. He reached up and touched the back of his head where he'd hit it, obviously checking for blood. When he was satisfied that he was uninjured, he looked over at Tyler. His eyes grew wide with terror. His lower lip quivered as he tried to muster the courage to speak.

Tyler's heart sank. He knew the man wasn't terrified about what he had just seen inside the engine compartment, no, but what he...*was seeing presently* behind him. He pointed over and above Tyler's shoulder.

Tyler froze. He suddenly realized the danger he was in. Out of the corner of his eye, he could see coagulating shadows, and a thin form that appeared like a wafting mist.

Tyler ground his teeth and tried hard to steady his breathing.

"Whatever you've done..." the man panted, "I want no part of it!" He turned around and ran away, screaming.

Anger swelled up inside Tyler. He shouted at the fleeing man, "You have no idea!"

He closed his eyes. It was then he heard them. Whispers rising and falling all around him, chanting in some obscure language long lost in the annals of history. The black shadow the man must have seen moved around the car and stood there in the vacant parking lot. Tyler didn't feel threatened, but he did feel his strength waning. "Blessed God," he shouted, "free me from the snares of the Devil!"

A deep solid tone took hold inside his ear and resonated in his left eardrum. The volume of the ambient noises all around him decreased with every beat of his panicked heart. Tyler called out again, "Hail Mary, full of Grace..." All he could hear were hollow sounds of nothingness.

Tyler gasped. He dropped to his knees which struck the pavement hard enough to cause him a good deal of pain. But it didn't matter. He wrapped his fingers together tightly and evoked the august presence of Jesus Christ before him, and then visualized the four Archangels manifesting all around him in blinding, shining white armor, brandishing glittering silver swords and ornate golden shields. He continued visualizing them swiping their swords beside his body and cutting away any darkness the demons were using against him. He began to hyperventilate and just when he thought he would lose everything, the tones and the sudden inexplicable deafness subsided.

Tyler felt as if a great weight had relinquished its hold on him and as it did so, it shot up and above him into the sky, and he heard what he could only describe as a sonic boom – perhaps signifying that the demons had left this dimension for yet another.

Tyler twisted around. He sat on the cold pavement and

leaned back against the car bumper. He wasn't physically attacked, but it was a confrontation to be sure. He blinked several tears away and whimpered, "Thank you, God Almighty!" He held his head and wept. He felt the icy grip of the pavement spreading through his backside. He sprang to his feet and rubbed his hands against his jeans in an effort to dispel the cold.

Tyler ran across the parking lot and reached the pay phone by the mall entrance. He dug into his pockets and pulled out only a crumpled chewing gum wrapper and a small piece of blue lint.

"Damn!" he shouted.

He snatched the receiver off the mount and pulled it up to his ear. The metal cords on the pay phones were never long enough and he cursed whoever designed them that way. Then he pressed the zero button and entered his family's seven-digit telephone number.

After a moment, a voice came on and said, "Operator."

"I'd like to place a collect call from Tyler, please."

"Thank you, please hold," replied the voice.

Tyler fought the cold and stomped his feet trying to get his blood moving. The chill in his buttocks and his legs from sitting on the ice-cold pavement hadn't quite yet been dispelled. The phone began to ring on the other end. "Finally!"

His sister answered, "Hello?"

"This is Northeastern Bell. I have a collect call from Tyler, will you accept?"

"Yes," Sarah answered.

"Thank you," replied the distant voice.

When they both heard the sound of the Operator disconnecting from the call, Sarah asked, "Tyler? Are you okay? This isn't like you, what's up?"

"Sarah! I'm at the Trumbull Mall. I need your help!"

"What's wrong?"

"You'd better put Dad on the phone. The car is totally messed up."

Sarah gasped. "You wrecked Mom's car?"

"No, I didn't," Tyler boomed. "The demons did!" He snorted.

"What do you mean?"

"Sarah, you'd have to see it to believe it. Will you *please* get Dad for me?"

"Dad went upstairs to lie down..." Sarah countered. "He's sick!"

Tyler paused, rolling that last sentence over and over again in his mind. He recalled the horrific chain of events that had led to the drastic decline in his father's health that ultimately led to his possession. Finally, he asked, "How sick?"

Sarah also paused. She too was pondering the unthinkable. "I don't think it's *that* kind of sick, meaning anything spirit-related, but he's not feeling good. He has a pretty bad headache."

"Well, what am I gonna do? The car won't run. I'm stranded!"

"I'll come get you, don't worry!"

"Good, that's good!" Tyler began shivering in the cold.

"Where are you exactly?" she asked.

Tyler fought another chilling breeze. "I'm parked by Circuit City."

"Wait for me inside the store. I'll be there in twenty minutes."

"Great! Thanks, Sarah!"

"See ya soon. Bye."

Tyler heard her disconnect. He hung up the phone and cupped his hand over his mouth. He shot three sharp breaths into it to try and warm it up, then stuck his hands inside his jeans and trudged back across the parking lot toward the car. He became more and more apprehensive as he drew nearer to it. His eyes darted back and forth as he scanned the area. He stopped and made the sign of the cross over his forehead and left and right shoulders and his breast. Once he reached the car, he pressed his palm down on the hood and slammed it shut. Then he opened the door, reached inside and retrieved his shopping bag and his keys. He closed the door and inserted the key. He looked over the roof of the car as night's full gloom fell upon the parking lot. He turned the key and expected to see the pneumatic door locks slide down into place.

Nothing happened.

"Well, I'm a dope," he said aloud to himself. "The battery is shot." He opened the door, leaned inside and pressed each door knob down with his index finger. Then he backed out and pushed his door closed. He tried the door handle. Satisfied that the car was secure, he started walking toward the bright red Circuit City sign and the welcoming warmth he knew was waiting for him inside.

He waited there against the glass until Sarah pulled up in front of the store almost exactly twenty minutes later as promised. Tyler walked over and climbed right in. Sarah gave him a quizzical look. "Well, the car doesn't even look damaged. What's happened?"

Tyler rubbed his forehead and said, "Sarah, you won't believe me until you see it with your own eyes."

Sarah scoffed at him and gave him a disappointed look. She didn't have to say a word.

Tyler extended his upward facing palm toward the windshield in the direction of the Mercedes and said, "Go ahead! Have a look, you'll see!"

Sarah pressed down on the accelerator and they navigated through the parking lot. Tyler said, "Aim the car so they're facing head to head, so we can see using the headlights." Sarah did as he suggested and she shifted the car into *Park*.

Tyler opened the station wagon door and popped the

hood. Sarah got out in her trench coat and stuck her hands in her pockets. Tyler walked around and stood before it. "Ready?" He opened it. Sarah gasped and whirled around toward her brother. Tyler held up his hands and just shook his head. "Explain *that* one!"

Sarah never even turned around. She just walked backward until she'd passed her door. Then she got into the car. She had lost all color in her face.

Tyler gave her a knowing glance. Sarah studied him from the confines of the car. A tear rolled down her cheek. When it appeared that Tyler had finished, he slammed the hood shut. Tyler locked the station wagon's doors again and stood there quietly.

When he got in, Sarah didn't waste time shifting the car into gear. She hit the gas and veered away from the disabled Mercedes as fast as she could. She drove up the steep hill of the mall exit. When she could contain herself no longer, she said angrily, "I thought the haunting was all taken care of!" She looked at Tyler as if it were her right to demand an explanation.

Tyler grunted and replied, "You and me both!" He sat on his freezing hands. He looked at his sister and said, "The dark spirits attacked me, Sarah!"

Sarah hit the brakes. Everything that was resting on the back seat that was not secured, flew off onto the floor. She looked at him with panicked eyes. "Were they the same..."

Tyler interrupted her. "How do I know? They all appear the same, don't they? I have to assume it's the same bunch as before..."

Tyler tried to be brave by offering Sarah a comforting smile, but tears were plainly welling up in his eyes. There seemed to be nothing that either of them could do about it, and to Tyler and his sister, that was the most troubling and terrifying aspect of all.

When they pulled into the garage, neither of them knew what to say or do. This was uncharted territory. The demons had only ever seemed to be interested in them, not their property. They both got out and walked inside. Tyler said, "We have to tell Mom and Dad!"

Sarah rolled her eyes and said, "Well, of course, we have to tell them, but we should wait until morning. There's nothing they can do tonight besides worry, and Dad isn't feeling good, so we shouldn't stress him out."

"Yeah, you're right." He grabbed Sarah's arm. "I'm pretty scared."

Sarah hugged him. "Me too."

"I'm just gonna go to bed early. Good night."

"Come get me if anything happens," she said.

"You know I will." Tyler went up into his room and closed his door.

The next morning, Sarah and Tyler were dressed for school and were seated around the kitchen table waiting for their father to come into the kitchen. When they heard his footsteps coming down the stairs, they gulped and waiting for the inevitable confrontation they both dreaded as much as they dreaded facing a demon.

Matthew shuffled into the kitchen and stopped in his tracks before his children.

"Hi, Daddy," Sarah said. She smiled at him.

Matthew eyed them both and put his hands on his hips. "Why do I have a bad feeling you're going to tell me something awful?"

"Oh, it's more than awful," Tyler said, nodding. "It's freaking *crazy*!"

"Are you feeling better today?" Sarah asked.

Matthew rubbed the bridge of his nose between his thumb and forefinger. "I'll tell you after you tell me what's wrong."

They heard a quick double-knock on the door and then Vincent walked in.

Tyler made a funny face and shot his hands in the air. "Thank God!"

Matthew looked over at him. Tyler addressed them both. "Are you two ready to see something freaking unbelievable?"

Matthew said, "It's all unbelievable, isn't it?"

Vincent cocked his head, which signaled that he was interested.

Tyler leaped to his feet. "This is gonna blow you away, c'mon."

Matthew huffed, put on his jacket and shoes and followed him outside into the driveway.

Tyler opened the front door of Vincent's car for his father and waited for him to get in. When he had done so, he closed the door and crawled in the back seat.

"If we're going anywhere," Matthew said, "The first place we need to go is a coffee shop. I don't do mornings without my caffeine."

"I second that motion," Vincent chuckled. "And I vote for Dunkin' Donuts."

After they got their coffee and breakfast sandwiches, Matthew asked, "So what's at the end of this mystery tour you're taking me on?"

"You'll see, Dad," Tyler said. "You'll have to see it to believe it."

Tyler blurted out the directions, turn by mysterious turn, until they reached the mall entrance and drove down the hill. They pulled in front of the Mercedes.

"Son, did you leave the car here last night?"

"I didn't really have any choice, Dad! You were asleep and not feeling well, so Sarah came and got me." They all got out of the car.

"What is it, a dead battery?" Matthew set his coffee cup down on the pavement.

"Worse!" Tyler said. "Wait until you see this one!" he grinned. Vincent raised his hands in the air as though he had no clue what was wrong.

Tyler opened the door and popped the hood, while Vincent and Matthew waited patiently. Tyler propped the hood open and Matthew stared at the engine compartment without saying a word.

"There *is* no battery," Tyler said. "It's melted to shit!"

Matthew regarded his son and then looked at Vincent. He didn't flinch. Tyler seemed to be in the habit of swear-ing, and he was old enough and used to doing it, so Matthew knew he'd be wasting his time by trying to ask him to tone it down. Swearing around his mother, though, is where Matthew would draw the line.

"You have got to be kidding me!" The battery had burned away to a molten pile of plastic. He reached in and poked at the wires. "Do you have an explanation, Vincent?"

Vincent shook his head from side to side. He took a sip of his coffee and said, "I've only seen or heard of this type of activity once before."

"My wife is going to be crushed! She loves this car!"

"*Loved*," Tyler corrected him. "Past tense." He shook his head and said, "This car is cooked!"

"How did this happen?" Matthew pleaded.

"I don't know!" Tyler replied. Matthew raised his arms in the air. "After I finished shopping, I came back to the car. I got in..." He glared at Vincent because he was sure he'd have the answer he was seeking. "I saw her..."

"Who?" his father begged. "Who did you see?"

"That woman!"

Vincent studied him. "What woman are you talking about?" He needed more information.

Tyler waved his hands in the air. "Okay, okay. Remem-ber when I told you about when Kyle, Jimmy and me were in the toy store about to buy the Ouija board?"

"Yes," Vincent said. "You didn't tell me first-hand, but I

watched the video recording of the preliminary investigation."

"Well, I saw her again after I finished shopping. She was standing back where that light pole is."

"You're sure it was the same woman?" Vincent asked, his eyes narrowing.

"Absolutely. There's no doubt in my mind," Tyler said excitedly. "She was even dressed the same. I got out of the car and when I looked up, she was gone without a trace. Poof!"

"And then what?" his father asked.

"I ran over to where she had been standing and called out to her."

"What did you say?" Vincent asked.

"I told her I wanted to speak to her." Tyler studied the ground. "But she didn't come back."

Tyler went through the events in his mind. Then he said, "I was mad, so I kicked a rock and it skipped off the pavement and hit the windshield and caused this crack." He pointed at it. He turned around and stuck his hands in his pockets. "I'm sorry."

His father snorted.

Vincent studied the engine compartment while Tyler continued. "I got in the car and thought I'd get out of here and go home. I turned the key and nothing happened."

"This isn't a natural occurrence," Matthew warned.

"No, it isn't," Vincent added.

"So now what do we do?"

"You're going to need to call a tow truck," Vincent said.

"It's a good thing we have AAA," Tyler added.

Tyler watched as his father dug into his wallet. After he slid the Emergency Roadside Service card out, he stormed off toward the payphone.

Vincent knelt and looked under the car. He noticed there wasn't a trace of battery acid on the pavement directly underneath it. He groaned as he supported his weight by holding onto the edge of the car to pull himself upright. He slid his hands together to wipe away any dirt and said, "This is very serious."

Chapter 13 – Seduction

JIMMY READING SPAT THE LAST REMNANTS of tooth-paste into his bathroom sink. He pulled a small paper cup from the dispenser attached to the wall, filled it with water and swished it around in his mouth. He admired himself in the mirror as he did so. He spat out the water and wiped his mouth with his wrist. Then he extended his arms before him, squeezed his hands together, and flexed his chest. He smiled. Then he squeezed his arms together to make his pectoral muscles bulge even more. He bent his arm at a ninety-degree angle and examined his perfectly rounded bicep. He studied his reflection in the mirror and said, "Yeah."

Jimmy flicked off the light switch and entered his bedroom. He was all alone in the house, but he closed and locked his door anyway. He opened his closet door, reached to the top shelf and pulled down a board game. He carried it to his bed, pulled off the top and set it down on the floor. He dug his index finger into one corner, pulled out the game board, and set it inside the box cover. Inside the box, he moved the game rule booklet away from a Penthouse Magazine and a tube of KY Lubricating Jelly. He smiled.

An hour spent in the privacy of his own bedroom doing what teenage boys do was the only logical thing to do, as far as he was concerned. Jimmy took off his jeans and underwear, carried the magazine and tube of lube over to his bed and climbed in. He opened the tube and squeezed gently until just a pearl-sized drop came out. He was careful not to squeeze out too much. A little bit of lube went a long way and he wanted to delay the embarrassing ordeal of having to go to the store to purchase a new tube as long as he possibly could. That was just about the most embarrassing thing ever.

He put the tube between his thighs to hold it upright so he could use his free hand to screw the odd-shaped white cap on, but then he decided against it, because he just might need more than he anticipated. It was going to be a long, fun night. He smiled to himself.

He set the tube down on the carpet beside his bed, scooted back against his pillows and lay down. He opened the magazine with his free hand and held it open, resting it on his chest. He reached behind the magazine and smeared the gooey lubricant onto himself and his eyes quickly rolled back into his head. He moaned in delight gazing at the perfect models on the pages of the magazine. He laid the magazine down in order to turn the page and admire himself, and then he held it up again so he could continue to fantasize about them. He squeezed and stroked himself slowly, enjoying every second.

Even though he found the women in the magazine extremely sexy, he closed his eyes and thought of Tyler's sister, Sarah. He visualized, in perfect detail, a secret midnight rendezvous with her, as he often did, and he imagined what her body must be like under her clothing. He lay there for several minutes, pleasuring himself.

Oddly enough, he heard his door open. Jimmy let the magazine fall flat onto his chest and he frantically tried to pull his clothes over his naked torso. To his amazement, Sarah McLaughlin walked into his room wearing her long coat.

Jimmy shook his head in disbelief.

She smiled at him seductively. He slapped himself on the cheek to determine whether he was dreaming, because this could not possibly be real.

Sarah turned the lock on Jimmy's door. He let the magazine fall away and close over on itself as it came to rest on the bed.

Jimmy couldn't believe his eyes. "How is this possible?" he thought.

Sarah unbuttoned her coat from the top and revealed her slender neck and her collar bones. Jimmy's jaw dropped. Sarah smiled. She walked toward the far end of his bed and opened all the buttons one by one. She licked her ruby red lips and asked, "Is this what you want, Jimmy?"

"Oh, my God, yes!" He threw aside the clothes he had bunched up and was using to cover himself. They landed on the floor. Jimmy felt his heartbeat intensify. He grabbed hold of himself. It was all he could do. He traced Sarah's eyes as they moved away from his own, down his neck and chest, down further to his abdomen, and down to undulating hips. Her eyes opened wider. He knew that she was impressed with what she saw. He looked at her perfect, beautifully round breasts. He studied her perky pink nipples and he knew that she was as turned on as he was. Sarah walked closer and slowly knelt on the carpet before the end of the bed.

"Oh, sweet God in Heaven!" Jimmy panted as she reached forward and wrapped her delicate fingers around his ankles. Her hands were warm and moist. They felt exactly as he'd imagined they would feel. She opened her mouth and licked her lips as she slid her hands slowly and forcefully up the front of his legs and the fine black hairs on his lower legs, over his knees and up inside his smooth inner thighs. She slid up and hovered over his waist.

Jimmy grinned from ear to ear. He had wanted her for years, since he first saw her really, and even though he was feeling like the lucky one, he didn't want to come off as being too easy, so he said, "Is this what you want, Sarah?" He pushed his throbbing erection toward her.

Sarah opened her mouth and smiled deviously. Her

chestnut-colored hair spilled down upon his abdomen and tickled his inner thighs as her head slowly descended upon him. He couldn't see her face, but he heard her moan in delight as she went down on him. Gentle slurping sounds echoed inside his mind – a teenage fantasy every boy hoped would come true.

"Oh, yeah," Jimmy moaned. He closed his eyes and savored every second of it. He'd been wanting this for as long as he could remember. He basked in her slurping and groaning, so he clutched the sheet on each side of his body, arched his back and moaned in pure delight. He was lost in a realm of unadulterated bliss where nothing else mattered but Sarah, his true love, his only desire – fulfilling his deepest fantasies just the way he'd imagined them being fulfilled.

Ten minutes into the rapturous encounter, Jimmy savored not just the feeling any longer, but the sounds of Sarah's satisfaction. She was definitely enjoying it as much as he was. He had always known, if given the chance to show her, that he was by far a better lover than her boyfriend, Bill. Sarah's moans and groans were all the confirmation that he needed.

As the encounter continued and the minutes passed, Sarah's moans became louder. They started to resemble growling noises rather than moans of delight. He smiled. He knew she was really getting into it. Then she emitted a deep, guttural growl, similar to the sound a large dog would make when chewing on a bone.

Jimmy frowned. With his eyes still closed, he reached one hand behind him to flex his bicep. He reached the other hand forward and touched her shoulder. Jimmy flinched. Her skin was ice cold, and it was...bumpy.

"*What the hell is wrong with this scenario?*" Jimmy thought.

A beastly growl issued forth that sent every tiny hair on

his sixteen-year-old body standing straight up on end. Jimmy shot his eyes open and looked at her.

What he saw was not Sarah at all – but a filthy, withered, wart-covered, ancient – hag. The matted black and gray hair on her head, where there was any hair at all, looked soiled and slippery wet in some places, and dried and brittle in others.

Jimmy gasped. Her shoulders were scabbed and festering

Jimmy tried to pull back the hand that had touched her, but it wouldn't budge. His every instinct was desperately to shove her off him, but he was paralyzed. Utterly paralyzed.

He focused on his breathing. At least his lungs were working. He inhaled so deeply, he thought they would burst. He couldn't move any other part of his body. Then she...*it*...stopped sucking. She paused.

Jimmy was frozen in terror. It was going to look him straight in the eyes. Any second. What was it waiting for, he wondered. He exhaled sharply. Then as expected, it shot its head up and stared into his soul with piercing, blood-red eyes. Ooze dribbled down from its warty, mole-covered lips.

Jimmy could barely move his eyes. He traced the thick, clear streams of phlegm oozing out of the corners of its mouth, down to his genitals.

Jimmy was aghast. He didn't even dare to look at his groin. He couldn't. He tried to move. He willed every muscle fiber in his body to fire, but he could not budge. He wanted to move as far away from the vile, repulsive creature as he possibly could. He focused his feelings down at his crotch. Even though he was full of revulsion, he could feel that he was still rock hard and throbbing as though it actually craved more from her.

Finally, he had the courage to look down at himself.

He cried out in horror.

His torso was covered in thick green and yellow bloody pus. It saturated his small patch of black pubic hair, filled his belly button and dripped down the sides of his hips and onto his sheets, soaking them. He began to hyperventilate.

He looked up. Her impossibly long, serpentine tongue slipped through her lips and hung down eight inches or so, well beneath her chin. Jimmy could not move away, but he could do the next best thing, so he looked up and stared at the ceiling. He felt his jaw muscles become free of whatever spell it was that was paralyzing him, so he inhaled as deeply as he could. He screamed in desperation.

When he looked up seconds later, he was astonished to see that the thing – that incredibly horrid thing – had dispersed in a cloud of black sooty smoke and then was completely gone without a trace.

Jimmy lay in his bed, violated, panting, and weeping. He looked down at his naked body. It was covered in foul, slippery slime. Jimmy bellowed, lunged toward his right side and rolled off his bed onto the floor. His knee landed on the tube of KY Jelly. The clear fluid shot out of the tube. What remained spilled continuously out onto the carpet. He could not care less about the mess on the carpet. When he made it to his knees, he looked down upon his body and screamed.

Jimmy walked into the bathroom in a daze. He couldn't bear to look at himself in the mirror. He slid open the glass shower door and turned on the water. As he stood there waiting for the water to heat up, he could do nothing but hang his head and weep. Seconds seemed like minutes. He thought of Sarah – the real Sarah. He'd fantasized about being with her more times than he could count and now he didn't know if he could ever look at her in the same way. He felt the slime drying and hardening on his naked flesh. It was tight and it caused a pinching sensation. It was revolting. This was not the way he'd imagined losing his virginity.

He closed his eyes and tried to force the image of the

hag out of his mind. He reached out again and found that the water was hot enough, so he stepped inside and slid the door shut. He leaned into the shower head and let the water soak his face. He moaned in delight. He imagined, he willed the water to wash away all traces of the filthy, evil scum that covered his body. He refused to touch it with his fingers. He was willing to wait as long as it took for the water alone to wash it away completely. He leaned forward and let the water soak the back of his neck.

He waited and waited, basking in the hot steam. He didn't want to think about or look at his abdomen, but after at least ten minutes, he still felt the uncomfortable pinching sensation on his skin, as if the scum was still there. The thought vexed him. He shook his head and said, "C'mon already!" He leaned back so the jets of hot water struck his navel directly. Then he backed away slightly so the water showered his groin.

There was no change whatsoever.

He gritted his teeth and quickly touched his abdomen. His finger stuck to the slime there for a second. He momentarily panicked, believing his finger would get permanently affixed to his body. The slimy residue felt hot and viscous.

"What the freaking Hell?" He shot his eyes open and looked down. He gasped.

He was still fully erect, but he never knew it, nor did he feel it. He wasn't stimulated in the least. Quite the opposite in fact. He was filled with revulsion and disgust about what had happened to him, and about the creature that had seduced him. All the slime was still there. It was still pooled into his navel and the overflow was still affixed to his left and right sides and down into his pubic hair. He wailed.

When he had caught his breath, he reached for a white washcloth. He snatched a bottle of shampoo from the hanging metal shelf beneath the shower head and squirted it all over the washcloth. Then he squirted the shampoo directly onto his chest and down his abdomen and down to his knees. He crushed the washcloth in his fist and pressed it against his flesh. He scrubbed his skin as hard as he could, back and forth in a frenzy. He yanked the rag away and studied it. When he saw the residue clinging to the cloth, he sighed in relief and said, "Thank God!"

He groaned as he scrubbed his thighs and groin and his abdomen and his chest. When he'd finished, he looked at the washcloth in disgust. He set it in the corner on the ledge and flicked the drain lever with his big toe and sealed it so that the water was now filling the tub, rather than flowing down the drain. As the water began to rise over his feet, he took another bottle of shampoo, squirted it all over himself and scrubbed for a full minute. Then he took a bottle of conditioner and lathered himself up with a hefty squirt into his palm. He took yet a third bottle and squirted it all around his legs into the water and swooshed it around with his foot. He set the bottle back into the rack and watched as the bubbles began to form.

Several minutes later, he turned off the faucet and slid down into the tub full of hot soapy water. He moaned, leaned his head back, and closed his eyes.

Before he knew it, he was drifting away into a realm of peace and stillness.

Then the image of the fetid hag blasted into his mind as if she had crawled in there like a burrowing insect. Her eyes were red, with reptilian irises and her flesh was rotting off her brittle, festering body. Her tongue shot out and flicked before him.

He opened his eyes.

She was not there, at least not physically, but her image seemed to be burning deeper into his mind.

Jimmy wailed.

He slid open the glass shower door and crawled out of the tub. He reached over and flipped the drain lever and saw a burned, clawed hand reaching up to snare his wrist.

Jimmy lunged backward and struck the sink cabinet

with the top of his back. He jammed his neck with a drawer knob. He heard a shuffling sound in the water of the bathtub as if something were wading furiously inside.

Jimmy panted and scrambled out of the bathroom on all fours, slamming his bedroom door behind him. He searched the room frantically for his clothes, snatched them in his arms and put them on as quickly as he could. Then he tugged open his door, ran down the hallway and ran out of his house as fast as his legs could carry him.

Chapter 14 – Coming Clean

TYLER WAS LYING DOWN ON HIS BED READING when he lifted his face from the pages and squinted his eyes. He wrinkled his nose and looked around him. He laid the book down on his bed and sat on the edge. Then he got up and went to his window. He leaned over and peered through the glass. It was as cold and white as death. The clouds rolled away against the light of a silver moon amidst a blanket of stars. He scanned the property from left to right.

"Humph," Tyler grumbled to himself. Seeing nothing, he turned away and then he froze.

A feeling of dread crept over him. He whipped back around and pressed his hands down on the window ledge. He scanned the yard again with his midnight-blue eyes. He could not believe what he saw approaching in the distance.

The black wolf leaped off the frosted, mossy boulders lining the property, stopped beside a tree, and studied him from beneath its brown scraggly branches. As it panted, small white puffs wafted out from wolf's gaping maw. Tyler was overcome with fear. He swallowed hard and backed away. He prayed silently to himself, and reached his trembling hand out toward the window shade. When he grabbed hold of it to pull it down, he looked outside. The wolf was gone. Tyler drew the shade anyway and sank down against the wall beneath the window. He ran his fingers through his hair, locked his hands together and prayed as hard as he could. "Not again! Please, God, spare us!"

The sudden sound of the doorbell forced Tyler away from the window. He leaped forward and landed face first on the carpet before his bedroom door. He trembled with fear. He could make out the feet under the edge of the door as they rushed down the hallway, obviously making their way downstairs to answer the door. He held his jaws clenched tightly together, agonizingly waiting for the next resonant clang of the doorbell. He knew that the evil had returned. It had revealed its presence in the form of the wolf just a few minutes earlier in order to taunt him, and now it was announcing its arrival – just as the spirits did that one fateful evening before Halloween. He wondered if this was going to be any different.

The doorbell rang again. He sank his head down until his forehead was resting on the carpet. He raised and lowered it three times, chanting, "Go away, go away, go away." Then he yanked his head up and opened his eyes. He dug his fingers into the carpet, leaped to his feet, tugged open the door and scampered down the hall to the landing. He paused, waited, listening...for anything, for everything. Then he clutched the black wrought-iron hand rail, squeezed tightly and raced down the stairs.

His mother and father were standing before the door, peering out the windows. The doorbell sounded five times in succession as if someone was pressing a finger against it over and over – desperate to get inside.

"Don't open it!" Tyler pleaded, as he leaped off the landing into the foyer.

Matthew turned his head toward him, wide-eyed with terror.

"Tyler! Help!" came the voice from outside.

Tyler grimaced. "That's Jimmy!"

"Oh, my God!" Linda cried out. "Yvonne was right!"

Matthew yanked open the door.

Jimmy Reading rushed forward and pressed his hands against the glass of the storm door in a panic.

Linda looked down the foyer and called out, "Yvonne! Come quick!"

Matthew opened the storm door and Jimmy stumbled inside. He reached out and wrapped his arms around both Linda and Matthew and hugged them tightly.

"What's wrong, Jim?" Tyler pleaded.

Yvonne came rushing down the hallway asking, "What happened? What's going on?"

Jimmy looked behind him. He swung the door shut and locked the deadbolt. He looked out the windows, panicked.

"What is it, Honey?" Linda begged him.

Jimmy leaned back against the door and whimpered. "I..." he looked down at the floor. Then he looked up at Tyler and then to the others. "I was attacked..."

"Where? How?" Matthew demanded.

Tears welled up in Jimmy's eyes and his lower lip trembled. "I was sexually attacked!"

"What?" Linda asked, horrified. She couldn't imagine what could have happened. Jimmy was like a member of the family; she felt at times that he was one of her own children. She was aghast.

Yvonne grimaced. She came in and touched his face. "Where, Honey? Tell me everything that happened, every last detail. It is all critically important."

Jimmy continued, "In my house! In my bedroom!"

"I was right!" Yvonne said. "I'm always right."

"Wow!" Tyler shouted.

"Yeah, wow!" Jimmy agreed.

Tyler wondered who or what could have sexually attacked his friend, anywhere in general, much less in his own house and in his own room. It was just too much to comprehend.

Yvonne took Jimmy by the hand and led him down the foyer, into the kitchen and down into the living room. She eased him down onto the sofa and sat next to him. She took his hand and asked, "Tell me what happened, Jimmy!"

Jimmy wept as he sat there, surrounded by the bewildered McLaughlin family. Linda wept as well, and Matthew held her firmly.

Tyler's heart sank. He had never seen his friend emotionally collapse. It was beyond disturbing. He began to question everything that he and his friends had done with regard to the Ouija board, and the binding ceremony in the cemetery. Everything and anything.

"I...can't go into all of the details! It's beyond embarrassing."

"You can tell us, Jim. We are all in this together," Matthew said.

Jimmy sank into the sofa. He wiped the tears from his eyes. "I was..." He grimaced. "I was beating off in my room..."

"It's okay, Jim," Matthew interjected. "It's completely normal..."

Tyler rolled his eyes and guffawed. "Oh, God, Dad!" His friend certainly didn't need to hear "the talk" and especially not now.

"We are all sexual..." Linda added.

Tyler slapped a hand over his eyes. It was worse than seeing bare breasts on the screen when sitting next to your mother in the cinema. He felt for his friend. But he was terrified to hear the details and the circumstances of his account of dealing with the dark spirits. And why, Tyler thought, did Vincent warn him that they were in danger, too?

"I was...taking care of business," Jimmy continued, like it suddenly didn't matter anymore, because obviously, it didn't. "And I swear to God, out of the blue, I heard my door open..."

They all waited with bated breath.

"In walked Sarah..."

Linda gasped. Surely she misheard what he had said.

Tyler parted his fingers so he could look at his friend.

He couldn't believe his own ears and he stared at his friend in shock.

Matthew's jaw hung slack.

"Sarah..." Jimmy continued.

"Or the likeness of Sarah..." Yvonne continued for him. "I can tell you for a fact that this attack was not perpetrated by Sarah!"

"Yeah," he looked up at her concerned parents. "It was definitely not Sarah. I mean it *couldn't* have been her!"

"I was with Sarah just like an hour ago," Tyler added calmly, as if defending his sister in a courtroom before a jury.

"Continue, please, Jimmy," Yvonne encouraged.

"She..." He swallowed hard. "*It*...undressed in front of me...and crawled onto my bed and..."

"You can say it," Linda encouraged, intrigued.

Jimmy covered his eyes. He was ashamed to even say it, but out it came anyway, "It...went down on me."

"Holy crap!" Tyler shrieked.

"It felt so amazing, but I didn't know it wasn't really her."

Linda shuddered and covered her face with both hands. "I can't visualize this. This is my own daughter!"

Jimmy's expression showed her that he empathized with Linda and he grimaced when he said, "I know...I'm sorry!" He started to cry.

"When did you realize it wasn't her?" Yvonne asked. She squeezed his hand. "After it had already seduced you, right?"

"Yes, exactly!" Jimmy nodded. His eyes glossed over as he relived the experience in his mind. "But not for a long time afterward."

Tyler sat there in shock, worried for his friend, but he was even more worried for himself. He couldn't even imagine being seduced by a demon, but by a demon masquerading as his own sister? That was just the most sick and twisted thing he had ever contemplated. He couldn't stand hearing Jimmy talk about how much he wanted his sister, and now he had to visualize it in the worst possible way. It looked like Jimmy finally got what he wanted; sadly, it was not the way he had intended.

"When did you know something was wrong?" Yvonne asked.

"I mean...*it was all wrong*! There's no way that it was ever Sarah who had walked into my room. She doesn't even like me at all. She can't stand me. She detests me..."

Linda interrupted him, "She doesn't detest you, Jimmy."

Jimmy sighed. He knew he had no chance with Sarah, ever, and that the biggest obstacle came in the form of her six-foot-two, rock-solid eighteen-year-old boyfriend, Bill Miller.

"When, exactly?" Yvonne insisted. "It's vitally important!"

"It was when I reached up and touched her shoulder." He whimpered and cringed. "It was all bumpy...and hairy... and cold and clammy!"

Yvonne asked. "Jimmy, are you..." she paused to come up with the right words, but no words would ever be chosen that could convey her intention for asking the question she wanted to ask, and it would be impossible to ask it without damaging his pride, so she said it as politely and as respectfully as she could anyway. "Were you...a virgin before this happened?"

Jimmy winced. Yvonne expected as much. To Jimmy, the embarrassment of disclosing the attack itself before his best friend and his parents was overwhelming on its own, but the idea of discussing the most private, intimate details of his personal sex life, or lack thereof, was just unfathomable. No teen ever wanted that. Even so, Jimmy simply nodded. It was all he could do. He looked up at Tyler and then the others. "Yeah! I was a virgin."

"That's what it was after," Yvonne tried to explain to them.

"What do you mean?" was the general group response.

Yvonne thought for a moment, trying to decide how best to explain it to them. She wished that Vincent were there to take over. She knew he shouldn't have left when they got home from the mall. For some reason, she knew it was easier for a man to discuss things of this nature. She didn't like it any more than Jimmy did, she was sure. "It was after your virginity, your purest life force essence."

They all gasped.

"Not so much for anything...permanent. But, to the demon, the energy cast off of a virgin during orgasm is like purest energetic food."

"Sick!" Tyler said.

"But..." Jimmy countered. "I didn't have one."

Yvonne was shocked. "You didn't...orgasm?"

"No!" Jimmy said. "It all ended well before then!"

"You're very lucky!" Yvonne said. "I mean...you know what I mean. I'm troubled for you truly. What a terrible experience!" She covered her mouth. "But you are extremely fortunate that it hadn't taken that from you!"

"I asked for Jesus' help and it just vanished shortly afterward."

"Well, I'd say you can count your blessings, given the alternative," Linda added.

"There's more," Jimmy confessed.

"Oh, God!" Tyler hooted.

"Go on," Matthew encouraged him.

"When I looked down, I was covered in this disgusting slimy goop."

"Oh, man, Jim!" Tyler interjected.

Yvonne nodded. She knew the activity.

"Pus and blood and slime!" Anger seethed within Jimmy. "I can't even tell you how disgusting and revolting it was. It wouldn't even come off in the shower until I scrubbed and scrubbed."

"And then, what?" Linda asked.

"After about...after a long while, it was just gone without a trace, just like she...just like the demon was." Jimmy recalled the horrific scene in his mind. His voice was reduced to a robotic, monotonous tone. "And then, I just jumped on my bike and came here..."

They all sat in uncomfortable silence until the telephone rang and Linda stood and shuffled off into the kitchen. She answered quickly.

"Hello? Yes, this is she." The others stared at her from the living room. "That's the best news I've heard all day. Can I speak with her, please?" Linda waited. "Oh, okay then, let her rest. Please call me here as soon as she's ready to be discharged." Linda held the phone to her chest, mumbled the words "*Thank You*" to the angels above, and finally set the phone back into its cradle.

When she walked back into the living room, Linda sat down next to Jimmy and hugged him. It was all her protective mother's instinct could encourage her to do.

Matthew rubbed Jimmy's forehead and Tyler just lay back down in awe.

Chapter 15 – A Call to Arms

TYLER SHOT HIS EYES OPEN AND SAT UP. His eyes grew wide with terror. He gasped and looked at Jimmy and Yvonne and then at his parents. "We have to warn Kyle!" Jimmy dropped his hands into his lap and Yvonne narrowed her eyes and nodded.

Matthew regarded him and shook his head. "I can't even believe this is happening! I thought this was over!"

Tyler ran into the kitchen and dialed his friend. A busy signal sent shivers down his back into his legs. "It's busy!" He walked quickly back into the living room and started to speak. "Hey..." He wanted Jimmy to go with him, but he understood that he was in no condition to go anywhere, and he'd be safer if he didn't. Tyler said, "I've got to go over there!"

"It's ten thirty in the evening, Tyler," his father warned.

"What difference does it make?" he growled. "If he's in danger, he has to be warned!"

"He's right," Yvonne nodded. "We'll both go!"

Tyler nodded as Yvonne stood and fished her keys out of her pocket.

"Be careful, please," Matthew warned.

Yvonne smiled at him and touched his shoulder. "He's in good hands."

Linda sat up and adjusted the pillow on the edge of the sofa. She patted Jimmy's shoulder and said, "Lie down, Jimmy. Rest your head, Honey." Jimmy moaned and turned around. He didn't say a word as he slid up and rested his head on the pillow.

Tyler and Yvonne came down the hallway in their coats. She handed her keys to Tyler, who opened the garage door and slapped the button on the inside wall. The automatic door rolled up in its tracks and they closed the door behind them and got into the Trans Am. Tyler adjusted the seat to accommodate his long legs. He turned and smiled at Yvonne, who obviously knew how much he liked to drive. He grinned from ear to ear and turned the key. The radio came on blaring Def Leppard and Tyler started to bang his head. Yvonne grinned as they backed away and then drove up the driveway and turned onto Route 111. When Tyler hit the gas pedal, the car lurched forward and snapped their heads back. "Wow, this car has some serious balls!" He smiled broadly and punched it all the way down the meandering roads toward Kyle's house.

A single light shone inside the gray one-story house. Tyler pulled into the driveway quietly, letting the car idle its way up to the front door. He put the car in park and saw Kyle peeking out his bedroom window. The shadow in the room told them that he was rushing toward the front door to see who it was. He obviously didn't recognize the car. Tyler ran up to the front door and Yvonne walked up slowly behind him.

Kyle opened the door and smiled brightly. "Tyler!"

His smile quickly faded when he saw Yvonne walking up and standing beside his friend.

"What's up?" he asked. "Hi, Yvonne!"

Yvonne gave a curt smile and said, "Hello, Honey."

"We came here to warn you..."

Kyle stepped out onto the landing and closed the door behind him to conserve the heat inside the house and to ensure that his mother wouldn't hear what was going on.

"Warn me about what?"

"I've tried calling you twice..."

"And all you got was a busy signal, right?"

"Exactly!"

"Ever since my younger sister got a phone for her room, she's on the thing every waking minute, talking to her friends. No one who tries to call can ever get through."

"Kyle, Jimmy's been attacked!"

Kyle gulped. "Attacked?" He rolled that statement over in his mind and stared at his shoes. Then he looked up at them and asked, "By what?"

"By demons!"

Kyle gasped and said, "Oh, shit!"

"You wouldn't even believe what happened!"

"Try me, Tyler!" Kyle countered.

"My mom's friend Julie's car got smashed right in front of our house. Kelly was taken over by an evil spirit, and now Jimmy's been freaking molested in his bedroom by a creepy old freaking night hag right out of the Dungeons & Dragons Monster Manual!"

Kyle's tongue shot out of his mouth and his face wrinkled up like a prune. "A night hag? Are you serious?" He turned his attention to Yvonne, crumpled his shoulders, raised his hands and implored, "How does that even happen?"

"It's a serious assault, Honey! We came here to warn you to be on guard."

"I haven't experienced anything odd since everything was stopped the last time. I've really read up on not giving anything any thought whatsoever and not giving it any recognition."

"That's good, man. But you gotta get your sister off that phone. We need to be able to get through to you, if something crazy happens. I can't just fly over here late at night like this."

"Honestly, Tyler, I'm pretty confident that I'm not going to get attacked. I've really been practicing my faith more and more as the weeks have gone on. I feel really safe."

Tyler eyed him with suspicion. He knew Kyle had never been much of a regular church-goer, but if he'd found new inspiration after all they'd been through – then great...good for him.

Yvonne studied the house. She walked up to Kyle's window and stood there silently for a moment. The two teenagers watched her. Tyler reached over and gave his friend a hug. Yvonne turned around in time to see them. Her eyes widened a bit and she smirked and brushed against the snow with the tip of her boot until they'd let go of one another. Tyler knew she was discerning whether there was any trouble with the house. "Find anything?" he asked.

"I sense nothing at all wrong with the house." She looked at Kyle and touched the back of his head. "I think Kyle's right." Kyle smiled.

"Well, we'd better get back home. Jimmy is really shaken up." He looked once more at his friend and said, "Be careful, Kyle. Call my house if anything weird happens."

"I will. Okay, see you later. Thanks for the heads-up."

Yvonne waved at him as Kyle walked back inside and closed the door. When they got in the car, Yvonne studied Tyler intensely as he watched Kyle walk back to his bedroom and peer out from behind the curtains. He waved at him and Kyle waved back.

"You two have a special bond," she smiled. "It's very sweet."

Tyler gave her a weird look, started the car and backed out of the driveway.

When they arrived back at the house, the lights were dim and there was a note on the kitchen table. It was from his mother:

Jimmy's sound asleep.

Yvonne, you can sleep in Tyler's room if you want to stay.

Tyler, I made a bed for you on the floor in the living room.

See you in the morning for breakfast.

Linda/Mom

Chapter 16 – Skinned Alive

WHEN TYLER WOKE UP IN THE MORNING, his mother was propping a pillow under Jimmy's head and adjusting his blanket. He was sleeping soundly. Clearly, the horrific events he'd endured had taken their toll. Tyler rolled around onto his side and noticed his mother looking down at him. Her eyes were bloodshot. She'd been crying; from what it looked like, she'd been crying all night long. Yvonne came down from upstairs and shuffled into the kitchen. Tyler noticed she was wearing his mother's purple zip-up sweatshirt.

Linda said, "Good morning, Yvonne. How did the pajamas fit? How did you sleep?"

Yvonne concealed a yawn as she felt the fabric. "They fit surprisingly well, considering I'm several sizes larger than you are. And they're as soft as silk. Thank you! I slept well." She walked up to the kitchen window and smiled as the sun struck her face, as Linda walked back into the kitchen. Yvonne continued, "As I said, I sense absolutely nothing wrong here at all." She turned toward Linda. "I meditated for a good thirty minutes upstairs and everything is peaceful and as it should be."

Linda said, "You don't know what a relief that is!"

"Oh, sure I do, Dear." She chuckled. She wove her fingers into her long brown curly hair and scratched her scalp. "This isn't my first rodeo."

Linda grinned and poured two cups of coffee.

Tyler stirred, inhaled deeply and just sank back down

into his sleeping bag. He hadn't the energy to lift a finger yet, let alone get up and start his day. He closed his eyes and lay there for close to a minute.

Suddenly, he heard a long, horrific scream come from outside. It was a female voice.

His eyes shot open. He panicked, going through a list of women and girls in his mind and ruling them out one by one, until he hadn't a clue who it was who could be screaming outside. Linda and Yvonne shared the same shocked expression. The scream came again.

Jimmy snorted, still in a daze, and kept his eyes closed as he lifted his head. When the scream came a third time, Linda joined Yvonne at the kitchen window and tried to see where the scream was coming from.

Tyler slid out of his sleeping bag and scrambled to the sliding glass door on his hands and knees. Another scream erupted and a then a desperate call for help. It was the neighbors. Tyler dug his hand into the metal seam and slid open the living room door. The cries of anguish were clearer now and were coming from the right. He stuck his head out. The wind whipped his hair in his eyes and they began to tear. The faint rays of the sun beat down upon him and his freckled face as he tried to see what was going on. He heard his father's heavy footsteps behind him as he stormed into the kitchen and asked, "What's wrong?"

As he peered outside, Tyler saw two silhouettes leaning down over the doghouse just across the property line in the neighbors' yard. It was a man and a woman, his neighbors, looking into Cinnamon's doghouse.

Tyler's heart sank. He heard the man shouting as he backed away from it.

Matthew pulled open the sliding door and stuck his head out. Yvonne and Linda looked through the kitchen window at an angle trying to see what was going on. Finally, Matthew ran into the foyer and put on his shoes. Tyler slid the sliding door shut, scrambled to his feet and followed his father. Still groggy and drained, Jimmy could barely make sense of what was going on, let alone be of any assistance. Linda and Yvonne scurried into the foyer after Matthew and Tyler.

Matthew and Tyler went out through the front door and trudged through the snow around to the side of the house. As he turned the corner, Matthew saw his neighbor drop to his knees in front of the doghouse and grab the sides of his head. His wife continually shrieked and covered her mouth with both hands.

"Scott?" Matthew called out.

The man, in obvious shock, turned sharply, and when he understood who had called his name, he hurriedly waved Matthew and Tyler over.

Tyler grimaced. Something terrible had happened to the golden retriever, he just knew it. Tyler's heart sank deeper as he drew nearer. When Matthew and Tyler knelt to see what was going on inside the doghouse that panicked their neighbors, nothing could have prepared them for the horror they were about to experience.

"No, God!" Tyler moaned. His head sank and tears streamed out of his eyes.

The golden retriever was skinned alive, as if it had been split down the middle with a machete and its innards spread as far and wide as possible, so that the fur was on the outside and the splintered bones and cartilage, veins, and corded muscles were severed and splayed open like a skin fastened to a drying rack.

Linda hadn't the heart or the courage to look. Instead, she went right up to her neighbor and hugged her. But then, she had to look. She peeked inside and coughed, immediately sickened to the point of heaving. Yvonne took one look at the poor creature. She closed her eyes and turned away.

"What the hell could have done this?" Scott pleaded.

Tyler wept and reached in to touch the dog's head. He

whimpered when he tried to touch him, and pulled away because he didn't have the stomach to touch the mutilated corpse.

"A wolf, maybe?" Scott suggested.

"Oh, man, I am *so* sorry," Matthew exclaimed.

"He hadn't come up to the house for his breakfast this morning, so I went to check on him and this is what I found," the woman explained.

Linda hugged her and cried with her. She hadn't the stomach to tell her what had been going on inside their house or on their property. She didn't have the courage to reveal their plight.

Yvonne studied the doghouse. She sensed the seething hatred all around it. She backed away. She visualized violet flames consuming the doghouse, in her own way of transmuting the negative energy. She saw Cinnamon's spirit lying down beside the doghouse and she felt its grief. She used her telepathy to tell the dog that everything was okay and that he didn't have to be afraid for his human friends and family. She told him he could go on into the spirit world.

Her eyes welled up with tears. She loved all animals and to see proof time and again that they too survived the death of the physical body filled her with satisfaction that what she was doing was right.

The neighbor dragged a blue tarp from the garage and spread it out on the grass. He put on long rubber gloves, knelt down and reached inside the doghouse to retrieve the remains of their lost pet. Tyler covered his mouth and wiped the tears of anguish from his eyes. The neighbor folded the tarp over the dog and secured the edges. Matthew bent and picked up one end and they hauled the carcass over to the garage and set it in the back of his pickup truck. He, too, was crying. "What the hell could have done this, Matt?"

Matthew shook his head. He couldn't respond with any

words that would suffice. He patted him on the back and simply shook his head. Linda hugged Scott's wife and the two families went their separate ways. Yvonne knelt and seemed to pat thin air. She whispered to Linda, Matthew, and Tyler. "He's right here!" They whirled around.

Tyler tried to smile, but he was too distressed. Losing a pet dog was as hard as losing a human friend or family member. Even though it wasn't his own dog, he loved him dearly. He would miss him terribly.

Tyler turned and moped back toward the house, followed by his dad, who held Linda's hand, and finally by Yvonne, who studied the clouds in the sky and the make-shift patterns of light cast down from the sun overhead.

Once inside, Linda and Yvonne started cooking break-fast together. Tyler sat down next to Jimmy, but this time, it was Tyler who was crying and needing the consolation. Jimmy patted Tyler on the ankle and shook his head. Tyler loved that dog. He ached inside because he had never known death before. His grandparents were all in perfect health and were far from the grave. He had never felt such permanent loss before.

Yvonne stepped down into the living room with a tea cup and saucer in her hands. She sat down next to Tyler and handed it to him. Tyler's eyes were red and swollen. Tears streamed down his cheeks and his lower lip quivered. "I'm sorry, Honey." Tyler grimaced in pain and rested his head on her shoulder. She patted his head and face and closed her eyes. Jimmy leaned his head over and rested it on Tyler's shoulder. They were all in need of some serious consolation. After many deep breaths, Yvonne looked over at the glass door and fluttered her eyelids. She opened her mouth, intending to tell them what she saw, but she knew that – despite her psychic sight, and the appreciation and admiration most people gave her because of it – telling them that the spirit of the dog was completely unscathed –

even though its body was so brutally mangled – would offer them little real comfort.

"Drink some of your tea, Honey." She reached for it and handed it out to him. Tyler rocked himself forward and took a sip. He smiled a bit when he swallowed it and nodded at Yvonne for being there for him and going out of her way to help him – and his family and friends. He leaned his head back against the wall and studied her for a moment. She always seemed so peaceful and at ease – well, aside from the time he nearly scared her out of her mind the previous evening. Tyler chuckled. It created ripples in the tea as his subtle laughter shook the cup. He admired her.

"Thank you, Yvonne!" He smiled warmly at her. She returned the smile and tapped him on the leg.

Shortly after, Linda called everyone to the table for breakfast. Matthew had squeezed two folding chairs around it, so everyone could fit fairly comfortably. With Sarah already gone on her way to her boyfriend Bill's football game with her friends from school, it left only Linda, Matthew, Kelly, Tyler, Yvonne, and Jimmy to make room for.

The meal was eaten in silence. Jimmy and Tyler pouted and felt sorry for themselves. Linda and Matthew were both emotionally shaken by the tragedy in the neighbor's yard. Yvonne just kept to herself, but being highly sensitive, she felt the pain of those around her as if she were experiencing it herself.

Kelly finally waddled into the kitchen and said, "I'm hungry." Linda turned her swivel chair around and held out her hands for her daughter. She came right up and received a hug. "What's for breakfast?" she asked. Linda reached over to pull the lid off the platter of pancakes she had been keeping warm, when Kelly gasped and put her hands over her mouth.

Tyler, who had been sulking, looked up and saw her

pointing into the living room. He spun his chair around and grunted. He didn't see what she was so excited about.

Yvonne's eyes narrowed and she smirked.

"Cinnamon!"

Linda and Matthew gave each other an uneasy glance and stood up and moved behind Kelly. She walked cautiously into the living room beyond the sliding glass door. Matthew and Linda followed her slowly.

Yvonne turned in her chair and said, "She can see." She nodded. "She's clairvoyant."

Jimmy's jaw dropped and he spun around in his swivel chair as well. He gazed at Tyler who returned the same stunned expression. Jimmy leaned forward, placed his arms on the black metal railing and rested his chin on his hands.

Kelly inched closer and held out her hand. "Honey, do you see something?" Linda asked. Kelly nodded. She smiled broadly.

"Weird," Jimmy said.

Tyler got out of his chair and stood next to Yvonne. She looked up at him, reached up and held his elbow. "She can see him. I could too, but I didn't think anyone would find comfort in that, because they couldn't see him and wouldn't find any real solace."

Tears flowed down his cheeks. "He's okay, then?"

Yvonne smiled and said, "Wait and see! Kelly will tell you." She stood up and walked into the living room. Kelly was bent on one knee, reaching out as though patting the dog the way she would if he were really there. He *was* really there, she knew, but not in his flesh and blood body that she was used to, but in a finer, translucent spiritual form.

"He's really sad," Kelly said. She pouted and cried for him.

Yvonne said, "You can feel his sorrow, Honey?" Kelly nodded. Yvonne looked around at the astonished family. "She's empathic too!"

"What does that mean?" Matthew asked.

He was surprised to hear Tyler call out from the steps in the kitchen, "She can sense emotions – empathy."

Yvonne smiled at him. She was happy that he knew what that was.

"As I've said, Kelly is a sensitive. She has been for a very long time." The family gathered around her as she knelt next to Kelly and held her hands in the air over the area that the dog's body usually occupied.

"He's quite frightened. He was brutally attacked without warning as he slept." Kelly gasped. Yvonne looked down and gave her an apologetic glance.

"I'm sorry if that scared you, Honey. Cinnamon has been through what we call a tragic death experience."

"But..." Kelly protested. "He's not...dead."

"No," Yvonne rushed to say. She held Kelly's back and chest with both hands, gently squeezing her. "His body died, but his personality didn't." Kelly nodded as though she knew intuitively what Yvonne was explaining to her. "His spirit is still here with us."

"He's still scared, though."

Linda and Matt held each other.

"Yes, he is, Dear," Yvonne told her. "But you can see him, so you can also talk to him and comfort him." Kelly gasped and looked up at her. Yvonne smiled. "Yes, you can tell him that he's all right. You can make him so he isn't sad anymore."

Kelly reached over and acted as though she was hugging the dog. She looked at Tyler and called out to him, "Tyler!" Tyler didn't know what to do. "He wants you to come be with him and pet him."

Tyler looked at Jimmy, who just shrugged. Tyler knelt beside Yvonne and Kelly. He looked down at his little sister as if she were now the wise older sibling about to teach him the secrets of the world. She took his hand in both of hers and gently eased it forward so it was extended over where the dog would be lying. Tyler smiled.

"You take your hand," Kelly said, "and you pet him like this." She moved her hands as though touching and caressing his physical body.

"Do you feel anything with your hands, Honey?" Yvonne asked.

Linda and Matthew looked on affectionately.

"Yes, I feel a heat. I feel Cinnamon's fur."

Linda whispered to Yvonne, "But he no longer has any fur. He's energy now, I get it..."

"In a minute, Linda," Yvonne smiled. Yvonne studied Tyler interacting with his sister. He was holding his hands above the carpet.

"Do you feel anything, Tyler? Close your eyes, don't reach out with your eyes, try and discern his energy by identifying any sensations in your palms." Tyler's eyes fluttered.

"Don't worry if you don't notice anything at first. This is new to you and I believe that you have the ability to feel just like Kelly does..." Jimmy gasped.

"But she's been practicing longer than you have." Kelly looked up and smiled at her.

Matthew leaned back against the wrought-iron railing separating the living room from the kitchen. Linda watched them intently. "What do you feel, Son?"

Tyler kept his eyes closed even though he turned toward his mother. "I see a purple light even with my eyes closed. It comes and goes. It's weird and kinda cool."

Yvonne nodded. "Tyler has 'the sight' too, he just needs to open it fully and to practice with it. It's like an entirely new sense that is lying dormant and just waiting to pop open like a flower ready to bloom at the onset of spring." Yvonne beamed. Then she looked up and said, "You have it too, Linda." Linda gasped.

Matthew looked deeply into Linda's eyes. "Linda, you

saw the spirit of Brock Manning for the first time in your kitchen because you were open and receptive."

Linda stared at the carpet and recalled those events, exactly as they unfolded back in October:

Linda had finished cleaning up the dishes, started a pot of soup on the stove, and brought a load of clothes hangers down from upstairs. She opened the laundry room doors and reached for the ironing board. Then she saw it. A gray, smoky shadow hovered silently behind and between the washer and dryer. Her jaw dropped. She could not believe it. Then, as if it knew that it had been discovered, it whisked past her with blinding speed. Linda screeched, whirled around and stared as it faded away in the brightly lit kitchen. She jolted her head back and forth trying to focus on whatever it was that she had just seen. She scanned the edge of the kitchen, then down into the living room. She knew it had to be a reflection or a shadow or something.

When she saw nothing more, she calmed down and shrugged. After a few seconds she turned around and started to pull out the ironing board. It was stuck on the side of the dryer, and she nearly fell backwards when it finally slid free. She slammed it down onto its edge and felt for the release. When she hit the lever, the ironing board sprung open, and Linda sighed with satisfaction.

After several moments, Linda plugged in the iron, opened the dryer, and pulled out a half-dozen of Matthew's shirts. When she returned to the ironing board she started on the first shirt. A sudden jet of steam shot out of the iron and scalded her arm. "Ouch!" Linda backed away and grabbed her wrist. She picked up the iron, raised it to eye level, and noticed that the temperature dial was turned all the way to steam setting. "Who in the heck?" She had always made it a point to turn off the iron. She thought about her mother, who had warned her too many times when she was a young teen about the danger of leaving appliances on and the many ways in which they could accidentally burn down the entire house and, apparently, the entire neighborhood.

A gray shadow came out of the wall behind the stove, moved directly through its center and passed right through her. Linda felt the icy cold grip of death throughout every fiber of her being. She gasped, turned around and leaned back against the stove. She wrapped her arms around her chest and held herself as if she had just been violated. She felt a chill in her core. She carefully examined the kitchen. There was no trace of any shadow. She looked around. Then she spotted the iron, sputtering and shooting out jets of steam. She realized that she hadn't turned it off yet. She stood there, frozen nearly a minute. "Am I losing my mind?"

Linda walked toward the laundry area, grabbed the iron, yanked the plug from the wall, rotated the dial to the off position, and set it down on the ironing board. She stared back at the stove. Her arm was throbbing. She backed away and then approached the kitchen sink carefully. She turned on the faucet and held her arm under cold running water.

Just then, the telephone rang in the kitchen. Concerned, Yvonne looked over into the kitchen as Linda rushed in to answer it.

"Hello?" Linda asked. "Yes, this is she." Yvonne nodded and tended to Kelly. "Yes, I can come pick her up, that won't be a problem at all." She smiled and said, "I'll be there then. Goodbye." Linda walked back and said, "That was the hospital. Julie's being discharged. She's going to be just fine."

Tyler looked at his mother with smiling eyes and said, "That's terrific, Mom. That's the best news I've heard in a long time." He looked at Yvonne and they exchanged wordless smiles. Finally he said, "Ya know, I *could* feel something."

Yvonne grinned and said, "I know, Honey."

Chapter 17 – A Clash of Titans

CROWDS ROARED IN THE BLEACHERS at Rentschler Field on the University of Connecticut Campus as the UConn Huskies football team ran onto the field for their final game of the season against Boston University. Sarah McLaughlin and her friends cheered for them and especially for Sarah's boyfriend, Bill, when they saw him run down the field hoisting his helmet into the air and waving it at the raucous crowd with a broad grin. The star defensive lineman ran up to the sidelines and grabbed hold of the hand railing. He leaped up, balanced himself there, and kissed Sarah on the lips. Then he hopped back down.

Sarah looked down at him and winked. "Good luck! Go get em, Tiger!"

Bill smiled brightly. "There will no luck involved. It'll be an utter annihilation!" He pressed his hands against his chest and continued, "And only through sheer athletic excellence!"

Sarah grinned and called out to him, "You're confident, I like it." Bill nodded and came back up for another kiss. "See you after the game, good lookin'." He backed away, turned and sprinted off to his team's sideline.

While they prepared for the game, Sarah and her giddy friends pointed at and admired some of the other players on both teams. They were high school girls, after all, and Sarah encouraged them, because perhaps they could find would-be suitors for themselves.

Soon both teams lined up and squared off against each other and the much-anticipated game was underway.

Bill studied his opponent intensely to try rattle his nerves, as he always did. The opposing player sneered at him, spat on the grass and put in his mouth guard. A line-man had only one job and that was to hold the line. He often didn't get to see what else was happening with the play and most times could only tell by the reaction of the crowd. It wasn't a glorious position like a quarterback or receiver or safety by any means, but it was equally impor-tant. Bill enjoyed his position and his contribution to the team effort. And he knew he excelled at it.

All of a sudden, the snap occurred and Bill's muscles fired instantly. He locked up with his opponent, dug his cleats into the grass, groaned against his opponent's weight, and turned him back in toward his own teammate, creating a gap in the defensive line so his running back could charge through. He knew he didn't get very far, because the whistle blew the play dead a moment later.

He heard the announcer call out the number of yards gained on the play on the blaring loudspeakers as he went back to his team's huddle so the quarterback could call the next play. After the team clapped and cheered each other, Bill returned to the line. Both men sized the other up again briefly before the next play was about to commence, trying to identify any weakness that they could exploit. Bill stared into his opponent's eyes. They were an unremarkable shade of brown. He couldn't detect any fear in them at all. Instead, he sensed a solid determination, even confidence and arrogance. Bill scoffed. This man actually believed he was better than Bill was. It enraged him.

Before he knew it, the snap occurred and the man colli-ded with him. The guy's strength was nearly double what it had been on just the previous play. Bill could do nothing to stop him and he was immediately and powerfully shoved backward forming a gap in the line. Bill could do nothing but growl in protest as he was pushed back right into his own quarterback, who was sacked just a moment later.

"C'mon, Miller," shouted the quarterback.

Bill gritted his teeth and shot his head forward in disgust. "How the hell did that just happen?" he thought. He went back to the huddle. He heard the play call and jogged back to the line. He looked at his teammates, both to the left and to the right of him. They nodded at him – clearly a message that, despite how big and how powerful his opponent was, they expected him to try harder, to try as hard as he possibly could. Suddenly, Bill went from being the dominating force to the underdog because he had been outmatched on that previous play. It wouldn't – it couldn't – be allowed to happen again. He looked at the man before him, whose face was surprisingly expressionless.

It was then that he sensed a feeling of pure, unadulterated hatred emanate from his opponent. It was a feeling of madness, of complete repulsion. He recalled the same sensation that he'd felt in Mrs. McLaughlin's art studio when the jet black specter came around the corner and paralyzed him with fear. He recalled what had happened when he pointed his flashlight at it. There, in that studio, before he could even attempt to understand what had happened to the beam of light streaking forth from the flashlight, the thing rushed right up to him. Now, here at the game, Bill had the unmistakable feeling that he was facing that dire spirit again, and this time it was flesh, bone, and solid corded muscle. And when he looked into its eyes, he knew that he was looking at something that wasn't human at all. He was looking straight into Hell itself. As he stared into the eyes, he felt pulled into the Abyss. Time seemed to slow to a standstill. It felt like two great hooks had punctured his helmet and ripped his mind in two. Once open and exposed, he felt as if he were being forced to recall the horrific events inside Mrs. McLaughlin's art studio during the investigation that he took part in:

Bill was sitting on the stool in the quiet darkness of the art studio. He knew, based on the testimony, that Linda had been viciously attacked in the room. Rather than let that fact fill him with fear, it enraged him. He was fond of his girlfriend's mother. She had always gone out of her way to make him feel welcome and at home when he visited Sarah. Bill took a deep breath and played with the flashlight the lead investigator had given him. He flicked it off and on several times and spun around on the stool he was sitting on to look at his reflection in the window. He shined the flashlight under his chin, just like he used to do as a boy. He laughed and spun back around. He listened carefully as the other investigators scaled the steps and walked upstairs to take their assigned positions. He leaned over to the right to see if he could see into the kitchen, but he couldn't, so he moved the stool forward and sat back down.

Satisfied that he had a clear view of the kitchen and both the garage and the living room beyond, he focused his attention on the unused formal living room before him. It was dark and uninviting. He could see the streaks in the powder-blue carpet that the vacuum cleaner had left. Every once in a while he saw a flash of light outside through the translucent white window panels, but he quickly understood them to be the result of cars passing by on the road. He heard a metal creaking sound above. Then he heard a solid thud. Then he heard the heavy footsteps up the ladder to the attic. He waited in silence, trying to make out what was being said. Suddenly he heard it.

"Oh, my God," he heard the lead investigator screech.

Another shouted, "What's wrong?"

"Back down, get back down," the lead investigator continued.

Bill's heart began to race. There were no more cars passing by on the road adjacent the house, so the room ahead of him was pitch black. Then, he felt the hair on the top of his head stand erect. The temperature in the room plummeted in *the blink of his astonished eyes. Bill shivered in the ice-cold temperature and wrapped his arms over his chest. That was when he saw it – the wafting mists of a jet-black spirit gliding backward from the deeper recesses of the living room. The shape and outline of its translucent, humanoid body appeared solid, yet the interior seemed to be fashioned out of rolling, moving mists. It was facing the stairs. It hadn't noticed him, yet. Each of his short and labored breaths shot white puffs into the room as his jaw hung open in silent terror. Bill was frozen, both from the frigid temperature in the room and from the panic he felt when the small clouds caused by his exhalations floated away from him and into the living room, dangerously close to giving his presence and his position away.*

"Holy shit!" The thing noticed those breaths, too, just as he feared it would. It spun around and stared right at him. He felt as if a million volts of electricity were coursing through his body, like he'd made the mistake of inadvertently allowing a screwdriver he'd been using to unfasten an outlet cover to stick inside. He didn't know which feeling was worse, the numbing cold, the dark and dreadful fear it caused him simply by being in its presence, or the long, stabbing pain of the electric current coursing through his nervous system.

Bill heard the heavy footsteps on the stairs as the investigators ran down to help him. The spirit whipped around toward the stairs. Then it looked in the opposite direction, toward the wall of the art studio, flitted past him and disappeared right through it.

When the investigators rounded the corner, the temperature began to normalize and the electrical shocks were becoming weaker and weaker until there wasn't any trace left of them at all, but the weighted thickness of evil lay all over the house.

With his attention once again focused on the football field, Bill shook his head and snapped back to the present. He blinked his eyes and then he cringed. He felt the same electric pulses surging throughout his body. A knot grew in his stomach as a sudden sickness overcame him. It was debilitating. His heart pounded in his chest. A bead of sweat dripped down from his brow, rolled down his nose, and fell past his gritted teeth and onto the short whiskers on his chin. He heard the cheers in the background as the fans eagerly encouraged the next play to commence. Dread consumed him. He visualized his girlfriend's smiling face. Then came the indescribable feeling that he would never see her again.

Time once again slowed to a standstill.

He heard a vicious roar emanate from the man – or *the thing* before him. The last sight he saw through his face mask was the number on his opponent's jersey coming at him like a runaway freight train. The massive, muscular hulk slammed into him, snapping his neck back and blasting him backward as though he were nothing substantial at all. And due to the agonizing slowing in the passage of time, he felt each painful moment as though each second lasted an eternity. He felt himself falling backward in the void until the juggernaut drove him into the ground like a hammer on a spike.

Bill yelped in agony. It sounded to him like a trumpet blaring in a vast, abandoned canyon. He felt each excruciating moment as his collar bone popped and splintered. Then he felt his ribs crack – one after the other – until he felt as though his sides were falling out. His right shoulder went numb, and he was consumed and smothered by the rank stench of rotting fish mixed with Old Spice deodorant. It overwhelmed him in a nauseating cloud that he knew he alone could sense.

From the dark place he found himself in, he could hear the muted calls of what he knew to be the announcer on the stadium speakers telling the tale of his demise. He heard the muffled calls of concerned teammates, the shrill sounds of nearby whistles. Most important, he heard the distant shrieks and screams of his girlfriend in the bleachers.

Out of the corners of his eyes, he saw his teammates, his coaches, and the team's physician rushing up to him, as if they could pierce the dark haze that held him prisoner. Their distorted voices did nothing but confuse him. His vision was growing darker by the second. By the time he saw the stretcher being wheeled in beside him, Bill faded out of consciousness and was sailing on a sea of numbing blackness, drifting further and further away from shore.

Chapter 18 – Reunion

OUTSIDE THE EMERGENCY ENTRANCE of the hospital, Linda helped Julie out of her wheelchair into the back seat of Matthew's BMW. An orderly wheeled the chair away as Linda fastened the seat belt around her waist for her. She was still obviously sore and stiff – especially with the neck brace on – but she got situated without any considerable difficulty. Matthew stood outside the car, clutching the door. He said, "You're such a trooper, Julie!"

"Oh, now, stop," Julie chuckled. She shot her hand out and laid it back down in her lap.

Linda got in and buckled her own seat belt.

When Matthew had climbed in and buckled his seat belt, an ambulance banked into the emergency entrance with its lights flashing. Matthew saw it in the rear view mirror and maneuvered the car clear of it, never knowing that the patient inside was his very own daughter's boyfriend. The ambulance came to a screeching halt just outside the emergency room. Its rear doors swung wide and the driver hastily worked his way to the back of the vehicle.

Julie regarded all the commotion from Linda's side view mirror. She said, "Oh, I hope whoever it is inside will be all right. Lord have mercy!"

Had Matthew known that Sarah's suitor was the patient being lowered out of the ambulance on that gurney, he would have pulled over immediately and rushed to his aid. He was fond of the athletic young man. He was worthy of his daughter. But he didn't know it was Bill, none of them

172

did, so he started driving toward the hospital exit, leaving him in the care of the medical professionals.

When he pulled out onto the road, Matthew called into the back seat, "Will you be okay at home, Julie?"

Julie nodded. She said, "I'm really looking forward to a nice piping hot lavender Epsom salts bath when I get home, I can tell you that."

Linda turned to regard her friend. She smiled at her tenderly. "Please tell us if you'd like to stay at our house. It is no bother at all."

Julie answered, "I've been alone for as long as I can remember. I'm used to making do, but thank you for the offer." She frowned. "Truth be told, I could use some peace and quiet." She chuckled and continued, "All those beeping and chirping monitors were driving me insane. Enough to drive me to drink, in fact!"

They all laughed. "Well, suit yourself, Dear," Linda said.

"Oh, goodness," Julie groaned. "What about my van?"

Matthew glanced at her in the rear view mirror. "I'm afraid it's totaled."

"Oh, my!"

Matthew nodded. "It's distressing, I know. Your insurance agent will take care of everything, don't you worry about a thing. You'll be getting a brand new vehicle, that's for sure."

Julie snapped her fingers and said, "Hot diggety dog!" She chuckled. "A new car!"

"Yes, and when you feel up to it, I can take you car shopping."

Julie smiled, then put a finger under her lip as she pondered that thought. "Hmm, but what kind of car shall I get? That's a tough one!"

Linda looked back and smiled. "Decisions, decisions, my friend." She turned toward the front again as they drove away from the hospital. She was so happy that Julie was in good spirits with all she had been through. Julie always had a way of seeing the silver lining.

"You know," Julie muttered. "Speaking of drinks, I can't even remember the last time I had an actual cocktail." She studied the houses whisking by as they drove down Main Street in Bridgeport. "I think it's time I had a Seven and seven!"

"Oh," Linda laughed. "Now I know your favorite poison."

"Poison is a good term for it, isn't it? What nutritional benefit does an alcoholic beverage really have anyway?"

"I can't think of anyone who has ever even considered that, Julie. All anyone wants to do when they drink is numb their pain and forget about their worries."

"I think I'll do just that! I'll numb my pain and forget my worries in the bathtub."

Matthew and Linda chuckled. Linda smiled at her husband, reached over and held his hand and forgot about her worries as well as they drove silently along. She didn't know why, but she felt safe.

Unfortunately, for the other poor souls who had interfered with the demon's plans back in October, their sense of safety was about to be irrevocably shattered.

Chapter 19 – Annihilation

KYLE FOSTER SAT AT HIS DESK IN HIS BEDROOM, applying glue to the edges of the plastic model's fuselage of a German Me-262 Jet Fighter. He set the tube of clear cement down on the desk, picked up the wing sections and pressed them into place perfectly. He studied the seam with precision and dabbed the excess glue away with his fingertip. He paused. Something was not right. His eyes darted to the left and to the right. Then he looked up and away from his model and his eyes grew wide with fear. He sensed the same unmistakably awful stench that he and his friends had smelled in Tyler's bedroom the morning after they had used the Ouija board.

Before he could react further, he felt the long, ice-cold fingers coil around his throat from behind and squeeze tightly. Then he felt the fingers literally start to freeze his flesh. He hacked and coughed. His tongue shot out of his mouth. He felt his head being squeezed by an overly large hand. Its fingernails dug into his scalp. Kyle tried to scream – tried to protest – but the thing had him. Out of desperation, he reached for his X-acto knife, but quickly realized that a material blade would be useless against a non-corporeal spirit. His breath was being cut off almost completely.

He knew that he had precious few seconds left, so he closed his eyes and visualized the august form of Jesus standing beside him in a blindingly white robe. The hold on his head and neck subsided instantly. "It worked," he thought. "I'm free!" Then he felt the hand swoop in again. Its fingers wound their way in and through his thick blond hair. It clenched its powerful fist, hoisted him up out of his chair and smashed his forehead down against the desk before him. The sound of his skull smacking the wood was bad enough, but the bright flash of white and violet light he saw in that instant stunned him just as terribly. Kyle recoiled, and sat back up. Blood trickled out of his nostril and he was suddenly thrown down head first onto the desk again.

And again.

This time, when he came out of his daze, his forehead was cut open. He drew a deep breath in preparation to scream, but he felt the blood flowing from his nose back into his throat. He recognized the metallic coppery taste in his mouth.

"Jesus, help me!" he whimpered. He felt the thing behind him dematerialize into a sooty black vapor and vanish at the precise moment his bedroom door opened unexpectedly.

He turned to see his friend Tyler rushing in. Tyler closed the bedroom door behind him and studied him.

"Tyler, I was just...attacked!"

"I know," Tyler replied.

"How'd you know to come save me?"

"Because we're connected!"

"Huh?"

"Yeah, we have a very special bond, you and I. It's strong. Don't you feel it?"

Kyle dabbed his bloody nose with a tissue. He pulled it away so he could examine it.

Tyler walked up to him, smiling gently. Kyle admired his friend smiling down upon him. Everything about his appearance, from his perfectly coiffed chestnut hair, the bone structure of his slender face, the set and sparkle of his blueberry eyes, to the tiny freckles on his nose and face showed that he was pure perfection. Kyle had never been so captivated before.

Tyler reached over and dabbed Kyle's forehead with his fingertip. He pulled his finger away and turned it around. He studied it intensely. Kyle frowned. Then Tyler opened his mouth and pressed the bloody finger against his own lower lip, smearing the drop of blood all over it. Slowly, he traced the contours of his lip with his tongue. The blood seeped onto it. Kyle cringed.

Tyler looked down at him, smiled, and said, "We're blood brothers now!" He licked his lip again. Tyler reached forward and dabbed his finger onto the wound on Kyle's forehead. It felt like it was already dry. The blood must have clotted. Tyler traced his finger down Kyle's head, past his temples, around his cheekbone and down to his chin. Then he traced his finger across Kyle's lips. Kyle began to breathe heavily. He felt a tingling sensation course through his body. Tyler cupped his hands across the back of Kyle's neck and squeezed it – massaged it gently. Kyle exhaled forcefully and his breathing became shorter and more intense. Tyler gazed down at his friend tenderly. He began working his fingers around his own shirt buttons.

"What is he doing?" Kyle thought.

Tyler unbuttoned the first button. Kyle knew that Tyler was studying him for the slightest, most minute response. He was mesmerized. He studied Tyler's fingers as he unfastened each button, which allowed his shirt to spread open wider and wider. He noticed that Tyler's silver ring was missing – the ring that his first girlfriend, Bethany, had given him. It didn't matter.

Kyle was in a trance...in a situation that, despite his deepest secret fantasies, he'd never believed he'd find himself in. He felt the familiar pressure in his jeans grow larger and fuller with each pop of the buttons. When Tyler's shirt was spread completely open, all Kyle could do was stare at Tyler's navel and the silver belt buckle hiding the button that would unfasten his jeans beneath it.

Tyler inched his body closer in between Kyle's legs so that his navel was just an inch away from Kyle's face. Kyle's trembling hands were resting on his knees. He wanted to reach out and touch his friend, but he was lost in uncertainty. Tyler reached over and traced his finger along the inside edge of Kyle's shirt collar. Then, so help him, Kyle could do nothing to resist what he did next. As much as he tried to fight the impulse, he opened his mouth and touched the tip of his tongue against the inside of Tyler's belly button. It was warm – salty. Kyle felt Tyler's hands on his shoulders, squeezing forcefully while Kyle finally kissed his navel. "I love you," said Kyle.

Tyler ripped Kyle's hands away, shot his fists forward, and shoved him back into the chair, which collided with the edge of the desk behind it. His head snapped back. Tyler sneered at him viciously with horrible squinted eyes. "What the *hell* did you just say? What the hell do you think you're doing?"

Kyle was stunned. Was he set up? He pleaded, "Tyler... I..."

"Shut your filthy trap!" Saliva shot out from the corner of his mouth, through clenched teeth. He grabbed Kyle's shoulders and practically crushed them in his hands. The strength was unbelievable. Before Kyle knew what had happened, Tyler threw him out of his chair and flung him around and onto his bed, head first into the wall. Kyle went limp. A second later, when he came to, he heard Tyler's belt buckle jingling...and his fly opening...and then he heard his friend taking off his jeans.

Kyle's ears began to ring. It was a low, dull tone. It was maddening. He tried to move, but he was paralyzed, not from fear or bewilderment, but simply paralyzed. Then, by-passing the tones in his ears, he heard the vicious snarling he could only compare to some of the most frightening monster movies he'd ever seen. He felt the ice-cold hands reach into the back of his shirt collar. They tugged violently and his shirt was torn in two halves. He heard them being flung away onto the desk behind them. Then he felt the razor-sharp fingernails dig deep into his flesh. He felt each agonizing sting and the warm sensation of a pool of blood form beneath each nail. He felt them rake down the length of his back.

Kyle screamed in agony.

He felt the pressure against his belt, and against his waist. He cringed and desperately visualized Archangel Michael holding a magical glowing golden rope that wound through each of his belt loops, securing his pants around his waist. The hands instantly released their hold on his belt. "Thank God! It worked!" he thought.

Then he felt like he'd been enveloped inside a nauseating cloud of the worst stench he could ever imagine – like being plunged headfirst and smothered in a week's worth of soiled, sweaty gym clothes. He heard the diabolical voice inside his head, the same voice he had heard when he and Jimmy burst through the front doors of Our Lady of the Rosary Chapel while the exorcism of Matthew McLaughlin was taking place. The demon inside Tyler's father had sniffed the air like a dog attracted to and tracking a scent. It had said, "I know your sins, Kyle Foster!"

Kyle was paralyzed with fear. He waited for the worst. Then he felt the seam of his jeans split wide open from the underside of the zipper on the front, all the way up the back side to the lowest edge of his belt. He heard the tearing sounds of his flannel boxers. He felt the open air on his exposed, vulnerable flesh. His pants and underwear split away to the sides. Kyle panicked. He whined and whimpered, but no sounds would issue from his lips. He felt an immense weight, and *the thing* climbing and sliding on top of him from behind, and slithering up the length of his body

– and he felt its horrid panting as its mouth hovered over his shoulder blade.

Kyle began to hyperventilate. "Oh, Jesus!" He felt the maw of the beast hovering over his shoulders and he gasped as the wet, tepid, hairy body slithered all over his exposed back. The putrid, sickening fumes that emanated from its throat and mouth permeated his nostrils.

He heaved.

Thick, slimy ooze dribbled onto his shoulder and neck as the thing moaned and salivated all over him. Kyle felt it bite into his neck, not deep enough to draw blood but enough to...Then Kyle gasped as he never had before!

He felt the stabbing pain in his rectum. It was huge, bumpy, and slippery as it penetrated him quickly and force-fully. Kyle tried to scream, but he felt the wet, cold, clammy hand coil around his mouth to silence him. The beast groaned as it shoved all the way inside him. Kyle tried to protest but it was no use. It pulled all the way outside of his body and just when Kyle thought it was over, it slammed right back into him.

The pain was excruciating.

It rammed him again and forced Kyle's skull into the wooden headboard. It did it again. And again. Kyle started to slip away. He hoped he'd pass out so he could escape the horror of the rape altogether. Then, in rapid succession, it pounded him and rammed the top of his head into the headboard mercilessly with over thirty thrusts. The visions of angelic intervention faded away – just as he did – into darkness and stillness, into unconsciousness.

With his first waking moments, he focused on the stabbing pain in his rectum. It was saturated and throbbing. With each beat of his heart, he could feel the pulse around and inside his devastated backside. His head was also throbbing, beaten in by a creature he never even saw. Sure, it appeared as his best friend and used that to gain his trust long enough to lure him into the situation that led to this most despicable violation, but he knew it was never Tyler at all. He opened his eyes. There was no sunlight coming in from the window. Instead, it was pitch dark outside. He heard his mother call from downstairs, "Kyle...it's almost time for dinner, Son."

Kyle closed his eyes and moaned. He heard the foot-steps on the stairs. Shortly after, he heard her approach his door. He knew he'd left it unlocked, but he couldn't move. This would be far more embarrassing than when his mother walked in on him while he was masturbating a few weeks earlier. "How am I going to explain this?" he thought. Then, unlike that time, he heard her release the doorknob, and out of respect for his privacy, he heard her knock two times on the door instead. "Kyle, Honey, dinner will be ready in fifteen minutes."

Kyle forced out a response. "Okay, Mom. I'll be down then." He heard her walk away. Kyle bent over and tried to sit up on the bed and immediately shot up onto his feet – the pain was excruciating. He regarded himself in the mirror. He had bruises all over his body, but from what? He couldn't remember being bludgeoned badly enough to cause the bruises he was seeing. Then he turned around to look at his back. Horrific scratch marks stretched from his neck to his waistline. Then, he glanced down slowly – afraid to examine the damage. He gasped.

His ass was red, swollen, bruised and...by God...covered in...

Kyle wanted to scream, but cupped his hand over his mouth and whimpered instead. Tears streamed from his eyes as he went into the bathroom and turned on the shower. How could he tell his mother what had happened? How could she ever come to understand the horror he and his friend's family had endured just a few months earlier, the same horror that led to this – the most debilitating and despicable attack upon him that he could possibly imagine?

Kyle stepped into the shower and sank into the soothing feeling of the hot steady stream of liquid bliss. He jolted when the water struck the back of his body. His head began to throb. Kyle leaned back and visualized holy water bathing his body. He felt his buttocks throbbing and a tight pinching sensation inside him. Then he sank into nothingness and focused on the hot water and nothing else.

For what seemed an eternity, Kyle enjoyed the peace and tranquility of the hot shower. The steam that filled the stall swirled around his body, coiled around his legs and torso and lightly and gently caressed him. He visualized this steam as being the Holy Spirit safeguarding him from any further violations.

When he was finished with his shower, he stepped out into the steam-filled haze of the bathroom. He could barely see his own reflection in the mirror, the faint outline of his blond mop-headed hairdo, the outline of his rounded shoulders and slender torso, a single pink nipple, and the top outside edge of his pelvis. The room was dead-silent. He waited and listened; his eyes darted back and forth. The last few water drops resounded inside the shower and Kyle could hear his own steady breathing. He leaned over the sink and looked at his reflection in the mirror – his green eyes, the few small freckles on his nose, and his nostrils expanding and contracting as he drew and exhaled each breath, as the terror inside slowly began to subside.

Kyle wiped the steam away from the mirror with a slow, steady swipe of his palm. The noise his fingers made against the glass made him cringe. It was just one of those uncomfortable sounds buried somewhere deep in the human psyche. He turned around slowly so he could see himself in the mirror, turning his head so he could regard himself. He tilted his head forward to examine the back of his neck. He jolted and scooted his body closer to the mirror. He turned sharply to expose as much of his back as he could. "What the..." The scratches he had seen before he started the shower were gone. He reached back and touched the center of the back of his neck and felt nothing out of the ordinary.

Relieved, Kyle smiled. He looked down at his ravaged buttocks and saw what appeared to be nothing but his perfectly round contours where, before his shower, they had been swollen and red. He hesitated to touch them, but he knew he had to. He grimaced and pressed two fingers against the outside edge of his right cheek. He watched as his fingers pressed into the side of his buttock. He felt nothing at all out of the ordinary. Kyle sighed in relief.

"Oh my God, thank You!"

He cupped his hand over one whole cheek and squeezed. Feeling no pain at all, he squeezed harder until he pulled his hand away. All he saw was the blood seeping back into the finger marks until his skin was a perfect shade of pink. He turned and faced the mirror head-on. Kyle inhaled deeply and held his breath as he examined his face and his body in the mirror. Then he exhaled fully. There was one thing left to do. His eyes widened because he was frightened about what he might feel inside his body and on his fingers. He reached slowly behind him and pressed his index finger on the small of his back. His breathing became shorter and more pronounced as his inched his index finger down into the cleft of his buttocks. Down it went into the moist warmer clefts of his cheeks inching closer to his anus. He felt nothing out of the ordinary in his nerves, and he reached out with the nerve endings in his fingers to sense anything out of the ordinary. He drew a final deep breath and closed his eyes. His lower lip trembled. He slid his finger onto his anus and pressed against it.

Kyle sighed.

He exhaled quickly and inhaled just as rapidly. He probed around the circumference of the most sensitive, most private part of his body and felt no pain, no swelling, and nothing at all unusual.

Kyle moved his hand forward and braced himself on the sink with both arms. He wept and finally broke down and fell to the bathroom floor and wailed in agony as he recalled the horrific events that had transpired. He sat there holding his palms over his eyes for over two minutes. Those two minutes seemed like two hours.

Kyle stood, checked himself in the mirror one last time and opened the door. He shrieked. His mother was standing right there in the doorway of his room. He realized that he was still naked and covered himself with his hands. "Jesus, Mom!"

His mother backed away and covered her eyes with her hand. "I'm sorry..." She turned her back to him. "I called you down for dinner over thirty minutes ago."

With his hands still cupped over his genitals, Kyle ran into his room while his mother waited for him in the hallway just outside his room. "How embarrassing," he thought. He tugged open the second drawer and pulled out a pair of his underwear.

His mother called out to him from the hallway, "Do you think you can handle your own 'private time' when it doesn't interfere with the needs of the rest of the family?"

Kyle's eyes bulged and he gasped. He knew what she was referring to when she emphasized the words "private time." He held his underwear before him, spread the elastic band and inserted a leg. He tried to feign ignorance and answered her, "My what?" He slipped his other leg into his underwear and pulled them over his hips.

He heard his mother's exasperated sigh. "You know what I mean," she replied. He heard her coming closer. Kyle panicked, and scanned his room quickly. He turned around and bumped into her as she walked further into the room. They gasped and moved away from each other. His mother said, "Can you please make an effort to come down for dinner when you're called?"

"I'm sorry, Mom. I lost track of time."

His mother smirked. She didn't know whether that was amusing or revolting.

He followed her eyes as they moved away from his own, past his shoulder slowly and down. Kyle took a deeper breath than normal and his mother's eyes opened up wide. Wider still went her eyes and she gasped. Kyle was paralyzed with fear. It was one thing to face the demons. It was another thing entirely to face the probing curiosity of a nosy mother. She lunged forward and eased him out of the way. Kyle whirled around, aghast. She bent down and picked up Kyle's rent jeans and underwear. She held them up before her and spread them out. The entire backside was torn down the middle as he expected.

"What in the name of God did you do?" She turned around and held them before her chest with a look of shock.

Kyle's tongue hung out past his lower lip as though he'd been knocked in the head with a two-by-four. "I...." Kyle tried to say. "I've been studying karate with Jimmy's dad and I tried to do the splits..."

His mother keeled over and laughed herself silly. She covered her mouth with the back of her hand and put his clothing on his dresser. Kyle felt an enormous wave of relief pass over him like a cool wave on a hot summer's day. He was pleased with himself that he came up with such a quick response, even though it was a total lie.

She walked closer to him and gave him an apologetic look. "That's why they wear those silly-looking white karate suits, Dear." She shook her head and chuckled as she walked away.

"Gis, Mom."

She turned around. "Jeez, what?"

Kyle huffed. "Gis," he corrected her. "They're called gis!"

"Jeez, gis, whatever." She started down the stairs and called out to him, "Just make like a *breeze* and *ease* into a chair at the table, *please.*"

Kyle snorted and shouted, "That was some serious *cheese!*" He heard his mother's laugh echo in the stairway.

After dinner, Kyle crept into his mother's office and closed the door behind him. He took the telephone receiver off the base and dialed. It didn't take long for someone to answer.

"Hello?" It was Tyler.

"It's me, Kyle!"

Tyler replied in his usual jovial way and asked, "Hey, what's up?" Then his tone became more serious because he knew these were serious times. "Are you okay, Kyle?"

"Yeah, well, no," Kyle answered.

"Well, what does that mean? You're either okay, or you're not."

Kyle paused. He had no idea what to tell him, or how to tell him, or what parts, if any, he should keep to himself, or what parts he should reveal.

"Kyle?" Tyler insisted. "Did something happen?"

"I...I'd better tell you in person."

"Sure," Tyler answered. "Do you wanna come here? Or do you want me to come to you?"

Kyle thought long and hard about that. To make him understand what had happened, he knew he had to reveal his special feelings for Tyler, but Tyler was one of his two best friends. He wasn't entirely sure how Tyler would take it. If Tyler ended up getting upset enough about it, Kyle didn't want to have to make him feel guilty about the need to kick him out of his house. Kyle also didn't want to have to guess, and then feel unwelcome enough to think that he should just leave on his own.

After a few moments, Kyle decided that it would be better to tell Tyler in Kyle's house, so Tyler could just leave – if that was what he wanted to do.

"Dude, you're wiggin' me out," Tyler said. "What's going on?"

Kyle said, "I think it'd be best if you came here. I have something really private to share with you."

"Well, okay," he replied. "But I'll have to walk, because we're short one car."

"Why not ride your bike?"

"It's too slippery to ride my bike. I don't wanna fall and bust my head open."

"Good idea," Kyle said.

"I'll see you in a little while."

Chapter 20 – Revelations

TYLER FELL FLAT ONTO HIS BACK when Kyle confessed what had happened to him, laughing so hysterically, in fact, that he both laughed and belched at the same time. On his knees facing him, Kyle dropped his face into his open palms. Kyle listened to him laughing for over a minute until he'd finally had enough and shouted, "Dude, it's not funny!"

Tyler wiped his tear-soaked eyes and sat up shaking his head. He looked over at the torn jeans and underwear Kyle had shown him, now crumpled in a pile on the floor next to his bed where he claimed the attack had happened. His lips quivered and he fell back down and broke out into another laughing fit. When he opened his eyes again and looked at his friend, Kyle just sat there pouting and when Tyler saw it, he snorted and burst out laughing again. He couldn't help it. He knew it was the most awful, disrespectful thing he could ever do, but when he visualized the attacks, something that he and his friends would laugh in hysterics about together if they had seen those same events unfold in a movie, or if they had heard about it happening to someone else, he rolled onto his side, which along with his shoulders, shook and convulsed as he laughed.

Disappointed, and clearly having enough, Kyle rushed over to his friend, snatched Tyler's sweatshirt hood, pulled it over his head, tugged on the drawstrings as tightly as he could, and squashed Tyler's face inside. When only Tyler's nose was poking through, Kyle shouted, "It's not fucking funny!"

Tyler wailed with laughter, more intensely than ever. When he found it possible to utter a response he said: "It's fucking hilarious, Kyle. I'm sorry, but oh, my God!"

Still kneeling and bent over Tyler, Kyle sat up straight, squeezed his thighs and arched his head back. The dark memories swirled around in his mind like deep-sea creatures in the dark, cold waters of the abyss. The recollections of the beast atop him, *and inside him*, filled him with fury. Amid the rage of that ultimate violation, there remained too much guilt about letting his guard down in a false sense of security, allowing himself to be caught in that vulnerability, even after Tyler and Yvonne had rushed over to his house to warn him. Kyle shook his head repeatedly.

Kyle wanted to strike back at the demons. The rape filled him with rage. Reliving the images as they moved in his mind fueled his rage like gasoline on a fire. He made a fist and rapped it on his thigh. As he felt his adrenaline course through his body, he suddenly felt ill at the thought of engaging those preternatural spirits. He was caught somewhere between the bile of hatred and the fear of falling victim to them again. Kyle lifted a hand to wipe the tears from his eyes. He could not contain them anymore from his best friend sitting there, now gazing at him intently, expressionless and at a loss for words.

But little did they know, the very act of recalling the horrific encounter and focusing his awareness upon the vile entity that had taken advantage of him, summoned a similar, if not identical, darkness right into their midst.

Without any warning whatsoever, the blackness swept over their heads from the ceiling and then down upon them, enclosing them both in a sooty black cloud of ash. The two teens scrambled, tripping and falling over each other to get out of harm's way. Tyler heard the sounds of the same buzzing black flies coming from the sink drain in his kitchen. He grimaced. But these weren't black flies, they were mosquitoes, stinging, blood-sucking bugs – the worst of them all.

All around them, the air hung thick with the smell of decay. The annoyance of stinging insects buzzed in their ears, and the sound of their own slapping became as annoying as the buzzing wings. They knew they weren't real, how could they be? They were part of the same demoniacal illusion cast upon them weeks ago, but it was just as convincingly real this time.

"What are we gonna do?" Tyler pleaded, punctuating his question with a resounding smack across his own face. He brought his hand out and held it up, expecting to see a squashed bug the size of his fingernail, and a splat of blood and pus. But there was nothing.

They ran down the stairs and continued right down into the basement. Kyle fumbled in the dark until he wound his way beyond the staircase. Tyler lost him and panicked.

"Dude, where'd you go?"

Kyle inched his way along the familiar wall into the next room. What little light shone in from beyond the glass sliding door allowed him to spot the long string affixed to the light bulb mounted on a small plank of wood nailed between the floor joists above. He tugged on it and the room was suddenly filled with a soft pink glow. Kyle poked his head around the corner and said, "In here!"

When Tyler rounded the corner, Kyle leaned a green bicycle over toward him. He rolled a second bike beside him, yanked open the sliding door and quickly moved outside.

"Where are we gonna go?" Tyler asked.

"Jimmy's house!" Kyle replied as though that was the most obvious answer he could have given him.

The terrified teens pedaled up the driveway as fast as they could, and screamed down the street a few blocks over toward Jimmy's house – even if it did mean "busting open their melons."

A moment later, Tyler and Kyle pedaled down Jimmy's road and when they saw what they knew to be Jimmy's house in the distance through the trees, they saw a column of gray smoke rising up into the sky. They coasted down Jimmy's driveway, dumped their bikes on the front lawn and ran up to the front door. Kyle pressed the doorbell over and over while Tyler pounded on the door with his fist.

Jimmy yanked open the door seconds later. His astonished expression quickly faded. "What is it, guys? You guys scared the shit outta me!"

"Wait till we tell you what happened," Tyler screeched. Kyle looked at his friends and was hesitant to continue. He had seen how Tyler reacted to the account of his rape, and Tyler had always been kinder and more sensitive than Jimmy was. Jimmy could be a complete dick more often than not.

"Come in, dipshits!" Kyle's jaw dropped. Realizing his uncouth summons, Jimmy tilted his head, sighed and clacked his tongue on the roof of his mouth. "Will ya just get in here?"

Kyle walked in. Tyler had already stepped down into Jimmy's man-cave, the finished basement complete with fireplace. It was nice and toasty warm inside. Kyle followed Tyler, and Jimmy was the last to enter the room. He waved his hands before them and asked, "What's up?"

Kyle's head sank and his shoulders drooped.

"Well, what is it?" Tears welled up in Kyle's eyes. "Aw, Jeez! What now?" He went over and sat down on the sectional sofa. He grimaced and reached behind him through the seat cushions and pulled out a Godzilla toy he'd sat on.

"Kyle's really been through the wringer, Jim," Tyler warned.

The tears from the horror, and the unrelenting anger – no, not anger, for that word hardly sufficed to describe the emotions pouring from him – streamed down Kyle's face.

Tyler nodded. He knew, but Jimmy, of course, hadn't a clue what was going on.

Tyler had come to understand that rape, for Kyle had painted for him a very dark scene indeed. He wondered what turmoil must be coursing through his friend's mind. Tyler could only imagine. He could equate nothing in his own past to the swirling storm raging within his friend.

While he had faced his own trials and trauma dealing with the vicious onslaughts of the demonic entities in his house, being choked paled in comparison to the rape.

He wanted to empathize, to understand and to offer some advice or words of comfort, but he knew that any words he might say would surely sound hollow. He couldn't truly understand. He knew now what a fool he had been for laughing at Kyle. The images of himself and his friend entwined in the passionate rendezvous he'd described was just too hilarious not to laugh about.

Though he always felt that Kyle had deeper feelings for him than he had ever let on, it felt to Tyler, at that awkward moment during that revelation, that the most natural reaction would be his own need to guard his manly pride and to simply laugh it off, at the expense of his friend.

Tyler dropped his head in defeat. He felt that he had failed an important test in his friendship, his relationship with Kyle. He scoffed and squirmed where he sat at the thought of the word "relationship." It was awkward to think about.

Kyle sat there with a distant, detached expression.

"Well, my God, I'm not Yvonne! Are you going to tell me what happened, or do I have to pull it out of thin air?"

Kyle looked at them both sitting on the sectional. These were his best friends, his only friends. How could he tell Jimmy the extent of the attack upon him the way it really happened? How couldn't he? He paused until Jimmy smacked his own thighs in frustration.

"Oh, my God! Are you gonna tell me or not?"

"Don't be a dick, Jim! This is gonna be really intense," Tyler warned.

Kyle forced a curt smile. Now, Tyler was finally understanding the seriousness of the situation. Kyle drew a deep breath and exhaled heavily. "Okay, here goes..."

Jimmy adjusted himself in his seat as Kyle paced the room in front of them, telling them exactly what happened.

"You were seduced by Sarah, right?"

Jimmy fidgeted. "It wasn't..."

"By the demon who masqueraded as Sarah..."

"Yep," Jimmy said. "It was the most awful..." He started to go into details, but they'd both heard it before. They didn't need any more clarification.

Tyler wrinkled up his face like a prune. Time and again Jimmy had made sexual innuendos about his sister and he hated him for it. Now, he had to think about the two of them in startling detail, and the whole thing made *him* as sickened as the ordeal was sickening for Jimmy. He was convinced that he had done something wrong in a former life and he was being punished in the form of Jimmy's taunting. But this wasn't about him at the moment. This was about Kyle, and Tyler knew he had to make amends for his rude behavior earlier when Kyle had confided in him.

"You were seduced by the likeness of Sarah because you have feelings for her."

"Had," Jimmy said with confidence. "I did have feelings for her, warm, moist, hard..."

Tyler smacked him across the chest. "Cut...it out!"

Jimmy belly laughed as Tyler held his face in his hand. When he was done joking around, he said, "I seriously can't ever look at her the same way again. I don't know what I'll do if I see her!"

"You're missing my point."

"Okay," Jimmy said, putting his hands up.

"This is serious," Tyler said.

"Wow, I'm feeling like I'm being raked over the coals here. Does either of you want to kick me in the balls too?"

"You're unbelievable, ya know that?" Tyler said. He shook his head.

"What?" Jimmy begged.

"This isn't about you, this is about your friend," Tyler said, holding his hands out toward Kyle. "Our friend..." He extended a hand toward Jimmy and curled the other toward himself. "And he has something to tell you."

"Okay," Jimmy said. "I'm sorry." He couldn't help but burst out with a laugh. "If this isn't in any way as serious as you both make it out to be, I'm gonna kick both your asses and throw you out into the snow."

Kyle huffed and whirled around. "I'm leaving!"

Jimmy said, "All right! All right! All right!"

Tyler sneered at him, "Continue, I won't say a word, I promise!"

Kyle paused and pondered how best to convey his message. He really didn't believe Jimmy was at all serious. "You thought of Sarah when you were 'slappin' the salami'..."

Jimmy started to make a wisecrack and Tyler held a finger up to him.

"When I was choking the chicken, yes!"

"Because you had feelings for her, right?"

"Yes. Obviously."

"It's been painfully obvious, for far too long," Tyler interjected.

"Well, this may or may not come as a surprise to you, but..."

Jimmy narrowed his eyes and rolled that statement over in his mind, concocting dozens of possible avenues this conversation could travel down, but try as he might, he didn't come up with anything definitive.

"I was sitting at my desk in my bedroom, building my

plane, when I thought of Tyler as I was holding the nose section and gluing it into place."

"Umm, care to elaborate?"

Tyler rolled his eyes and exhaled heavily. He glanced at Jimmy and rocked his whole body at him as though he was saying, "*You don't get it?*" without actually uttering the words.

"Ohh!" Jimmy said.

"Yeah, I thought of Tyler in a way I really don't want to discuss right at the present, and all of a sudden, I felt this freezing cold hand wrap around my hair, tug tight and slam my forehead into the desk."

"No shit?"

"Yeah! It hurt like a bitch. Then when I realized what had happened, I was still seeing stars, and it happened again. I got smashed into the desk. My head was split open and I was bleeding. As soon as I came to my senses, in walked Tyler." Jimmy looked at Tyler and then back at Kyle. "Only, it wasn't Tyler, any more than your attacker was Sarah."

"Whoa!"

"Yeah, but just like you, I didn't know it at the time. I couldn't believe my eyes, partly because I was totally out of it and I felt a gash in my head. Tyler walked up to me, really close, and then acted totally out of character, just like Sarah seemed to you."

"Then what?" Tyler covered his face in his palms. He couldn't even fathom how terrible this had been for his friend who genuinely felt strongly for him. Sometimes it happened, he knew. Sometimes, friends become more closely knit than others and feelings start to get convoluted.

"The demonic spirit tried to seduce me based upon my passions, just like it did you."

"Okay," Jimmy said.

"I'm going to use Tyler's name during the rest because to me, it was Tyler."

"Go ahead," he urged.

"Tyler pressed his finger on my bloody forehead and tasted the blood and told me we were 'blood brothers!' He rubbed my shoulders and told me everything would be okay. He started unbuttoning his shirt and told me we had a 'special bond.' Then he inched closer to me and unfastened his shirt until it split open."

Jimmy reached his arm back behind his head and propped his head against it.

"He squeezed my shoulders again and leaned in closer, smiling down at me. His belt buckle was right there in front of my face."

Jimmy grinned and grabbed his crotch. "Ohh, this is making me horny!"

Tyler slapped his own thigh and scoffed. He whirled around to face his friend. "Really, Jim? This is making you horny? Really?"

Jimmy looked taken aback. "Yeah, we're all hot young dudes in our sexual prime. We think about sex five times a minute, or something crazy like that. It's a sexy story!"

"What the fuck?" Tyler said. He just shook his head. His friend was a walking hormone.

"I stuck my tongue out and pressed it into Tyler's belly button and for some reason, I don't know why, because I wasn't thinking it – I said, 'I love you!' "

Jimmy smirked. "Aww!"

"All of a sudden, Tyler lurched back, sneered at me as if I had told him I hated him and wanted to kill him. His response was 'Shut your filthy trap!' "

"Well, that's not very nice," Jimmy said. He shot a disappointed look at Tyler.

"It wasn't me, that's for sure," Tyler interjected.

"Then he picked me up, threw me out of my chair, I mean like literally tossed me out and threw me onto my bed."

"Uh, oh," muttered Jimmy.

"I smashed my head into the headboard pretty bad and I was seeing stars. The next thing I knew I heard Tyler undoing his belt buckle. It's a pretty distinctive sound and I recognized it from that time when we all had to strip down to our underwear on Tyler's porch, and when we changed into dark clothes together before mischief night. Then I heard the sound of his zipper opening and of his pants coming off and then the sound of them thrown into the corner. I couldn't move, no matter how badly I wanted to move."

"Did you want him to stop or, ya know...were you looking forward to it?"

Kyle scoffed. "After he'd turned into that snarling monster version of himself, and after he tossed me out of my chair, I definitely knew it wasn't him! I definitely did not want to just lie there."

"It wasn't me," Tyler repeated. "Stop saying 'Tyler' this and 'Tyler' that!"

"Then, what happened?" Jimmy asked, intrigued.

Tyler buried his face in a pillow. He couldn't even imagine what Kyle was going through and he thanked God it hadn't happened to him instead.

"It ripped my shirt off and then it tried for my jeans, but I visualized an archangel tying a golden cord around my waist so it wouldn't be able to take off my belt and remove my jeans like I knew it was wanting to do."

"Oh, it wanted to get some!"

"Then I heard my jeans split at the seam, right down the middle."

Jimmy roared with laughter.

"I was terrified. I felt my boxers split, too. I knew my bare ass was showing through because I could feel the falling temperature in my room. Then I felt this grotesquely hairy, disgustingly fat, muscular, revolting body sliding up along mine. I heard it breathing over my shoulder and felt its putrid breath against my ear. It dug its fingernails into my neck and raked them all the way down to my waist. It bit me in the shoulder and neck and then it basically pounded me into the headboard until I passed out."

Kyle sat down cross-legged on the carpet and tapped his fingertips against his thigh while Jimmy stared at him in silence for a full, agonizing minute. Tyler looked at Jimmy several times, wondering what he was going to eventually say or do. Finally, he broke his uncomfortable silence.

"Does it still hurt?" the ever sarcastic Jimmy asked.

Kyle scoffed at him and stared incredulously. "Is this how you make yourself feel better, chiding me because I got my freakin' ass plowed when you got an amazing blow?"

Jimmy huffed. "Dude, I am not *poking* fun at you, honest!" He laughed. He leaned over and held out his hand for him. "I feel really, *really* bad for you."

Kyle shook his head from side to side. He wouldn't take his hand.

"Seriously, I can relate," he pleaded, recalling his own rape experience. "Sure, I can't relate in the *exact* same way, because your attack was much more severe than mine was."

He slapped his hands together like he was about to ay, looked at the ceiling, and said, "Spare me, Jesus! I can't even imagine what that was like." He shook his head and looked back at his friend. "But I *can relate* to the being tricked and violated part in pretty much the same way. I promise you!"

Jimmy was being honest when he finally said, "I'm trying to say the right things, so you'll understand my sincerity."

Without looking at him, Kyle reached his hand out toward Jimmy who took it instantly, squeezed it tight and held it for several moments. Tyler added his own hand on top of theirs and said, "We are all in this together. Nothing is going to screw up our friendship." Kyle's head sank. Tyler wanted to reach out and hug his friend who was obviously hurting inside. Kyle looked at the carpet before him. He looked utterly defeated.

"Screw it," Tyler said. He leaned over, wrapped his arms around his friend and hugged him tight. Kyle reached his hands around Tyler, but he held them in the air, not knowing what to do with his feelings – now that he had revealed them to Tyler.

"You're one my best friends, Kyle. I mean it." He wrinkled his brow. "You know it."

To Kyle, Tyler's grin told him that he recognized his true feelings all too well. The timbre of his voice told him that he was more amused than upset. He appreciated the embrace and returned it wholeheartedly. The two friends hugged tightly.

"Aw, come here and give me hugs, too, ya big softies," Jimmy said. Tyler chuckled and for the first time in days, Kyle actually laughed aloud also. The trio held each other for a while, and then they each scooted back and took the spots they had occupied before.

The crackling fire shot embers exploding against the black metal fireplace screen. The pale moonlight coming in from the great sliding glass door cast long shadows through the tree branches and speckled the carpet before them. It was a quiet night, full of self-reflection. Every once in a while, Tyler would look up to see if Kyle was looking at him, and more times than not, he wasn't. Their friendship from this time forward wasn't going to be at all awkward as he had feared it would be. It wasn't going to be uncomfortable after all. Rather, it made him feel special and he would find later that the loving bond between them was the greatest defense against the dark spirits that had campaigned against them.

Chapter 21 - Unwelcome Guests

IN THE MCLAUGHLIN HOME, JUST AFTER DINNER, the doorbell rang. Sarah looked up as she was scraping her plate into the trash and regarded her mother with a quizzical expression. The doorbell rang again. Linda raised a brow. Sarah answered her back with a wordless, unsure shrug of her shoulders. There in the kitchen they remained, in uncomfortable silence until...

The doorbell rang again.

Linda braced herself on the table and was about to get up, when Sarah finally broke the silence and said, "I'll get it." She walked into the foyer and shuffled down the slate floor in her socks. As she approached the front door, she glanced out the narrow windows on both the left and right sides of the door. She peeked through the opaque sheer white panels covering the windows to see who was there, but she could see nothing – or no one – outside.

The doorbell rang again. This time Sarah saw a shadow flit on the porch and identified it, in all probability, as the arm that must have reached out for the doorbell and had been retracted. Sarah switched on the outside light and pulled open the door. She stared through the glass storm door. She flinched and stepped away. Outside, two children, a girl and a boy, each no older than ten, stood on the landing shivering in the cold, rubbing their shoulders with their bare hands. Sarah's first, protective impulse was to open the door to let the children inside immediately, but something deep in her gut caused her to regard them with suspicion. She paused and studied them intensely, but as she did so, she felt herself being pulled toward them in a most peculiar and uncomfortable way.

The female child stepped forward. "Can we come inside?"

Sarah gasped. "Um!"

"Please, we need to call for help."

Linda called out to her from the kitchen and asked, "Sarah, who's at the door, Dear?"

Sarah felt stranger as the seconds passed. The longer she scrutinized them, the more difficult she found it to do so. She noticed that both of the children were fair-skinned. Studying them further, their skin appeared to be more translucent and pure white, rather than what a normal rosy-colored pinkish skin should appear to be. Their platinum hair was out of the ordinary also, and the boy's hair was cut short – too short.

"Please, it's cold," said the girl. "Can we come inside and use the telephone?"

Sarah winced and turned up the corner of her mouth. Something was far from normal.

Her mother called out to her again from the kitchen, "Sarah...who's there?"

The children wore gray button-down, long-sleeved shirts and their pants appeared to be made of an old-fashioned wool. They did not seem to fit right at all. When she looked down through the glass at their feet, both of the kids were wearing what she could only describe as the black shoes a businessman would wear back in the early fifties.

"Sarah," her mother called, walking now into the foyer. "Who's *there*?"

Sarah turned slowly back toward her mother. For some reason, she found it hard to speak. Her mother had asked her a question and for many heartbeats, that question spun in the air before her. She tried to grasp at it, but each time, it seemed to move further and further away out of reach.

She honestly had no clue who or what had come to their door, but she knew they were affecting her ability to reply.

Suddenly, she felt forced to turn back and face the children. Everything before her, including the images of the children, seemed to pull and stretch away from her in an elongated cone. Even though the things up close seemed to be moving farther away, it caused things in the distance to appear nearer and to become more clearly defined. She could see all the way to the stone wall at the far edge of the lawn.

The bizarre crystal clarity led to a dizzying, almost magnifying effect on the grasses, the branches, and the fallen leaves far in the distance.

When she was able to focus again on the children, she noticed something even more substantially wrong. The images shifted in and out of focus when she tried to examine the minutest details of their faces. She flinched upon further examination, because she saw that they had no eyebrows at all. Then she noticed that though they stared at her incessantly, they never blinked once. Not once. In fact, to Sarah's astonishment, they had no eyelashes. And to make matters worse, their eyes also had no irises. They looked like solid black, shining marbles that absorbed the light rather than reflected it.

Sarah felt as though she were spinning away. Then she felt her mother's warm hand as she cupped it over her shoulder. It was soothing, something familiar in the alien environment she had found herself in. It brought Sarah's awareness back from the dark, foreboding place it was being drawn into.

Linda leaned in so she could see what was going on and who had come to their door unexpectedly in the dark early-evening hours.

"May we please come inside?" the little girl pleaded.

Linda was instantly mesmerized. She reached for the door handle. It was all she could do. The girl smiled at her and nodded. The smile was hypnotic, satiating, and comforting. She unhooked the lock release with her thumbnail and suddenly, a hand came from behind her, grabbed the small handle on the storm door and held it shut.

The little girl's face exploded with rage.

Yvonne had thrust her left hand in, accidentally shoving Linda away in the process. She tried to flick the lock shut, but the girl tugged on the much larger door handle from the other side. Yvonne was lurched forward each time the little one yanked on the door handle. She screeched. Her hair flew wildly with each terrifying thrust.

"Linda!" Yvonne cried out. Though she had been shoved just a step or two away, Linda hadn't moved since. Her face was locked in a silent scream. Yvonne shouted again, "Linda!" The door pulled away again and Yvonne yanked it back, but each time she reached for the lock, the little monster on the other side caused her to fly forward.

"Sarah," Yvonne called.

Linda was lost to her. She quickly realized that Sarah was also immobilized. Immobilized, paralyzed, she knew it was one and the same. Sarah seemed to be fixated on the children standing before her as if she were lost in some hypnotic trance. She stared at the children with a blank expression while her jaw hung slack and a thin line of saliva spilled out and oozed down from her lip.

The door shuddered. Yvonne tried not to look at them, for she knew that their hypnotic gaze was a very real danger. A deep Celestite gemstone set in Yvonne's silver ring glittered in the moonlight shining through the glass as she fought to control the tiny latch with her perspiring fingers. The little girl regarded the stone as if it were a threat to her. She growled and stepped back a pace.

"Help me please, Linda," Yvonne shouted.

Linda snapped her head around and regarded Yvonne as she stepped beside her and then studied the children intensely from behind the glass. Suddenly, Linda came to.

She covered her mouth with her hand and bellowed. "Oh my God!" Her eyes grew wide with terror and she screamed.

Kelly ran down the stairs. "Mommy?" When she saw the very same children she had drawn in her coloring book, she rushed up to the door. She smiled and pressed her hands up against the glass. The little boy, who had avoided all contact earlier, seemed to glide forward up to the door in an instant. He reached out to Kelly.

Finally, Linda looked at Yvonne and realized what was happening. She reached forward with both arms and maneuvered her fingers in over the tiny latch and slid it into place.

The girl sneered at her when she heard the click.

Yvonne let go and stepped back. She regarded the visitors briefly and then turned her head toward the eldest McLaughlin child. "Sarah, snap out of it."

Suddenly, the two children turned toward each other, but they never said a word. Yvonne gently but forcefully eased Sarah into the adjacent living room, out of the way. As Linda studied the little girl and then the little boy standing next to her, a third child, dressed exactly like the others, appeared out of thin air behind them. All three children approached the door together. They spoke in unison. "We're very, very cold. Can we come inside?"

Linda clutched her chest and gasped again.

"Why won't you let us inside?" said the second boy.

"Kelly!" Yvonne protested. "Come back away from the door please, sweetheart."

The boy reached out for her with his pasty white hands. He leaned in closer to the door.

"Kelly! Honey!"

Yvonne yanked Kelly away and her amethyst stone dangled on its chain. The boy saw it and sneered at her. Kelly screeched and backed away up the stairs. The boy snarled again as she scaled the steps.

Linda panicked. She knew he wasn't a human boy at all. He...*it*...had no teeth whatsoever, just smooth, gray, glossy gums that appeared more like a dolphin's skin than normal gums. Linda bellowed when she saw a fourth child appear, seemingly from nowhere, behind the others, standing in the middle of the lawn. A mist started forming all around the strange, black-eyed children and spread out evenly across the front yard like a fog bank off a lake.

Suddenly, out in the haze, the yard lit up in a bright flash of white light. The main group of children on the porch landing paid no attention to the light at all, but the fourth child turned his head slowly in the direction of the driveway, where Yvonne now realized that a car was slowly turning in. The high-beam headlights passed right through the children that were standing before the door, confirming Yvonne's intuition that the children were never physical beings at all. She squinted her eyes at them and chanted silently to herself.

Sarah, who had been staring at the scene through the living room windows, suddenly unleashed a deafening scream. It frightened Kelly so badly she scurried back upstairs. Both Linda and Yvonne regarded her and then quickly turned their attention again to the yard. The fourth child they had seen earlier was gone.

The lead female child, however, turned her head in the direction of the car as it made its way down the driveway. She flitted away in an instant, and as soon as she did so, another child walked up immediately, seamlessly, to take her place. He stared into the glass door as if he were analyzing them all with silent, unmoving, jet-black eyes.

As paranormal investigator, spiritualist, and empath Jason McLeod maneuvered his white Subaru Impreza down the driveway, he noticed that the children who had been facing the house were no longer doing so. Instead, they were facing...*him*. He knew he was a target because he had been the first investigator to arrive on the scene back when the McLaughlins first reached out for help. He had been responsible for performing the final suffumigation there – a Roman Catholic house cleansing ritual for driving away evil spirits. It seemed his intuition was right. It seemed that the spirits had not given up so easily, after all.

One of the children he saw when driving in, a girl, appeared right up against the passenger side window. As the car rolled farther down the driveway, the girl seemed to move effortlessly along with it, as if she were not walking at all but silently gliding alongside the car instead. Jason pressed the power door lock button and all four doors locked in unison. When he stopped the car, put it into *Park*, and looked back through the window, the girl had vanished.

Jason looked into the rear view mirror and shuddered when he saw that very same specter sitting in the back seat, staring at him with vacant black eyes. Realizing the demonic nature of the spirits who had manifested themselves into the likenesses of children, Jason closed his eyes and drew a deep breath.

He thought the words '*I AM.*' Upon his exhale, he reached out to sense the subtle vibrations emanating out of his own electromagnetic field and visualized a brilliant, blinding, golden golf-ball-sized sphere of energy in his core. Then he focused on the emotion of love and felt it emanating from this golden sphere, spreading out in all directions as the sphere grew in size to that of a softball, and then to the size of a basketball.

He kept his focus on his breathing while silently surrounding himself in a field of pure unconditional love. And he focused on and felt the effects of all the wonderful, warm emotions associated with that love.

He didn't pay any attention to the spirit in the car with him. He didn't care about it in the least. Instead, he visualized this brilliant golden sphere spinning and rising in frequency until it was pulsating in a harmonic waveform of pure, unconditional love. As it encapsulated his body, he visualized what he knew through his understanding of the Universal Law of Attraction. He knew that by its very nature, the positive polarity of his energy field was pushing the dark, negative entity away from him, and as the field expanded into the back seat, it pushed the negative spirit out of the car completely.

He felt as if a weight had lifted, and when he checked the rear view mirror again, he noticed that the spirit had indeed moved out of the car. It stood behind it in the exhaust fumes. The little girl's eyes were not eyes at all, but instead were dull black holes appearing to consume her face from inside her head. The girl vanished, and as the field of unconditional love spread out further, she reappeared farther away from the car and closer to the road.

"I AM the Light and the Love of God," he shouted within the confines of his car. He felt the field of energy expand further, so as to intersect the garage of the house to the right of him. Then he visualized it spreading out into the foyer and the front walk and the entire front yard of the house, and expanding all the way back to envelop the mailbox and lamp post at the edge of the property – pushing away all negativity. He believed, he knew without question, that the demonic spirits were powerless against the wave of love energy.

Inside the house, Yvonne smiled with satisfaction, because she too felt the shift in energy. The child that seemed to have presented itself as the leader reappeared, or rather, phased-over the male child who was standing in the place she had previously occupied before the storm door. Instantly, the two children – the two strange beings – melded into one.

Yvonne said to her, "You're not fooling anybody!"

The face of the girl appeared again. This time, instead of eyes, it had two gaping black holes in its face where the eyes should have been. It was revealing its true form. It glared at her and then it snarled and vanished, as if it had never been standing there at all.

Yvonne looked back at the bewildered McLaughlin women. They shared silent, uneasy glances. When Yvonne turned again to face the door, all the children had vanished.

Shortly afterward, an overly large shadow cast its ominous presence on the porch as it drew closer, but this shadow was from a real, living person rather than the essence of yet another spectral intruder.

When Linda saw that it was Jason, she sighed in relief and said, "Oh, thank God!" She reached out, turned the small lock on the storm door, opened it, stepped back to grant him entry and beckoned him inside.

Chapter 22 – Discerning the Truth

JASON MCLEOD FOLLOWED LINDA AND YVONNE into the kitchen. Linda was shaking as she stood there. Yvonne smiled delightedly at the sight of her friend and colleague. She hugged him and said, "It's good to see you, Jason!"

"Likewise, Yvonne! I came as soon as I heard what was going on."

"You've arrived just in time."

"As you did, I hear," he added. "As did Vincent and the bishop when they arrived here." Jason counted with his fingers and held them up for them to see. "As did Bishop Phelan when he arrived in the nick of time to save Vincent's neck by hauling him out of his museum."

Yvonne nodded and said, "Yes!"

"I have to believe," Jason continued, "it's divine providence."

Linda liked the sound of that. She beckoned them down the hall and into the kitchen. She sank into one of the kitchen chairs.

Jason and Yvonne followed her. Sarah walked into the bathroom and grabbed a tissue. Jason said, "We've all been *nudged* to be exactly where we needed to be at precisely the most opportune moment."

Linda motioned for them to join her at the kitchen table. When they were all seated, Sarah shuffled into the room. Her eyes were bloodshot. She'd been crying. Linda made a sympathetic face. Sarah stood in the corner. She was forlorn and deeply scarred by the events that had taken place just outside the front door.

"Hello, Sarah," Jason uttered. She looked at him and forced a smile. "I hear things have been quite hairy around here."

Sarah again forced a slight smile and said, "You can say that again."

"Jason, what's going on?" Linda asked.

"Why is this happening all over again?" Sarah added, sniffling.

"If you've been paying careful attention, as I have, you'll understand that the things 'going on' are not at all similar to what happened the first time."

"They sure seem similar to me," Sarah exclaimed.

"How do you mean, Jason? Isn't it all the same type of activity?"

"We were successful at driving the spirits away the first time!" Jason pointed out.

Linda scoffed.

"That's a laugh," Sarah snorted.

Jason paused. He understood they were upset but he tried to calm them, so he could continue with his explanation. "I mean, we were successful at driving the spirits *out of your home... and out of your husband.*"

Linda nodded. "But?" She seemed to be waiting for some kind of punchline.

Jason cleared his throat. He waved his hand briskly before Yvonne. "Yvonne here has had premonitions concerning a series of attacks the demonic spirits intended to orchestrate against your family, your friends, and anyone else involved who stood against them, or stood in their way."

Sarah asked, "So everyone is going to be attacked?"

"No!" Jason said. Linda looked at Yvonne, who stared at him blankly, eager to hear what he believed was happening. "I surmise...that everyone who was present in the chapel prior to the exorcism, who had confessed their sins, and then who had been personally blessed and prayed over by Bishop Phelan, is protected from any serious physical attacks...on their person."

Linda's eyes grew wider as she ran the moving images of that terrible day over in her mind. "You're right."

Yvonne belly-laughed and rapped her fingernails on the table. She, too, recalled those events as they unfolded. "Now, why didn't I think of that?"

"You should be a detective," Linda added.

"Really," Sarah said. She came in closer, eager to hear more.

Jason smiled. He sat back in his chair. "In a way, I am a detective." He looked at his psychic friend. "In many ways, we all are. Many cases I work on with Ed and Lorraine Warren and their other investigators, such as Andy, John, Joe and Donna, are quite mysterious indeed, and they require a good deal of detective work. In fact, you wouldn't believe the detective work involved in a case I worked on with my psychic friends, Barbara Doede, Valerie Crisp, and our scientist friend, Bruce Tainio, in Rathdrum, Idaho! It was incredible." He looked at Linda.

"You're a very interesting young man," Linda smirked.

"I'd like to meet your friends in Washington," Yvonne said. "I think we'd be very effective working together."

"I do, too," Jason added.

"So tell me more about this situation here," Linda encouraged.

"Every case we encounter has its own unique elements, but much of the activity these spirits manifest is quite similar."

"So the people who weren't in the Chapel," Linda said, "and who didn't confess..." Jason nodded at her repeatedly. "And the people who were not also blessed...and prayed over by the bishop...are the ones who are in danger of being attacked. Is that what you're saying?"

Yvonne interrupted her. "Many of them already have been attacked!" Linda turned her head sharply to regard Yvonne.

"Yes," Jason said. "And you're absolutely right, Yvonne!"

Linda gulped.

"So, let's go over my list!" He withdrew a piece of paper that was folded in thirds from his brown leather jacket. Yvonne rested her chin on her open palm and leaned over so she could see it clearly. Linda got up, walked over and stood between them so she could get a good view also.

Linda gasped.

Six names were written on the paper, in blue ink. Yvonne squinted to see them more clearly. Sarah walked over and slapped the paper down onto the table.

"Sarah!" Linda protested.

She studied the list and ran her finger over the names and shouted, "Thank God!" She didn't see her name on the list. Of course, it wasn't there, because she had confessed while inside the chapel and she had also been blessed by the bishop. Then she noticed her boyfriend's name written there as plain as day. She gulped and grimaced.

Beside the names were arrows pointing to boxes that represented certain locations based upon the words written inside the boxes. The first name written in overly large script was not at all a surprise.

"Kelly," Jason said, "never confessed her sins, nor was she blessed within the chapel. Nor was she blessed in Union Cemetery when we held the memorial service there."

"Well, who was?" Sarah asked.

"Brock Manning was."

Sarah turned her upper lip. "Well, who cares about him?" She realized her insensitivity. "Well, I mean...you know what I mean," she said, sounding agitated.

Matthew walked in the garage door, scaring everyone out of their wits. When he realized what he had done, he made a wry face. "Sorry," he pleaded. "I thought you'd hear me pulling into the garage." He studied the group assembled around the kitchen table and based on his expression, he was quite pleased to see the investigator who had been so instrumental in handling his family's plight, though he had never met him. "Jason McLeod, I presume!"

Jason stood and extended his open hand toward him. "It's very nice to see that you've made a full recovery, Mr. McLaughlin."

Matthew grinned from ear to ear. "Please call me Matthew." He took off his jacket. "I have you to thank for coming to my family's aid when we needed it most. It's a pleasure to finally meet you."

"Thank you."

Matthew hung his jacket on the doorknob. He gave everyone a confused look and asked, "What's going on?" He placed his hands on his hips.

"We had a harrowing experience out on the front porch less than an hour ago."

"Oh?" Matthew replied. "Care to tell me about it? Want to fill me in?" He kissed his daughter, Sarah, on the forehead. "Hello, Sweetheart."

Sarah moaned. "Hi, Daddy! We've had a really scary night so far."

"Well, I'd love it if someone would explain why this is going on! Why is this happening again?"

After a few moments of awkward silence, Linda looked at Jason, who extended a hand toward Matthew. "Please join us, we're going over that right now."

Matthew walked over and kissed his wife on the cheek. He looked at his watch and commented, "It's half past eight. Are we going to have dinner?" He glanced toward the kitchen and noticed there was nothing being prepared. "I can order some pizzas."

"That sounds really good, Dad," Sarah said excitedly.

"That does sound good, Sweetheart!"

Matthew looked at Yvonne and Jason. Yvonne smiled.

Jason said, "Count me in! That sounds great to me. I'm not picky either, so whatever you want on it is fine with me. I'll have a slice or two."

"That's what I like to hear," Matthew chuckled. He held up his finger and said, "Don't continue without me, I'll be right back." He walked over to the refrigerator and found the magnetic business card for the family's favorite Italian restaurant. He snatched the phone off the wall mount and quickly dialed and placed their order.

When he returned to the table, Jason pointed to Kelly's name again and continued with his explanation. "Okay, Mr. McLaughlin...Matthew, sorry!"

"Matt!" he said. "You can just call me Matt."

"Okay, Matt! I've deduced that everyone who hadn't confessed their sins in the chapel, and everyone who wasn't blessed and prayed over by Bishop Phelan just before your exorcism..." He looked up at him. It was never easy to discuss such things to someone who was unfortunate enough to have been possessed. He gave him an apologetic stare and continued. "I'm sorry."

Matthew raised his hand and said, "It's quite all right."

"Everyone who wasn't blessed prior to the...exorcism is..." He paused.

"Say it!" Sarah encouraged.

"It's okay, Jason. The facts are the facts," Linda added.

"We can handle the truth," Matthew said.

Jason took a deep breath and exhaled. "Everyone who was involved and who hasn't been blessed is now extremely vulnerable to demonic attack."

An uncomfortable silence fell over the room.

"I believe they are all facing what we in the field call, 'Demoniacal Retribution.'"

Matthew put his hand on his wife's shoulder. "Can you tell us what that is, please? In layman's terms?"

He looked at Yvonne, who urged him on with her learned eyes. "Simply put, the demonic spirits we'd expelled from this house – using suffumigation – and from your body – using rites from the Roman Ritual – are seeking you out to exact their revenge."

"Oh, that's just great," Sarah scoffed. "Where was this explained as a potential consequence?"

Linda scolded her. "Sarah!"

"That makes sense," Matthew agreed. He pointed to Kelly's name. "Kelly is the first one on this list. Does that mean she's in the greatest danger?"

Linda gasped, "Oh, sweet Jesus!"

Jason shook his head from side to side. "No, I don't believe so."

"Whew," Sarah moaned. "That's a relief!"

Jason continued, "She's done nothing at all to infuriate the demonic spirits..."

"Well, what was that horror show out in the front yard then?" Matthew complained. "They certainly seemed upset to me! She sure seemed like she was a target then! I don't see how your deduction holds water. I've never seen anything like that! Was she possessed?"

"Matt," Linda scolded him. "Let him finish."

Jason looked up at him and said, "It's okay, Matt. I understand your frustration. Please let me explain further."

"Go ahead!"

"She wasn't possessed, she was co-habitated," Yvonne interjected.

"What?" Linda begged.

"What does that mean?" Matt demanded.

"Co-habitation is not quite the same as full possession in the classical sense of the word, which is when a demonic spirit wears down the body enough to force the spirit inhabiting it out and away from it completely and therefore seizes control of it for itself and its own devices – as was the case with your body, Matt."

Matthew gulped. Linda squeezed his hand.

"But when there is a strong enough connection, usually

established over long periods of time, the spirit can most effectively affect the body when it is undergoing a great deal of stress, such as the case with Kelly on the front lawn, just before and after Julie's accident."

"I understand how she could feel stress after such a loud crash, but why would she feel stressed out *before it happened*?"

Jason raised his finger. "Because the terrible vision of the crash was implanted into her mind before it even happened, and I can guarantee those images the demons made her see were most unpleasant, especially for a six-year-old girl."

Matthew's face was quickly contorted with frustration. They all understood his protective instinct and his desire to keep his daughter safe from harm, spiritual or otherwise.

After everyone took a moment to gather their thoughts, Jason continued. "Because she was traumatized both before the accident and afterward, Kelly was in an especially vulnerable state of mind. The demonic spirit was then able to maneuver itself close enough and inside enough of her electromagnetic field not only to control her thoughts, which allowed it to control her body's movements, but also to seize control of her body, enough to move away from Vincent who was approaching her because it knew he'd quickly be able to discern what was really going on. That's why it appeared that Kelly was protesting his approach and was demanding he keep away from her."

"Fascinating," Matt said.

"It was a simple feat to knock Vincent away with just a quick shove."

"It's all just incredible to me," Matt said.

"Quite!"

Matt paced the kitchen. He checked his watch. "I'd never in a million years have believed this stuff, if it hadn't happened to me and my own family!"

"You're not the exception. Most people wouldn't."

Linda scoffed. "You *didn't* believe it," she said loudly. "I tried to tell you what was happening and you thought I was crazy!" Matthew turned his head and locked eyes with his wife. He knew she was right. Linda recalled the first time she had been sufficiently frightened to call him. Her eyes went out of focus and she replayed the horrific scene like a movie in her mind's eye:

With her steaming coffee cup in one hand and the cordless phone in the other, Linda entered her art studio off to the side of the kitchen. She set down her things, closed the glass French door, and smiled in anticipation of three hours of uninterrupted painting. She slid the new canvas onto the easel and sat down on her antique Shaker-built stool that she'd found at an estate sale in Westport.

After several minutes of mixing her oils, she finally dabbed her brush into the paint. Just as she made her first stroke, she thought she heard someone call out her name. Her heart skipped a beat. She spun around on her stool and checked the four corners of her studio. She heard her name again, though this time it was more pronounced.

"Linda!" The aged, female voice seemed distant, though frighteningly nearby.

Linda cringed. "Who's there?" She glanced at the security panel to see if Julie might have stopped by, but she saw nothing at all that was out of place or unusual.

"Linda," the voice came from behind her.

"Who are you? What do you want?" She spun around, jumped off her stool and backed into the corner of the room. Then she felt the slightest pressure against her arm. The tingling felt like an insect crawling along the length of her forearm. She quickly pushed up her sleeve, expecting to find an ant or even worse – a spider. She checked her arm and found nothing.

A faint hissing laughter came from nowhere, and then she felt three short, spine-tingling breaths like someone blowing into her ear. She squeezed her paintbrush tightly, held it in the air like a dagger and demanded, "Who's there?"

The rays of sunlight that found their way past the curtain and into the room were suddenly snuffed out as though a dark cloud had settled over the house. A chilling breeze swept in and surrounded her. She shivered in fear and then lunged toward the door. It was warmer there, as if she'd passed out of an air-conditioned space into one that was room temperature.

"Linda!"

She screamed and fumbled with the door. The handle wouldn't turn. She said, "Jesus help me!" She banged on the door and pleaded, "Help me!" She shook the door handle violently, twisting and turning, banging on the frame with her palm. "Help me!" The glass panes in the door began to fog up. She could see her own panting breath forming a fine mist. She turned quickly and stood with her back against the door, so she could face the unseen terror that would not stop calling her name.

Then through the mist that hung heavily in the air, she saw the phone on the shelf by the door where she had set it earlier. She had to call Matt. She reached out toward the phone and felt the cold air on her fingertips as if she had entered a freezing sphere. It was like being instantly frost-bitten.

"Linda."

Her heart pounded as she jerked her hand back. Then she lunged for the phone. As she grabbed it, she heard her name. This time it was coming from above. "Linda." She felt as though her heart would explode through her ribs. She focused on the illuminated keypad that was growing more and more indistinguishable in the thickening mist. She pressed the speed dial. At the precise moment that it began to ring, the door cracked open on its own.

Linda stumbled into the kitchen, holding the phone firmly against her ear. She spun around, closed the door and pressed all her weight against it. Behind her in the misty room she heard her name being called again. When she looked back, she saw a hand pressed against the glass. She backed away in terror. "What do you want? Get out of my house!"

"Matthew McLaughlin's Office. Hello."

Linda looked at the door to the studio, where she usually checked all her worries and concerns. She moved deeper into the kitchen. "Yes, Matthew McLaughlin, please." She felt sudden refuge in the calm sound of her husband's voice.

"Linda, what's the matter?"

"Matt! There's someone in the house!"

"What?"

"I couldn't see her, but I heard her voice. I mean, she wasn't there." She paused a moment and then shouted, "There's something in the house."

"Linda, you're not making any sense. Are you all right? Who is in the house? Tell me what's going on."

"I think Kelly was right," she panted. "I think she did see a ghost in Union Cemetery. I think it followed us home. There's a ghost in our house."

"Linda Tanner!" It was her maiden name and the one that Matt used only when he was clearly upset with her.

"Matt!" Linda pleaded. "Please come home!"

"I can't just leave work when I want to, Linda! I have three closings today. Just don't go back into the studio until I get home to check it out, okay? Have Julie come over to stay with you. I'll be home right after work. And call me if anything else happens. I have a meeting now. I have to go. Okay? Linda?"

She pulled the receiver away from her face and stared at it in disbelief. She was alone. Something terrible was happening in the house, and no one – not even her own hus-band – was coming to help her. "I can't stay here." She clicked off the phone. "I can't, and I won't."

She heard her name being called again, and she snapped out of her spell. Matt was tapping her on the arm and Jason was calling out to her. She shook her head and cleared her throat. "I'm sorry, I was recollecting the time I was attacked in my art studio."

Jason continued. "As I was saying earlier, I know Kelly was being co-habitated based upon the display of incredible strength she had when she knocked Vincent away from her as though he were a rag doll."

"I didn't see any of that, and thank God I didn't," Linda interrupted. "It was bad enough watching her turn into some kind of crazed animal and attack Julie as she did at the Friendly's restaurant." Linda gasped. She felt a strange sinking feeling as if she were being sucked down out of this world into another. Instantly, she found herself reliving the last terrible moments before Kelly transformed from a sweet little girl into...

Kelly licked her spoon for the last traces of chocolate and ice cream as Linda got up to use the telephone. Julie dipped a napkin into the water in the plastic glass and wiped the corner of Kelly's mouth. "I hope you don't have a tummy ache after so much ice cream, Sweetie Pie."

Linda held her hand out. "May I have that piece of paper, please? It's time that I made a phone call." Julie pulled the paper out of her purse and handed it to her friend.

"I've had lots more ice cream than this, and I didn't ever get a tummy ache, Auntie Julie," Kelly giggled. Linda walked over to the pay phone, slipped her quarters into the slot and dialed. The phone rang four times and then connected.

"Thank God! Hello..."

It was obviously a recorded message. All she could make out was: "...ello...s...chic...fai..." She waited until she thought she heard the tone that signaled her to leave a message. Linda studied Julie in the distance looking on with anticipation. "Hello, my name is Linda McLaughlin. I need to talk to you as soon as possible. We are in real trouble. I need to speak to someone who's psychic who can help me with ghosts. I have a really big problem in my house. Please call me back..." She left her address and home phone number and hung up. She looked at the floor in hopelessness. When she walked back, Kelly looked at her and smiled.

"Who were you calling, Mom?"

"I was calling someone who might be able to help us, Honey."

Kelly licked her finger. "Help us with what?"

Linda knelt beside Kelly and whispered. "With the ghosts, Honey. We found someone who can help us make them all go away." Kelly's appearance changed drastically. She clenched her teeth, whipped her head around, and snarled. Her blue eyes suddenly looked like black pearls. Her face appeared to shift and age in an instant.

"No!" she roared. She pushed her mother away forcefully. "I don't want them to go away!" Linda gasped. Julie tipped her glass over and the icy water spilled all over Kelly's lap. Kelly growled at Julie, though they knew that it was not Kelly at all. She reached over and clawed at Julie like some sort of wild animal.

Julie screamed, "Oh my! Kelly!" She grabbed Kelly by her wrists and tried to still her, but the little girl had ten times what should be her normal strength. She batted away Julie's arms, tore her glasses off, and dug her nails into Julie's face.

"Kelly! What are you doing?" Linda grabbed her daughter by the hair and tugged it sharply. Kelly's head snapped back. Then her appearance reverted to normal, as if some spell affecting her had been suddenly lifted.

When Linda came back to the present again, she gazed at the paper and pointed. She gasped. Her friend Julie's name was next on the list.

"We'll get to Julie in a minute, but first I want to finish with Kelly."

"Okay," Matthew and Linda said in unison.

"The first time the demonic spirits were able to manipulate Kelly was in the restaurant when you told her you'd found someone who would help make the spirits go away..."

"She didn't like that very much, I can tell you that," Linda said.

"The spirits are the ones who didn't like it," Yvonne countered.

"The second time happened just outside the house."

"She hadn't been blessed prior to either occurrence."

Matt interjected, "But she's blessed now."

"Yes," Jason agreed.

"So, is she safe now?"

Jason regarded Yvonne who folded her fingers together and said, "I believe so, yes."

Jason continued. "She's been blessed and prayed over by the bishop. In addition, Yvonne has employed her own spiritual methods to protect her further..."

Just then, the doorbell rang. Sarah turned toward the front door. She shook her head and said, "I'm not answering it!"

Yvonne reached out with her feelings and smiled. "Pizza's here!" She chuckled. Jason joined her and they shared a hearty laugh.

Matt dug into his back pocket for his wallet and rushed into the foyer. Yvonne leaped out of her chair and rushed after him, just as Matt was holding the door open for the pizza delivery man to come in out of the cold so they could settle up.

Yvonne called out, "We can't have any wet feet on the foyer floor, Matt!" The delivery man stepped back and apologized. Stunned at first, Matt trusted the woman's instincts as she came up to the door and held her hands out. "I'll take the pizzas, so you can pay the nice man." She leaned outside and the delivery man shrugged and handed her the boxes. "Sorry, young man, I just treated the floors."

"It's okay, I understand, Ma'am."

Sarah wrapped her palm over her face when she realized what could have happened.

Yvonne squished her face in a loving expression, backed

inside and waited for Matt to pay the man. Matt handed him the money and thanked him. "Have a nice night," he said to the delivery man. When he closed the door, Linda was leaning against the wall in the hallway with folded arms, patiently waiting to learn what had happened. "Well?"

Yvonne smiled and said, "You don't see what could have just happened there?" She shook her head and walked into the kitchen. Linda took the pizza boxes and set them down on the counter while Yvonne wheeled around and looked at Matt. "You were about to invite that man inside, or to..."

"Give him permission to enter your house," Jason interrupted, calling it out loudly.

Linda gasped. "Oh, shit!"

Yvonne nodded at her, "Yes, now you're seeing the bigger picture."

"I don't understand..."

"The demonic spirits want back inside this house," Jason continued. "You saw how they so easily manipulated Kelly to use her to trick you into letting them inside..."

Matt slapped his forehead and said, "Wow! I didn't even think of that!"

"Chances are they weren't influencing the delivery driver, but if they had attached to him when you had given him permission to enter, they'd have gotten in by default!"

Matt just shook his head. Linda handed him a plate with a slice of pizza. He folded the pizza in two with one hand and stuck it in his mouth. He raised a finger as he chewed, intending to say something more, but it had to wait. Linda laughed and called out to the rest of the group, "Come and have some pizza, everyone. We can pick this up in a few minutes."

When they had taken their places again around the table, Yvonne continued with her explanation about what she experienced when she first pulled into the driveway following Kelly's co-habitation. "When I first arrived and approached Kelly, I could feel the last traces of negative energy that had been affecting her wafting away. The bishop's prayers and blessings of course worked at driving away the demonic spirit itself, but the remnants of its energy had still been lingering."

Interesting," Matt said, between bites. "This is so damned interesting."

"I then examined her auric field. It was still intact and it was growing stronger in my mind's eye..."

"How, if I may ask, did it look? I mean, how could you tell, for those of us who can't see like you can?" Linda asked. Yvonne swallowed the bite she was chewing and set the crust down on the plate before answering.

"That's an excellent question, Linda, thank you. Imagine soap bubbles coming out of a plastic ring after you've blown into it. The first few bubbles of varying sizes float up into the sky. They're intact, and perfectly round. The soap that you're blowing through the ring seems to be shifting and contorting as it's moving through the hole. That bubble, under stress from its outside environment, is having trouble forming and taking on its natural shape. When the demonic spirit was attacking Kelly, it was trying to breach or break through her bubble. It couldn't quite do that, because Kelly wasn't worn down as was the case with Matt." She looked at him.

He stopped chewing and stared at her wide-eyed. Then he started chewing again and simply nodded in agreement.

"Kelly's aura would look like the bubble going through the ring would, it would be squished in one end and bulging in the opposite end, and shifting, expanding, contorting and so forth. Think of it as an invisible force field surrounding the body, two to three feet beyond the outline of the body, and picture a black spirit hammering it, poking at it, and trying to make a hole in it. Then visualize a holy man attacking the spirit with a high-vibration holy symbol to repel it and force it away, and imagine blessed, ultra-high-frequency holy water being cast upon it, to injure it and cause it to flee, until it could not bear to remain there and endure any more pain."

Yvonne took another bite of her pizza as the others digested those last comments. She looked at Linda and Matt to discern if what she said had made sense, or if she'd only confused them further. Then she looked over at Sarah, who just chewed her food and stared at her lap. Yvonne reached out with her senses. "Sarah, Honey?" She looked up slowly and regarded her with her big blue eyes. "I know you've been through a lot of trauma. I'm empathizing with you regarding what happened to your boyfriend, Bill." Sarah's head sank again. "We're going to do everything we can to protect him and see to it that this will never happen again."

Sarah forced a smile. She was as depressed as she had ever been. "I want to go see him, but I'm afraid to leave the house. What if they attack me like they did Tyler?"

Jason held up his list and said, "Your name isn't on here, remember?" Sarah's eyes started to sparkle. "You confessed and then you were blessed. I think you're completely protected."

"Well, what about Tyler? He did the same and he was attacked at the mall!"

"Tyler interacted with a second Ouija board," Jason said.

Linda begged, "What?"

Jason nodded and smiled. "Yes! This is how devious these spirits can be and how dangerous seemingly innocent interactions can be!" Jason sat up straighter in his chair. "Just by recalling the situation he and his friends had endured when he was warning those two boys about the Ouija board could have summoned those same spirits to him and they were just waiting for a chance to strike back against him. They couldn't really harm him, but they sure did a number on the car, didn't they?"

"I'll say!" Matt admitted.

Sarah seemed to be filling with new life and energy.

"Well, what about those creepy kids on the front porch? They affected me, really terribly."

"Those 'creepy kids' were definitely not kids at all. They assumed the form of children to trick you into letting them inside the house." Jason looked around and said, "Under no circumstances are you to let any stranger inside this house." He locked eyes with Matt and then Linda. "Am I making myself perfectly clear? I don't mean to sound authoritative or disrespectful by any means, but this is of paramount importance."

"I understand now," Matt said. He dropped his crust on the plate and wiped his fingers with a napkin.

"Back to Kelly again," Yvonne urged them. "I felt Kelly's crown chakra and it was intact and open as it should have been. Then, I evaluated the strength of her aura surrounding her body to seal any breaches if I found any. It was intact. I strategically positioned myself before her so my amethyst pendant would become visible to her, watching her very carefully for her reaction."

"Okay," Matt said.

"If she had any negative reaction or aversion to it at all, it would have concerned me."

"Why," Matt said, "it's just a rock!"

Yvonne chuckled at his ignorance as Jason said, "Oh, boy! Now you're gonna get it!" He covered his eyes because he knew what was coming. You don't tell a psychic medium that her precious gemstones are "just rocks." Linda's eye's darted back and forth and Matt pursed his lips as though he knew he was in for it. He raised his hands in surrender before Yvonne even began.

She leaned forward, rested her elbows on the table, fluttered her black, mascara-lined eyelashes and drew a long, sustained breath. "Crystals have incredibly beneficial, powerful natural abilities that we can take advantage of, should we only take the time to learn about them and use them as they were intended to be used, rather than discrediting their worth without studying their history or experiencing their power firsthand."

Matt felt like he was in grade school being lectured about his ignorance. He sighed.

"We are interacting with fields of positive and negative energy all the time: throughout our day in the places we go, and through the people that we interact with. One valuable assortment of tools we can use is the vast and powerful natural crystal formations that have formed for millennia deep inside the earth, that are capable of absorbing, conserving, storing, focusing, and emitting energy." Yvonne reached into her blouse and showed him her pendant. "Each type of crystal is unique, as are its abilities. They are living first-dimensional beings, each with their own memory, personality and capabilities. Each crystal has a color."

"Color is a function of frequency," Jason added.

"Yes, and color is vibration. If people want to protect themselves from negative energies, they should wear crystals that deflect or absorb those energies. One of the many crystals that have an especially powerful effect on deflecting negative energy is the amethyst." She tapped one of the flat edges of her pendant. "Amethysts are violet in color and violet frequencies found in lavender oil, meditating on a violet light, or wearing purple or violet clothing protect the wearer by deflecting negative energy."

"Roman Catholic priests hearing confession," Jason interjected, "wear purple stoles around their necks to deflect the negative energy that is projected upon them when sins are released to God. Catholic exorcists wear purple stoles to protect themselves against evil spirits. Wearing an amethyst crystal around the neck for protection is an excellent way to deflect negative energy."

Jason took a sip of water and drew a deep breath.

"There are multitudes of planes and dimensions that exist all around us simultaneously." Matt and Linda paid close attention. Sarah found it most interesting and perked right up as if her batteries had been recharged.

Jason continued, "It has been said that the first dimension is the mineral kingdom. It is the realm of the intelligent crystalline entities that live and grow and thrive in their own way. The second dimension is the plant kingdom. It is the realm of the intelligent plant life that lives, grows and thrives in its own way. We live in the third dimension. It is the realm of intelligent animal life. At least our conscious awareness here in this limited three-dimensional body is focused on the third dimension, so technically we say that we live in the third dimension, when in reality we live eternally and we exist in multiple dimensions simultaneously. The fourth dimension and those above it all have their own intelligences that live, grow, learn, and thrive, and so on."

Matt sat there with his head tilted to the side. Some of the information was soaking in, Yvonne knew, but she wanted to finish the topic, so she said, "Ancient cultures, world-wide, celebrated the unique qualities of precious gemstones and crystals. Many people cherished them and felt that they were more valuable than gold. Ancient people had much more access to esoteric information than we do today." She looked down at her pendant one last time and shifted it into her blouse again so that it rested over her heart.

Linda pointed at her. "You held that...amethyst when you stood in the spot where Tyler and his friends used the Ouija board."

"Yes, I did that to declare my intention to close that doorway that they had inadvertently opened. I do what works for me. Jason does what works for him, and Vincent and Bishop Phelan focus entirely on religious protocols. We all have our own approaches and when they're combined, it's a potent synergy to be sure."

"Well, how does a crystal close a portal?" Sarah asked. "How does that work?"

"The crystal is a potent deflector of negative energy. It all has to do with vibration, or..." Yvonne extended her hand for Jason to add what she knew he would want to.

"Sympathetic vibratory physics," Jason added with a smile.

Yvonne looked at her and smiled. "Your brother and his friends used their God-given free will."

"Or the Universal Law of Intention..." Jason added.

"I believe it's one and the same," Yvonne nodded, "but thank you for clarifying, Jason. They made the decision to initiate contact with the spirit world, and inadvertently opened a doorway to that dimension."

Matt shifted in his seat. He drew a breath and hesitated. Linda looked at him and furrowed her brow. "You know, I just have to say it." Linda looked at him, concerned, and Sarah frowned and looked at him as well. "I haven't ever spoken about it, but the fact that my son and his friends played with that Ouija board without permission really rattles me to the core!"

"Oh, Matt," Linda said. He gritted his teeth. Sarah's eyes widened.

"The key word you're misinterpreting there is 'played.'"

Matt turned to face him. "How do you mean?"

"The Ouija board is sold as a game, to be 'played with,' but it's most certainly not a game. You can't blame a bunch of young men for buying what in their minds was only a game. It's sold as a game in toy stores all across the world, unfortunately."

Matt grabbed the edges of his plate. He stared at the reflection of his face caused by the shiny surface and the overhead light. "Yeah, I guess you're right."

Linda touched his forearm gently and said, "Matt, please don't hold a grudge..."

Jason interrupted her, spread his fingers and pressed

them down on the table to emphasize his point. "It is absolutely imperative that you get rid of any negative emotions that you have been harboring for your son or his friends. You must love and forgive Tyler and his friends – unconditionally." Matt studied him.

"The demons will use anything and everything they can to drive you apart. They will use those negative emotions against you. We must not let that happen!"

They all reacted with surprise when a thunderous knock resounded on the garage door.

Chapter 23 – A Plan of Action

LINDA AND MATT LOOKED at each other, but it was Matt who got up and crept toward the door. Yvonne pursed her lips when the knock came again. "Who is it, please?"

"It's Vincent Decker and..."

Sarah's giggling broke the uncomfortable silence.

Yvonne chuckled and held her chest. "We sure are jumpy around here!"

Matt opened the door. He stepped to the side and allowed them to enter. He held his hand up and blocked Vincent who stopped suddenly and looked dumfounded. Matt looked at Yvonne and asked, most seriously, "How do we know it's really them?" Vincent gave them a stern scowl.

Yvonne smiled warmly, "It's them!"

He moved away and extended his arm as a sign of his warm welcome. "Come in, please."

"Thank you," Vincent said as he walked in and smiled at everyone. He stood before the kitchen table as Bishop Phelan walked in behind him and removed his black fedora.

Linda stepped up and hugged them, one after the other. Bishop Phelan took care to move his hat away from her, so that the melted snow water didn't roll off and dampen her clothing. She took the fedora and when he'd removed his jacket, he handed it to her and smiled with his eyes.

Jason stood and shook the bishop's hand and then Vincent's. "Hello, Your Excellency. Hello, Dr. Decker. It's good to see you again."

Vincent slapped Jason's shoulder and said, "Hello, Lad."

Linda took Vincent's coat and set them down on the kitchen chairs. She walked over and reached into the cabinet for some water glasses and said, "Let's all sit down in the living room. There's more room in there."

Vincent sniffed the air and said, "I smell pizza!" He sniffed around like a bloodhound.

"You sure do," Linda answered. "Would you like some? We have plenty."

Vincent chuckled. "Linda, I have never been one to turn down a slice of pizza. I would be a fool to deny your kind offer."

Sarah laughed aloud and said, "Good grief. You can be funny at times."

Vincent chuckled. "Laughter is good energy against the demonic."

"Okay, go and sit in the living room and I'll bring you in some pizza."

"That sounds like a good idea, Linda," Vincent said. "We have much to discuss." He motioned for the bishop to go down the three short steps into the living room.

"How about for you, Your Excellency?"

"Oh, no thank you, Linda. I've been fasting."

Matt opened the cellar door. "I'll get some folding chairs."

Jason decided to help him so he started to follow him, but stopped to examine the door frame. Matt had started down the gray-painted stairs, but turned back around as Jason called out to him.

"I see you've installed a new door." He ran his thumb along the door frame.

Matt smiled broadly and said, "I didn't really have a choice, did I? You did a number on it for sure." Jason recalled the time when he had to batter the door down to get to Vincent when he was being attacked in the basement. "Did you have to install a new shoulder?"

"Hazards of the job, unfortunately," Jason countered. He rubbed his shoulder. "It's fine."

Matt turned and continued down the steps. Jason followed. He avoided thinking about the horrific events that took place in the basement back in October. When Matt handed him two chairs, he turned and went right back up the steps. When he and Matt came back into the kitchen, they met Sarah who was still standing nearby. "Would you get the door, Sweetheart, my hands are full." Sarah closed the cellar door and followed her father and Jason into the living room where the others had gathered. Vincent and Bishop Phelan were seated on the sofa and Yvonne was wedging herself between them. Linda set a tray full of water glasses on the coffee table and went back into the kitchen to make up a plate for Vincent. Jason and Matt set up the four extra chairs and everyone sat down at last.

Yvonne addressed Vincent and Bishop Phelan, saying, "We've been discussing what happened with Kelly. We've also been talking about the color purple and its significance with regard to amethysts, stoles, and so forth." Bishop Phelan nodded and took a sip of water. "Kelly reacted positively to my amethyst pendant, so I felt confident that the spirits affecting her were gone. I asked if she'd like one of her own."

Jason interrupted her. "She needed to accept it by using her free will to do so..."

Yvonne slapped her thigh and gave Jason a friendly scowl. "Jason...Stop stealing my thunder, will you?" She chuckled.

They all laughed.

Sarah cracked a smile. "Jason's a lot like Tyler." She looked at her mother. "He loves to interrupt and showboat."

Jason frowned and said, "I'm not showboating! I'm just throwing in my own two cents."

Bishop Phelan added his own deep, commanding tone. "His contribution is worth far more than that..."

Yvonne tilted her head. "Of course, it is. I was just joking. We have too many chiefs and too few Indians around here."

Everyone laughed.

Matt nodded. Linda patted him on the thigh and smiled lovingly at him.

"Kelly accepted my positively-charged pendant I had made for her and there was no negative reaction whatsoever."

"That's good," Vincent added.

"I believe that – following Bishop Phelan's blessing and prayers for her protection, coupled with her new pendant's innate ability to deflect negativity, added to the fact that I personally charged it for her with my own energy – she is now completely safe from harm..."

"I disagree," the Bishop interjected.

Yvonne turned to regard him, stunned that he would challenge her before the others. The McLaughlins' jaws were hanging wide open. Vincent sat there patiently, his eyes drawn wide as if knowing what the bishop was going to say next, because he had been discussing it with him over the past several hours in the chapel.

"Kelly, and every other individual who was in any way associated with this case, who..."

As he was speaking, Jason reached over and handed his list to the bishop. Bishop Phelan studied it and said, "Talk about stealing the thunder!" He scrunched his face and handed the list to Vincent.

Vincent frowned. Then his eyes lit up in amusement. He traced his finger along the lines Jason had drawn from the people involved in the case since October, and the locations where they'd been present throughout it. He chuckled. He reached into his own pocket and withdrew a crumpled piece of paper. Everyone watched him carefully. He opened it, leaned forward and spread it out on the coffee table. Then, he laid Jason's list beside it. Everyone leaned in to examine them as Vincent ran his finger over every name. Jason smiled at him. "I'm impressed," Vincent said, looking up at the younger man. "The Warrens have taught you well."

Jason laughed. "Indeed they have. I've learned a lot about demonology and spirit activity from Ed, and I've learned much about psychic abilities and sensitivity from Lorraine. In my opinion, they're the most effective duo in the field." Yvonne smiled at him.

"But I've also learned a lot of things from you, Vincent, from the bishop, from Yvonne here, and from my dear psychic friends in Washington."

Vincent ran his finger over the first name. "We need to keep a close and careful eye on Kelly." Linda gasped and looked at her husband and then at Sarah.

"Next on the list is Julie."

Linda said, "My friend Julie was in that awful accident!"

"Julie could have been killed," Matt said firmly.

Jason said, "That was definitely no accident."

"But why?" Sarah asked. "Auntie Julie never did any-thing."

Jason raised a finger and said, "Au contraire, ma chérie."

Yvonne smiled and held her chin. She had always loved the French language and it was just another reason to admire the young investigator more than she already did. Again, he was clearly showboating, but she loved it. She even chuckled to herself.

Jason continued, "Julie was instrumental in taking Linda to the Monroe Public Library to find the Psychic Fair flyer she'd seen there that would ultimately lead to both Yvonne and Vincent getting involved."

Linda said, "Oh, wow!"

"When they went over the details of the case and had realized its severity, they in turn contacted the bishop and got him involved. So, you see, Julie single-handedly caused the most disruption to the demons' plans, and therefore did them the most harm, though she never even knew it. That's why they went after her as they did. To punish her for it."

"But you blessed her in the hospital," Linda interjected. "So why is she on the list now?"

"She is safe for now," the bishop warned. "But she and Kelly, Jimmy, Kyle, and Bill all need to confess their sins in the proper way, and they need to be granted absolution. They need to be blessed and protected in the House of the Lord. He took another sip of water. "And that goes for you, too, Mr. McLeod!"

Jason rubbed his chin and said, "If it's all the same to you, bishop, I can confess my sins in my own way. I have already been baptized in Christ. I know how to surround myself with God's love and protection..."

The bishop grumbled.

"He's right," Yvonne said. She looked at the others. "He has an understanding and a method with which to protect himself. There's no doubt about it, because it works."

Matt, Linda, and Sarah sat there in uncomfortable silence. It was like watching a bunch of wizards bickering about things they had no clue how to understand themselves. Finally, Linda asked Jason, "Can you teach us that method?"

Bishop Phelan interrupted her. "Another time, please, Linda." He became stern, serious. "The five people on this list need to be present in the chapel this Sunday morning. They need to confess their sins before God with me as their intermediary or witness. Then they need to participate in Catholic Mass. Afterward, they need to be blessed in the spirit of our Lord, Jesus Christ!" He spoke with authority. "Only then will there be peace! Only then will they be free of these spirits once and for all!"

Jason and Yvonne exchanged wordless glances at each other. "I agree," Jason said.

"What about Julie? What about Tyler's friends, Jimmy and Kyle, and Sarah's boyfriend, Bill?" Linda asked.

Vincent answered. "Jimmy and Kyle were in this very house helping Jason with the final suffumigation. They were not present at the chapel for the exorcism, because it was a private family matter. Therefore, they did not participate in confession, nor were they blessed. This makes them the most vulnerable, and therefore the most likely targets."

"And," the bishop added, "if you remember, when Jimmy and Kyle entered the chapel, the demon sniffed the air and shouted, 'I know your sins, Kyle Foster!' Because Jimmy has already been sexually attacked, I believe that Kyle is now in the greatest danger of all!"

Vincent added, "The devil always knows our sins and he will always use them against us."

"...Unless or until they are confessed before God through an intermediary who can then absolve them," the bishop added. "I need to be sure I do everything in my power to see that these poor people are safe from diabolical attack – especially Jimmy, who was sexually assaulted by a demonic spirit." Bishop Phelan wrinkled his brow and his look of concern was not missed by anyone in the room. "Attacks of this nature are the most despicable, sacrilegious blasphemy!"

Matt asked, "How and why was that even possible?"

"Lust!" Vincent said with confidence.

The bishop turned his head sharply toward him and said, "That is precisely the reason!"

Matt looked down at the carpet and folded his hands together. "That's why it's called one of the seven deadly sins?" he queried.

"Precisely!"

"What do we do now?" Linda asked.

"We arrange for the simultaneous suffumigation of all five houses, including this one – just to be absolutely sure," Bishop Phelan said. "Jason will conduct one here, just as he did last time. Yvonne will handle Jimmy's. Two priests I work with will handle Julie's and Bill's houses and Vincent will handle Kyle's. This will all happen, of course, while all the occupants are attending Mass this Sunday."

"Until then," Vincent warned, "everyone needs to be on guard. Leave no one alone."

"Be ever mindful of who's coming to your house and be on guard with any situation that could lead to someone asking to come inside," Yvonne added. "Demonic spirits need you to grant them permission. They cannot enter without it. That's why they appeared as the children outside. That was the danger with the seemingly innocent situation with the pizza delivery man."

"Well said, Yvonne," the bishop confirmed. "I think it'd be an excellent idea if Jimmy and Kyle spent the night here, so neither of them is left alone. I'd like you to make contact with Julie and with Bill this evening to make sure they're okay." He cleared his throat and added, "I'd also like to keep Kelly in the dark with regard to our intention to bring her to the chapel..."

"Why?" Matt interjected.

"It's just a precaution. I am not as thoroughly convinced as our dear psychic friend here is that Kelly is fully protected." Yvonne studied him intensely. "Just act as if it's any other Sunday morning. Once we've prepared everything, we'll come over for coffee after you've all had breakfast and we'll see how she reacts to our suggestion that we go to Mass."

Bishop Phelan cleared his throat. "I believe she will have a negative reaction..."

Linda cut him off and asked, "Why would she have a negative reaction? She loves to go to Sunday School. She's very fond of church!"

"We are not concerned with Kelly's reaction," Vincent added. Linda shuddered. "We believe that she might be under demonic influence. We're concerned with the demon's reaction."

Bishop Phelan interrupted him. "We are dealing with

wicked spirits, Linda. They almost always lie low once they've gained a foothold. They'll force the individual under..." He fluttered his eyes, and chose his words a little more carefully, considering the delicate nature of the subject.

"They'll force the individual who is being manipulated into seclusion." He paused and checked his watch. Then he waved his hand before the others.

"It's nine o'clock in the evening. There are people in the house whom Kelly is both familiar with and fond of. Where is she? Why is she not here?"

"He's right, Mom," Sarah said, turning to face her. "Kelly would normally be down here visiting with everyone, no matter how tired she might be. You know what an attention hound she is."

Linda looked around. "You think she's not herself. You think she's..."

The bishop raised his hands and gently placed them on Linda's. "It's not my intention to alarm you, or to cause you any duress, but we need to keep our intentions a secret – until the very last minute. Yvonne said she showed no signs of a negative reaction to her amethyst, but I believe that it is highly probable that she will react negatively – and violently – when she's informed about our intention to take her to church."

"Jason, what do you think?" Linda asked.

Jason tilted his head. "I'm an investigator. At this stage, in cases like this one, when the investigation phase is over and when we know we're dealing with demonic spirits, I always defer to the clergy." Vincent nodded at Jason's words.

"Thank you, Jason," the bishop said. Jason smiled and nodded respectfully, then continued.

"We all have our own methods. I like to teach people how to protect themselves by knowing and believing that they are inseparable from God and how to locate, identify, and expand what I call the 'God-Spark' within them. This enables people to shield themselves in a field of God's infinite love – the highest frequency and the greatest power in the universe." Jason looked about the room.

Linda said, "Can you teach us..."

"I can teach you all how to do that, but only after the bishop resolves the current situation as it stands for everyone concerned. My methods work to help prevent people from attracting spirits as Kelly did in the first place, when you two drove past Union Cemetery last October. When demons are actively hunting people down, and we are lucky enough to have the clergy involved, I defer to the clergy first and teach people how to defend themselves second. At this point, the rest of us are here to offer our skills and support, but the bishop is running the show – and we should all be extremely grateful that he is."

"Indeed," Vincent agreed.

"Thank you, bishop," Sarah said. "I can't imagine going through this without you."

The bishop set his water glass down and stood. He motioned for Vincent to follow suit. He placed his hand on his chest and said, "I am merely doing the Lord's work. Please forgive me, but I'm fatigued and there is much that I need to do."

Linda and Matt stood in unison. Linda folded her arms. She didn't know what to believe or what to expect. Matt could only trust in the bishop's plan. He held out his hand and said, "Thank you for all your help, Your Excellency. I am grateful." Linda looked around at the group and amended, "We are grateful for all of you."

"We all are," Matt said.

The bishop shook Matt's hand and smiled at him and at Linda. He made the sign of the cross over their foreheads and whispered a prayer as he did so. "Everything will work out according to God's will. This time, we'll leave no stone unturned. Everyone involved will be given a deliverance.

Their homes and their cars will also be blessed. We shall soon be rid of these demons once and for all." He looked them all in the eyes and said, "I guarantee it!"

Vincent handed the bishop his coat and fedora. Within a minute, they were standing in the door. "Good night and God bless you all."

"Good night," Matt said as Sarah whisked by them and ran up the stairs.

As Vincent and Bishop Phelan were passing down the front walkway, a car started to turn into the driveway. Vincent proceeded toward the driveway while Bishop Phelan stopped and looked up at the second story of the house, specifically at Kelly's room and her window. Over in the driveway, Tyler got out of the car and Vincent bent his head down to regard and wave at his two friends, Jimmy and Kyle. Tyler rushed up to Vincent and grabbed at his jacket. "You won't believe it!"

Vincent chuckled and said quite frankly, "I probably would believe it, Tyler." He looked back at the bishop but he was still watching Kelly's window. "What is it, young man? Try me." Vincent leaned down again. Tyler's friends seemed hesitant to get out.

"It's Kyle!"

Vincent narrowed his eyes and asked, "What about Kyle?"

"Kyle was attacked in his house. His clothes were ripped off his body and he was freaking raped by the spirits..."

Vincent whirled around toward the bishop, who was still standing before the house, studying Kelly's room. Vincent spun back around and motioned for the boys in the car to come out and approach them. They all heard the doors opening and Vincent went over and tugged on the loose edge of the bishop's jacket around his elbow. The bishop turned and saw the group standing before him.

"It's as we suspected." Vincent wrapped his arm around Kyle, who sank his head against the bishop's chest and nuzzled the soft fabric of the jacket. Kyle wept. The bishop pressed his hand against Kyle's jaw and eased his face up so he could see him clearly. Tears rolled down his face and the bishop made the sign of the cross over his forehead.

"Tell me everything that happened..."

Linda stuck her head outside and studied the five of them conversing. She was sure they were discussing the events they had planned for Sunday, and it was cold out, so she closed the door and walked back into the kitchen. Matt was in the process of collecting the water glasses and plates, so Linda wet a rag and started cleaning and tidying up.

A few minutes later, she decided to go upstairs and check on Kelly. As she climbed the steps, she had a sense of foreboding. As she walked toward her daughter's door, she experienced a thickness in the air; it seemed harder to pass down the hallway than it normally would be. She heard Matt start up the stairs. She stopped next to the closed bedroom door. She was concerned because Kelly rarely closed her door completely. Linda pressed her ear against the door and listened carefully. She winced. She thought she heard Kelly talking in her room. When Matt stepped onto the second level, Linda beckoned him over with several rapid waves of her hand. Matt's eyes grew alarmed when he came close enough to hear Kelly talking behind the door in her room.

Before he had a chance to ask Linda what she thought was going on in there, she turned the doorknob and the door creaked open. Linda thought she would find some reason to panic, as did Matt, she knew, but Kelly was lying down on her bed and nestled in her comforter as if everything was completely normal. The noise they'd made when entering didn't even cause her to stir. Linda turned slowly to face Matt, who stood in the doorway. She saw the lights in the driveway through the window signaling that Vincent and Bishop Phelan were on their way. As the light shone inside, something caused Linda to focus her attention on the pink desk beside the door. There was the glittering silver necklace that Yvonne had given Kelly, and affixed to it – the remnants of the now shattered purple amethyst crystal. Linda pointed at it. A knot formed in her stomach. Matt swallowed hard. They knew the potential seriousness of the situation, and the plan they had all agreed to, so they wisely said nothing.

Linda looked at her husband, who backed out of the room and waved at her to follow him out into the hallway. She closed the door softly behind her. She looked over Matt's shoulder and saw that Tyler and his friends had come up the stairs. Linda could tell they were all hurting. She wrapped her arms around her son and kissed him on the cheek. Then she saw Kyle and noticed his bloodshot eyes. She hugged him also. She kissed Jimmy on the forehead and hugged him as well. Matt placed his right hand on Tyler's shoulder. They all exchanged forlorn, wordless glances.

"We have a big day tomorrow and hopefully that will be the end of it," Matt assured them.

Tyler said, "I sure hope so, Dad." He fought tears and opened the door to his room. His friends passed silently inside and the door closed behind them.

Linda rested her forehead against Tyler's door and then turned toward her husband. She felt badly for Jimmy and the horror he had experienced. She feared for all of them. She had no idea what had happened to Kyle, however, and at his request, she never would. The devastating sexual attack upon him would remain a closely-guarded secret between the bishop and the three friends all the remaining days of their lives.

Chapter 24 – Unleashing the Beast

SUNDAY MORNING CAME AT LAST, AND KELLY LAY ASLEEP in her bed. Her sleep was restful now, her breathing rhythmic and even, but shortly before, she had flailed about in the last phases of a lucid dream. Gradually, as the morning light shone on her face, Kelly stirred, especially when her mind became increasingly aware of the voices nearby. They were familiar to her, as she was coming out of her deep sleep and slowly becoming aware of her presence in the brightly-lit room. She opened her eyes and rubbed them. She jumped off her bed, and ran up to her window where she parted the white curtains and peered outside. She gasped and ran to her door, opened it quickly and scampered down the hallway and downstairs.

The front door was open, so Kelly pressed her hands against the glass of the storm door and peered once again outside. Her eyes lit up like sparkling diamonds. She pushed herself off the door and ran into the kitchen where Linda, Matt, and Sarah were seated around the kitchen table enjoying their coffee.

"Tyler and Jimmy and Kyle are making a big, big snowman!" She extended her arms as wide as they could be and smiled from ear to ear.

Matt set his cup down and held his arms out for her. She ran up and slapped his knees like bongo drums. "I want to build it, too!" She hopped up and down excitedly. Linda smiled at her. "Please, Daddy!"

"Sure, Princess, go have fun!"

"Yay!" Kelly ran off toward the foyer, but stopped short and came rushing back. "Help me open the closet, Daddy. The closet!"

Matt came right up behind her and followed her into the foyer. He opened the closet door and handed Kelly her boots, mittens, and coat. Kelly sat down and put them on and within a few minutes, she was reaching up and pressing open the storm door latch.

Once the door was open, Kelly grinned and shouted, "I wanna help! I wanna help!" Tyler turned and waved her over. Kelly laughed and ran down the front steps. The guys had already rolled the bottom third of the snowman and Jimmy crouched under the second section and nodded for the others to come help him. Tyler and Kyle both reached underneath it.

"Ready? Hoist!" The teens struggled with the weight, but they held it firmly in their arms. Kelly ran in, reached her hands underneath and groaned as if she were actually helping instead of getting in the way, which is all she was really doing. The guys smiled at her and set the gargantuan snowball into place.

Kelly let loose with an exasperated "Whew!" She sank down in the snow and leaned back as though she were completely sapped of all her strength and energy. She laid her head back and the guys chuckled again at the sight of her.

"All right, that's how it's done," Jimmy cheered. He looked around the snowman and regarded their new helper. "Good job, Kelly." He smiled at her.

"Yeah, way to go, Kelly!" Kyle added. "We couldn't have done it without you." Kelly didn't move.

Tyler thought it odd. He turned to help his friends start on the third and final piece, but then looked back at his sister to make sure she was okay. "Kelly, are you all right?"

"I need to go back inside now," Kelly said softly. She

looked up at her big brother and asked, "Can you carry me like you used to do when I was little, Tyler?"

Jimmy laughed and said, "Well, you're a big help!"

Tyler guffawed and countered, "We're nowhere near done yet." He held his palms face up. "You said you wanted to help us out. Help us finish the rest, silly." Kelly stood and looked all around her. Then she turned her head toward the front door.

Linda admired them all from inside, brandishing a huge grin. She waved at her daughter. She heard Kelly shout, "I want to go inside!" Linda thought about the scene that had unfolded the previous evening outside on the front porch and on the lawn. She started to panic. All the warnings she'd heard came flashing through her mind.

Kelly walked slowly over toward the door. Linda felt tiny electrical tingles coursing throughout her body. She locked the storm door and Kelly stopped short. She stomped her feet and shouted, "Someone let me go...inside!"

Jimmy put his hands on his hips and he and his friends looked down at her as though they were disgruntled school board members listening to a trouble-making kid throwing a tantrum. "What's gotten into her?" Kyle asked.

The boys turned their backs toward Kelly and started to roll the third piece of the snowman. They had no idea what was happening to her. Nor did they see Linda as she cupped her hand over her mouth in terror. Kelly suddenly bent her hands in, twisted her torso around and bent over like an old, arthritic woman. Linda knew, of course, that what she was looking at was not her beautiful six-year-old daughter at all, but something despicable, vile, and ancient.

She found it impossible to speak, as though the words she was intending to use were erased from her mind before she could attempt to utter them. Because their backs were turned, the boys were still oblivious to what was going on behind them. That is, until they turned around.

Jimmy saw Kelly first. He leaped back as if he had

bumped his nose on an invisible wall he had inadvertently walked into. He shrieked, "Holy shit!"

Tyler regarded him and turned, unsure what had spooked his friend. Tyler cocked his head to the side and stood there frozen as his sister twisted and contorted before their eyes. Kyle gasped, covered his mouth and slowly backed away.

An ungodly wail issued from Kelly's lips that was so unnatural and so horrific, they were all forced to cover their ears and cringe. "Inside!" Kelly screamed. "I need...to...go...in...side!"

Then, much to their relief, the familiar blue sedan pulled into the driveway, and as usual lately, just in the nick of time. Linda saw that the two men in it were stricken with as much awe as the rest of them when they saw Kelly hunched over like a cripple.

Bishop Phelan made the sign of the cross before him and parked the car. He exited, reached into his pocket and drew out a silver crucifix. Vincent got out and waved the teens off and away from her. The trio did as they were signaled to do and backed away closer to the stone wall as Vincent uncorked a bottle of holy water and held it securely in his hand. He looked over at the bishop before either of them proceeded further. When the bishop finally nodded at him, the two men started to walk over toward Kelly cautiously. She pulled her gnarled hands in closer to her body center and then thrust her arms out and lashed out at them.

When Matt joined his wife at the storm door and saw his little girl as she was, he jolted back in shock. He couldn't believe the scene unfolding before his eyes.

Kelly whipped her head around wildly.

Vincent shouted at him. "Lock the door!"

Matt flinched and moved back for an instant. He watched in horror as Kelly quickly moved toward him and the door, holding her fingers out as though they were talons capable of ripping the door out of its framing. Matt slammed the wooden door shut before his shrieking, wailing daughter. His heart sank as he turned the lock. He was terrified of what was influencing her, or controlling her for its own evil purposes. He heard the storm door open and heard Kelly scratching and clawing at the door. Her wails from the other side were as potent and as clear as they would be if she were standing right next to him in the foyer.

"Let me in!" she shrieked. "Let me in!"

As Vincent approached her from behind, she turned violently and growled at him. Then she saw the bishop circling in as well. She couldn't react fast enough when Vincent sprayed her with holy water with a swift swipe of his hand. She bellowed and sank back trembling. Vincent splashed her again and she dropped to her knees.

Linda opened the door and gazed at her through the glass of the storm door. Linda shrieked. "Her poor little knees!"

Mathew watched powerlessly as the horrific scene unfolded before him. Adrenaline coursed through him. This was his daughter – his own flesh and blood. Vincent rushed down before the porch and held out his open palm to signal Matt to stay put.

Bishop Phelan leaned in and thrust his crucifix before Kelly's eyes. The holy symbol mesmerized her. As he was studying her, he noticed that her eyes – her beautiful blueberry-colored eyes – were shifting.

A strange blackness formed in the outside corners of each eye and rapidly spread across them like ink until it had blotted her eyes out completely. The bishop found new determination and he came closer to her, brandishing his silver crucifix before him. Then she...*it* looked at him and the crucifix flew away from his hand by some invisible force and disappeared into the snow behind him.

"Matt, come help me! We need to restrain her and get her to the chapel."

"No!"

Screams bellowed forth with an intensity none of them would ever expect could come from a little girl. She stared at the house and then up at her mother.

She screamed again. "No!" It lasted for five long, terrifying seconds.

"No!" Each scream was more terrifying than the previous one.

Bishop Phelan was seemingly the only one unbothered by the deafening volume. Matt and Linda ran out and knelt in the snow. Kelly just stared at them with vacant eyes. Matt knew that his precious daughter wasn't even there. Linda maneuvered in such a way that she held Kelly so that the child's head was resting against her chest and her legs were wrapped around her waist. She looked at the teenagers, who just shook their heads and backed away still further when they saw her regarding them with her forlorn gaze.

Bishop Phelan gritted his teeth and called out to Tyler and his friends. "Open the back seat of my car. We have to take Kelly to the chapel immediately!"

"No!" Her scream cascaded out into the trees and the surrounding countryside, causing several birds to take flight from whatever they were perched upon. The scream was most certainly not of this earth.

"Kelly, Sweetheart, you're not well and we're going to take you to the chapel!"

"No!" Kelly roared in defiance. She shoved her father away from her. He fell back off the landing and into the bushes. Linda panicked. Matt rolled off a bush and got to his feet in time to see his wife clasp her hands together in prayer and drop to her knees in the snow. As he brushed the snow off his clothes, he watched his wife as she moaned and wept and prayed and wailed, and with each syllable, he sank further and further into despair.

Tyler opened the door and moved everything off the back seat. The bishop took off his purple stole, splattered it with holy water and wrapped it securely around Kelly's hands, securing them tightly. He stood and splattered Kelly in the face. "In the name of the Father..." He sprayed her again. "In the name of the Son!" He doused her again. Kelly's face crinkled. "In the name of the Holy Spirit, I bind you, unclean spirit. The power of the Lord Jesus Christ, the Savior of all Mankind or all God's precious children binds your hands, saps your energy and renders you impotent!" He nodded and Vincent wrapped his arms under Kelly's armpits and hoisted her up. The bishop grabbed her legs. Kelly kicked and screamed, but Matt ran in to assist. Jimmy unclasped his belt. He ran in and wrapped it around Kelly's legs. When he was trying to get the end of the belt through the buckle again, she looked at him sharply and stuck out her tongue and wiggled at him.

"Ready for some more, Jimmy?" Jimmy leaped back in horror. Her serpentine tongue writhed and curled at him, coated in long, dense hairs.

Tyler rushed up and secured the belt that Jimmy had let fall from his hands. The demon looked at him, for it certainly had to be the demon, and its eyes softened. "Take me inside, Tyler. I want to go to sleep..."

Matt dug into Vincent's pocket for the vial of holy water. He uncorked it and the demon snarled at him. "Oh, we will have you again, Matthew Henry McLaughlin!"

Matt winced and felt a biting pain in his chest.

"Don't listen to it!" Bishop Phelan pleaded.

Matt uncorked the bottle and cast the holy water down upon its face. The demon screamed. Matt didn't know what to say, and he was sure that he lacked the conviction of any words that would come to him if he managed somehow to assemble and utter them into any form of coherence. He moved along with the bishop and the demonologist as they carried Kelly's body closer to the car.

"Douse her again!" Vincent commanded.

Matt complied. Rather than feeling any pain, he knew

he was affecting the demonic spirit that had invaded his daughter's body. He wanted it out of her.

"Do not challenge it, Matt!" demanded the bishop. "Back away! Far away!" He groaned. Vincent backed into the car and pulled Kelly headfirst into the back seat. Bishop Phelan pushed her inside and sat down with her ankles across his lap. "My crucifix!" He patted his pocket. He was shocked he hadn't remembered.

Vincent realized the danger they were in. He pointed at the teens and said, "Find the Bishop's crucifix in the snow..."

The boys scrambled into action, but the bishop shouted, "There's no time!" He splattered the demon with holy water. "We'll get another!" Vincent got into the back seat with them and rested Kelly's shoulders and back on his thighs. He made the sign of the cross on her forehead.

Regardless of what they were told, Jimmy and Kyle began pacing the yard where the bishop last knelt before the crucifix flew from his hand. They scanned the snow for the slightest indentation and dug their hands into the snow and came up empty-handed each time they tried.

Vincent waved the McLaughlins over toward him. Linda came rushing over and peered into the glass. "Linda, I need you to drive!" Linda opened the driver's door and hopped in. Matt reached for the handle of the passenger side door and the bishop held open his palm. "Not you, Matt!" Matt grimaced. "Not in this car anyway! It's far too dangerous for you. The demon is desperate." Tyler and his friends waited in a huddle beside the car. The bishop pointed at them and said, "Take your own car and bring the others with you to the chapel."

Matt nodded and pointed at the garage. Tyler ran over to tell his friends. Just as he approached, Kyle withdrew his hand from the snow and revealed the snow-covered silver crucifix. "I got it!" He turned around smiling and ran off to the car as Linda was turning it around. Kyle startled the bishop when he held the holy symbol up against the glass. The bishop smiled with relief. It was special to him – a potent reminder of his faith.

Then the demon opened its black shining eyes and stared at the crucifix and at Kyle, whose face suddenly went deadpan. The bishop saw this and held his hand up on the glass to block Kyle from seeing her, from making a connection with the demon.

"Kyle, get out of here, now!"

Kyle couldn't move. He sensed his soul being pulled forth, as if the demon drank of his very life essence. He felt the coldness of obliteration, the emptiness of nothingness. Tyler yanked him away and the crucifix fell from his hand, ricocheted off the window ledge and fell to the driveway.

Vincent shouted, "Linda, drive!" She pressed down on the accelerator, spun out on the snow, and moved up the driveway. The bishop looked back at Tyler and Kyle lying in the snow. He watched as Kyle covered his eyes. Kyle's mouth was agape and he knew that he was crying out in pain, forcing away the thoughts that the demon had projected into his mind. He shook his head against the unnerving and unholy power of the demon's gaze.

Chapter 25 – A Perilous Journey

THE POWDER BLUE SEDAN MOVED SWIFTLY beneath the tall, white-frosted evergreens and along the snow-littered, icy back roads of Monroe, Connecticut. Crows cawed in the distance as the car passed by; their piercing calls echoed all around them. Kelly's eyes were closed and her chest rose and fell with each breath. Though the demon was most assuredly there, it was being held at bay – for now.

Soon, however, the demon shook and convulsed. Vincent doused it with his holy water and Bishop Phelan subdued it with his prayers and psalms. When Linda looked back in the rear view mirror to check and see whether Matt and the others had caught up to them and were following, she accidentally veered too close to the side of the road and drove into some deeper snow there. The car shuddered to a halt.

"My God!" the bishop shouted. "No!"

Linda shifted the car into reverse and hit the gas. The rear tires spun without any traction at all and the car didn't move an inch. "Oh, no!"

Vincent hopped out of the car, made sure Kelly's head wasn't in the way of the door and quickly closed it. He moved in front of the car, stepping from the pavement into the deeper snow pack. Linda watched him intently through the windshield.

Vincent wrapped his hand around the tree and saw the black wolf stepping through the brush, crouching and snarling through yellowed fangs. Vincent's heart skipped a beat. He reached into the neck of his sweater, unclasped his crucifix, and held it before the wolf, dangling on the golden chain. The wolf snarled and stepped back. "Be gone!" he commanded. He saw that it was never a wolf at all, but a projection in his mind, because it vanished instantly without turning into smoke and without leaving a trace of its presence where it had stood. Vincent moved in front of the tree and then leaned back into it. It was solid and strong. He pressed the bottom of his boot against its trunk and leaned in to steady his hands on the front hood of the car.

Linda studied him and knew what he was thinking of doing, so she checked to make sure the car was still in reverse and grabbed the steering wheel so she would be ready. She stared into his eyes waiting for him to signal her to apply the gas.

Bishop Phelan checked Kelly and saw that her eyes were still closed. When he turned away, he noticed lights approaching from behind. In his peripheral vision he saw that they were headlights. Vincent saw them, too, over the roof of the car. He started to nod at Linda when she saw the silver gearshift lever suddenly move down by itself two notches into the *Drive* position as the approaching car drew nearer. Linda gasped.

Kelly's lips curled.

The accelerator pedal depressed fully as though a heavy foot stomped down on it. The wheels spun wildly but had no traction at all in the snow. Vincent dove safely out of harm's way as Linda slammed her foot down on the brake pedal.

Kelly's eyes opened. The demon roared in protest.

The bishop knew that it had lain low and had waited for the opportune moment to strike out. The tires chewed the uppermost edges of the snow, but never connected with the pavement beneath them. Linda quickly turned off the engine. She rolled down the window and Vincent tried to calm his nerves as the other car pulled up beside them. Tyler got out quickly. Good luck alone had saved Vincent's legs and quite possibly his life.

Bishop Phelan made the sign of the cross over the front seats and prayed, "Bless this vehicle with Your holy right hand. Direct Your holy angels to accompany it, that they may free those who ride in it from all dangers, and always guard them."

The demon came through and its eyes opened wide. Black voids studied the roof of the car as its nostrils flared and suddenly the thing began to hyperventilate. The bishop showered it with holy water, and again, and yet a third time until it finally sank back down into the seat and became still.

"Now," the bishop said. "It's safe! Move the car, now!"

Vincent got out in front and prepared himself to push. Bishop Phelan showered the front dashboard and shifter with holy water. Linda wrapped her hand around the gear shift and shoved it up into the drive position.

"Shift into *Neutral*, Linda!" Vincent shouted. Linda nodded, understanding that to be a very good idea, just in case the demon had found a way to come through again.

Tyler joined Vincent at the front of the car. Vincent heaved. Tyler tried to push as well, but slipped in the snow with nothing to use for leverage. He studied Vincent's position and looked around to see if he, too, could use anything planted in the ground for his own advantage. He saw nothing.

Linda saw Vincent's face turning red. She held her hand up and suggested she shift into *Reverse* with a wave of her arm. Vincent nodded and she switched gears and hit the gas ever so slightly. Vincent pushed again and the tires spun loosely in the snow. Tyler quickly went around the car, climbed on and added his weight to the back end. Jimmy got out and did the same.

When Linda next hit the gas pedal very softly, the car lurched, and coupled with Vincent's help with a quick shove, and the added weight on the rear trunk, the tires were able to gain the traction needed to move the car back into the road. The boys high-fived each other and hopped off to the sides. Vincent exhaled heavily and leaned over to hold his knees while he caught his breath.

"Quickly, please," the bishop urged them.

The boys got into the car and Vincent crawled in the front of the Buick so as not to disturb the demon any more than he needed to. Kyle ran up and rapped on the window. Vincent rolled it down and Kyle handed him the bishop's crucifix which he gladly accepted with a smile.

Linda stepped on the gas pedal and they started once more on their way to the chapel. When she saw that Kyle had safely reentered her husband's car, she continued down the road and turned onto Route 111.

Even though they had finally turned onto Pepper Street in Monroe, and they were nearing the chapel at last, they knew that their ordeal was far from over, because they also knew that they would soon face the demon's greatest resistance.

Just as those thoughts left their minds, Kelly's eyes rolled up in the back of her head and her body buckled as though something was pushing her up and away from the seat below her back. She drew in a deep, ghastly breath that sounded like the outcry of a trio of diabolical voices. Bishop Phelan quickly went to douse it, but found that his vial of holy water was empty. Vincent went scrambling in his own pockets for his vial and then the car began to vibrate.

Linda screeched. She turned into the long, narrow driveway of the chapel as the car began to shake and rock back and forth. She came to a halt by the tree-line and turned off the engine and got out as fast as she could. In the blink of an astonished eye, all four door locks slid down in unison.

Matt pulled his car in beside the Buick and everyone got out, terrified about what they were seeing in the other car. Vincent rolled down his window and pulled himself up and out until he was sitting on the window ledge. He propped himself up with his arms and hands, placed all of his weight on his right leg, swung his left leg out, eased himself down onto his side and then leaped onto the pavement. He moved away and saw the door locks open by themselves. All four doors opened at once, shocking everyone.

Bishop Phelan knew this to be yet another attempt to disrupt their egress and to cause them as much fear and foreboding as possible with the intention of injuring anyone that got in the way.

When Vincent leaned in, the door slammed right before his eyes, as did the driver's door, then the left rear door and then the front passenger door. Then they opened one by one, and began slamming shut and opening back up again in rapid succession.

Inside the car, Bishop Phelan covered his ears and screamed. The sound of the slamming doors became deafening. All the while, the demon's belly rose and fell with each laughing fit. How it savored the distress of others. It cackled so loudly that the windows inside the car began to tremble.

When the door beside the bishop opened again, Vincent wedged himself inside it. He fought against the incredible weight of the door as it was being forced closed, but Vincent gritted his teeth and held his ground. He propped it open enough to grab the bishop by the arm and drag him out. Once the bishop was outside, the doors stopped opening and closing altogether and just hung open as if they were waiting for them to come nearer again.

Linda buckled over and wept. That was her daughter's body in the car. Kelly wasn't there, she knew, but she was her youngest child – her baby. Matt held her from behind and Sarah hugged her from the front. Tyler and his friends stood together in a tightly-knit pack and peered into the car as close as they dared to, while avoiding interacting with the demon in any way.

Bishop Phelan inserted his key into the trunk and it popped open with a creak. Vincent reached in and propped it open just in case the demon would force it down upon him. Matt followed suit. The bishop opened his brown leather case and retrieved a bottle of holy water. He smeared some into his palm and dipped his fingers into it and made the sign of the cross over his forehead and before the car. He motioned for the men to back away and he closed the trunk. Then he cautiously walked around to Kelly's door, which was resting wide open. Vincent stood against it and held it open and the bishop poured some holy water in his palm and made the sign of the cross on Kelly's forehead. Her skin sizzled. The water created two pink discolorations where his fingers had passed over her flesh. He stood and watched them grow deeper and redder. He showered Kelly's forehead with holy water and then splattered her entire body. Red splotch marks dotted her face. She didn't move, but her body was reacting. The bishop knew that there was precious time left before the demon would gain enough strength to attack them again. He backed away and motioned for Vincent to retrieve her and pull her out of the car.

Vincent pulled her out by the arms. He twisted under her, hoisted her up and draped her torso over his shoulder. He held her legs securely so she would not fall. The bishop showered her again with holy water. Linda and Matt came up to steady her and they rushed her in the back door of the chapel, followed by the others. Vincent called out to those behind him, "Follow me!"

Vincent rushed inside and carried Kelly up the back steps. Bishop Phelan also climbed the steps and instead of following Vincent down the narrow hallway deeper into the chapel, he disappeared into an adjacent room.

The others came in, first Linda, then Matt, Sarah, and Tyler, and walked in single file down the hallway.

Because Jimmy and Kyle were last, they lost track of where the others had gone. They heard a clamor coming from an adjacent room and opened the white-painted door and walked in. Candles burned throughout the sacristy, though it was dark with wood paneling and exposed beams that supported the ceiling. They spotted the bishop's reflection in a wall mirror. He walked over to a closet, kissed the likeness of the Virgin Mary in the center of the door and made the sign of the cross over his forehead. He opened the door wide and reached for his purple cassock. He removed it from the wire hanger and inserted his arms into the robe and pulled it over his head and down over his body while the boys watched. He wrapped a reversible stole around his neck. They saw that one side was purple, the other was gold. Then he quickly inserted his head into a large gold chain and positioned a large gold pectoral cross over his chest. He walked over to a grand table, picked up his bible and kissed it. He noticed the teens staring at him. He snatched a silver aspergillum from the table and submerged the first two thirds of it into the aspersorium beside the table.

Jimmy and Kyle stood there frozen as the bishop gave them an imposing point of his long and crooked finger. The bishop warned, "Under no circumstances are you to interact with the demon. Never listen to what it's saying. Never engage it in conversation, no matter what it says! Am I perfectly clear?"

"Yes, Your Excellency," Kyle said.

Jimmy nodded. "Yes, I hear you loud and clear."

When he checked and saw that his aspergillum was full, he retrieved it and walked hurriedly toward the door. He grumbled and said, "I think it best if you stay right here." Kyle gulped and looked at Jimmy.

The wide wooden planks squeaked when the bishop

walked into the nave. He wound his way around the corner and stepped over to a cloth-covered table, as Jimmy and Kyle peeked out from the sacristy door and crept a little closer. They saw Kelly's blond hair splayed over and hanging off the table. Her body was still bound. For the two frightened teens, it was all too unbelievable to behold. It was all their fault, they knew. Everything that had happened was because they made the stupid mistake of buying the Ouija board. They snapped out of their recollection when they heard the bishop's booming voice echo throughout the chapel.

"Blessed Father, we are here today to pray for the soul of Kelly Alyssa McLaughlin and for her deliverance from the demonic spirits now affecting her."

The bishop cast his aspergillum forward and splashed Kelly's body with it. Baleful moans emanated from all around them, though not specifically from Kelly alone. Vincent turned around in full circles, he, too, identified the many voices.

None of the three pairs of people could take their eyes off little Kelly on the table. Not Matt and Linda, nor Tyler and Sarah, nor Kyle and Jimmy. Nor could they look away from the bishop who was busily tending to her body.

The door on the opposite side of the chapel opened and out walked three priests – the same priests, Linda knew, who had participated in the exorcism of the spirits that had possessed her husband back at the end of October. Their stern, serious expressions meant that they were fully prepared to fulfill their duties according to the plan that the bishop had set in motion.

Jimmy and Kyle looked around at the scene unfolding before their eyes, a scene they had missed in its entirety the first time when Tyler's father was the focus of the bishop's attention. A fourth priest acting as the thurifer followed the other three out of the room where they had been preparing and passed down the outside edges of the pews, waving a brass thurible before him on chains. Clouds of frankincense and myrrh rose up unhindered toward the great arched ceiling and candles flickered all around the table. The bishop prayed over Kelly's body and examined it for a reaction. As if sensing their scrutiny, Bishop Phelan pointed to Jimmy and Kyle and then pointed to the sacristy. Jimmy patted Kyle on the arm and they walked over to the door quickly and silently.

As they passed by, Kelly's lips turned in a wry smile. The demon called out to them, "We'll give you some more, Kyle Foster, when the time is right." Kyle felt the stabbing pain again in his rectum. "We know how much you liked it the first time!" Kyle grimaced. The memories of the savage rape came swirling back into his already fragile mind.

Kyle backed away as Bishop Phelan swept in and cast holy water onto the demon, shouting, "Be silent, vile spirit! Bind your tongue in the name of Jesus Christ!"

The demon inhaled. Kelly's belly rose and fell with each powerful fit of laughter. Bishop Phelan showered it again and this time, the demon cringed and growled in opposition.

"Get out of this room," the bishop shouted.

He pointed toward the door and said, "Now!"

The teens practically fell over each other as they scrambled for the door to the sacristy. They slammed it shut behind them. The bishop stooped over Kelly's body and made the sign of the cross over her forehead with his thumb.

"In the name of the Father, and of the Son, and of the Holy Spirit, I bind you here! I strip you of all your preternatural power and I command you to reveal your name! Speak it," the bishop roared. "Speak it now!"

Vincent made the sign of the cross over his own body and then pulled out his vial of holy water. He showered the demon with it. He growled, "You will reveal your name, and you will surrender your power to God Almighty and to His one and only Son, the Lord and Savior of all mankind – Jesus of Nazareth!"

"Yeezhala!"

The demon bucked and rolled and twisted and convulsed. The bishop knew it had just given its power away. Saliva spewed from Kelly's clenched teeth in waves, flowing continually out of the corners of her mouth and rolling down her cheeks and finally collecting in bubbling white pools of thick mucus-filled slime.

Bishop Phelan cast his arm forward three times, showering the demon with holy water.

"I cast you out, Yeezhala!"

With each wave, the demon sank further down onto the table. "Be gone and trouble this girl and this family and their friends no longer!"

Bishop Phelan pressed his crucifix against her forehead and splattered her with holy water again. "In the name of the Blessed Virgin Mary; in the power of Jesus Christ, I command you to vacate the body of Kelly Alyssa McLaughlin now and forevermore."

Finally, Kelly's body fell limp and the back of her head struck the hard surface of the table. Remembering what could have happened if the demons that were possessing Matt had succeeded in smashing his head against the exposed metal railing of the hospital bed, Vincent quickly took off his jacket, folded it up and placed it under Kelly's head. He double-checked the stole around Kelly's wrists and he pointed toward her legs. The bishop understood and tightened Jimmy's belt around her knees. He stepped back and showered her again with the holy water.

Bishop Phelan quickly realized that because the demon had never truly possessed her and because she had been recently assisted by Yvonne and because she was young and strong of faith, the demon had a far lesser hold upon her than the demon that had identified itself as Azandrathuu had on Matt's body. Though the demons did everything in their power to prevent themselves from being exiled, they could not resist the bishop himself – a conduit of Christ's power – nor could they resist the bishop's prayers and his commands – especially when it all took place on sanctified ground and in the chapel.

Vincent exhaled in relief.

Bishop Phelan loosed an exasperated sigh as well. It was not nearly as terrible as it could have been. He reached over and began to unclasp Jimmy's belt that had been tied around Kelly's knees.

The first phase of the deliverance was complete. Kelly was now free of the demonic influence. There was only one thing yet left to do.

Chapter 26 – Absolution

BISHOP PHELAN WAITED ON THE FRONT STEPS of Our Lady of the Rosary Chapel for the imminent arrival of the entire McLaughlin family and their friends, who had all individually and collectively stood defiantly against the evil spirits that had laid siege to them over the past several months. The sun was shining high in the sky, beaming its golden rays down upon the front of the chapel. Bishop Phelan glanced down at the majestic white marble statue of St. Michael the Archangel. He smiled. He knew that the hour of deliverance was at hand.

Three cars rolled up and parked in a single line in front of the chapel. One by one, the beleaguered McLaughlin family and their friends exited and stood before it, gazing up at the bishop with reverence and appreciation for all that he and his Church had done to help them.

The bishop was vested in a white and purple surplice and he wore a double-sided purple and gold stole. He held his Roman Ritual firmly against his breast and extended a welcoming hand toward the group gathered on the lawn. He nodded at them as they scaled the steps in single file and stopped before him. Kelly was first.

Bishop Phelan knelt and smiled lovingly at her. He made the sign of the cross over her forehead and gently patted the side of her face. She was free of the demons and he intended to ensure that she stay that way. Then he stood and greeted the rest of them in order, beginning with Linda, followed by Matt, Julie, Bill, Jimmy and Kyle and Tyler and

Sarah. He made the sign of the cross over each of their foreheads and welcomed them, one by one, into the chapel.

As they proceeded inside, a priest in a white surplice smiled at them, held out his extended arm and directed them to walk down the right-side aisle. As they went down further, they saw a second priest who directed them to proceed down before the first pew and to sit in the order in which the bishop had received them outside. Behind them, they heard the clamor of the front doors closing and locking from the inside. They looked up and noticed a third priest standing before them on the red carpet of the sanctuary behind a wooden railing.

One of the priests who had directed them earlier carried in a tall wooden table with a neatly-folded white linen cloth draped over his arm. Once the table was set into place, he unfolded the cloth and draped it evenly over the table so that its edges hung precisely to the ends of the table's legs, just barely skimming the wooden floor. He turned and waved a second priest over who carried with him a silver tray on which rested a tall glass fluid-filled decanter, a series of white cotton balls, and a piece of bread. He set the tray down upon the sacramental table. A third priest walked in with an oval-shaped white porcelain bowl and a clear glass fluid-filled pitcher.

The family and their friends sat in reverence and examined the huge crucifix hanging on chains against a blue-painted wall and between two bright red curtains that were drawn and tied with golden cords. Two altar boys in white robes entered from the sacristy. They walked to two different alcoves, one to the left and the other to the right side of the sanctuary. They proceeded to light two rows of candles in red glass. Each set was arranged before a different statue of the Blessed Virgin, which was surrounded by varying assortments of fresh flowers.

Bishop Phelan rounded the corner and stood before

JASON MᴄLᴇᴏᴅ

them. He extended his hands and said, "God's peace be in this place."

Linda and Matt smiled and regarded the rest of the group who had assembled there and who sat patiently on the same pew. The bishop revealed his silver crucifix and displayed it before them. He approached Kelly slowly and held it out before her.

"Kiss the crucifix, my dear." Kelly leaned forward and pressed her lips against it.

Bishop Phelan thrust his aspergillum forward and showered her with holy water. He raised his head and his voice and said, "Purify me with hyssop, Lord, and I shall be clean of sin. Wash me, and I shall be whiter than snow. Have mercy on me, God, in Your great kindness. Glory be to the Father, and to the Son, and to the Holy Spirit." He studied her for a few moments and then, satisfied that there was no negative reaction, he proceeded across to Linda, extended the crucifix for her to kiss and then showered her with holy water and repeated the same prayer. He continued until he had completed the same process on all nine of them.

"To make ourselves pure before the Lord God, we must confess the sins we have committed against Him. The Lord is always ready and willing to forgive. I will act as his intermediary and you may purge yourself of all wrongdoing, of all iniquity, of all impurity." He looked at Kelly and extended his hand toward her. "We will begin with you, Kelly." She gasped out of bewilderment more than hesitation. "Are you ready?" Kelly nodded and hopped off the pew and took the bishop's hand. He led her away into the sacristy.

After Kelly returned, he extended his hand toward Linda and then he followed suit with each and every one of them until they had all confessed and were seated in the first pew before him. He spread his arms before them and said, "By the power vested in me by our Lord and Savior Jesus Christ, I absolve you of all your sins. Our help is in the name of the Lord."

They answered by saying, "Who made heaven and earth."

"The Lord be with you."

"May He also be with you," the group chanted.

"Lord Jesus Christ, as we, in all humility, gather here together in Your house, let there enter within us abiding happiness and God's choicest blessings. Let serene joy fill us and let our health never fail. Let no evil spirits approach us, but drive them far away. Let Your angels of peace take over and draw away all wicked strife. Teach us, O Lord, to recognize the grandeur of Your holy name. Sanctify us and bless what we are about to do; You who are holy, You who are kind, You who abide with the Father and the Holy Spirit forever and ever."

The group responded with "Amen."

"Let us pray and beseech our Lord Jesus Christ to bless our dwellings and all who live in them. May He give them each an able guardian angel. May He prompt those who dwell in them to serve Him and to ponder the wonders of His law. May He ward off all diabolical powers from them, deliver them from all fear and anxiety, and keep them in good health in their dwellings; He who lives and reigns with the Father and the Holy Spirit, forever and ever."

The group again responded with, "Amen."

"Hear us, holy Lord, Father, almighty everlasting God, and in Your goodness send Your holy angel from heaven to watch over and protect all who are assembled here today and to watch over and guard their dwellings and their conveyances, to be with them and give them comfort, encouragement, and protection; through Christ our Lord.

"May almighty God have mercy on you, forgive you your sins, and lead you to everlasting life."

The group responded with "Amen."

"May the almighty and merciful Lord grant you pardon, absolution, and remission of your sins."

The group responded with "Amen."

"As you all sit here in quiet contemplation of your sin-free life from this moment, center your thoughts around the person I lay my hand over and bless and offer the Lord your prayers for their salvation, for their protection and for their well-being through Christ our Lord."

All three priests walked around to join the bishop. One stood directly behind the table and the others stood to either side of it. The priest behind the table poured anointing oil out of the decanter and into a small white, gold-rimmed porcelain dish. The second priest took a cotton ball and waited patiently for the bishop to begin.

Bishop Phelan extended his hand over Kelly's head and said, "In the name of the Father, and of the Son, and of the Holy Spirit; may any power the devil has over you be destroyed by the laying-on of our hands and by calling on the glorious and blessed Virgin Mary, Mother of God, her illustrious spouse, St. Joseph, and all holy angels, archangels, patriarchs, prophets, apostles, martyrs, confessors, virgins, and all the saints."

Bishop Phelan dipped his thumb into the anointing oil and made the sign of the cross over Kelly's eyelids. "By this holy anointing and by His most tender mercy may the Lord forgive you all the evil you have done through the power of sight." The priest holding the cotton ball came forward and wiped Kelly's eyes with it. The third priest came up behind him holding a straw basket into which the cotton ball was deposited.

"By this holy anointing and by His most tender mercy may the Lord forgive you all the evil you have done through the power of hearing." He made the sign of the cross over each of Kelly's ears and rubbed them with the anointing oil. Just as before, the other priests wiped the oil clean and discarded the cotton ball into the basket.

Bishop Phelan and the priests repeated the process on the nose for the sins committed through the sense of smell; on the lips for the sins committed through the power of speech; on the tops of the hands for the sins committed through the power of touch; and on the soles of the feet for the sins committed through the power of walking.

Over the next thirty minutes, they repeated the same process and the same prayers on each of the people seated in the pew before them.

When the bishop was finished with all of them, the priest behind the table filled a white porcelain bowl with the water from the glass pitcher. The priest set the pitcher down and draped a towel in his open palms. The second priest handed the bishop a piece of bread and the bishop rubbed his own thumbs with it. Then the bishop threw the bread into the wicker basket, dipped his hands into the water and cleansed them. Then the bishop pressed his hands together into the towel that the priest held out for him and the priest dried the bishop's hands for him.

"Lord, have mercy. Christ, have mercy. Lord, have mercy. Our Father Who art in Heaven, hallowed be Thy name. Thy Kingdom come, Thy will be done, on earth as it is in Heaven. Give us this day our daily bread and forgive us our trespasses as we forgive those who trespass against us. And lead us not into temptation..."

The entire group prayed in unison, "But deliver us from evil."

Bishop Phelan said, "Save your servants."

The group replied with, "Who trust in You, my God."

"Lord, send them aid from Your holy place."

The group replied with, "And watch over us from Heaven."

"Let them find in You, Lord, a fortified tower."

The group replied, "In the face of the enemy."

"Let the enemy have no power over them."

The group replied with, "And the son of iniquity be powerless to harm us."

"Lord, heed my prayer."

The group replied with, "And let our cry be heard by You."

The bishop spread his arms wide before them. "The Lord be with you."

The group replied with, "May He also be with you."

"Let us pray. We beg You, our Redeemer, to cure by the grace of the Holy Spirit this group's vulnerability. Heal their wounds, and forgive their sins. Rid them of all pain of body and mind. Restore them in Your mercy, to full health of body and soul, so that having recovered by Your goodness, they may take up their former duties. We ask this of You who live and reign with the Father and the Holy Spirit, God, forever and ever."

"Amen," said the group.

"Let us pray. We entreat You, Lord, to look with favor on Your servants who were weak and who were susceptible to the devil, and refresh the life You have created. Chastened by suffering, may they know that they have been saved by Your grace; through Christ our Lord."

"Amen," said the group.

"Holy Lord, almighty Father, everlasting God, in pouring out the grace of Your blessing on Your humble servants, You show Your loving care for Your creatures. And so now as we call on Your holy name, come and free Your servants from their oppressors and restore them; reach out Your hand and raise them up; strengthen them by Your might; protect them by Your power; and give them back in all desired well-being to Your holy Church; through Christ our Lord."

The McLaughlin family and their friends had finally completed the necessary steps to ensure their salvation and their protection from the agents of evil who had come to prey upon them. At long last, they were free from the snares of the devil and his demons. Their reign of terror had come to an end.

Chapter 27 – Requiem

WITH THE MCLAUGHLIN FAMILY now protected and free from diabolical attack, Bishop Marcus Phelan closed and locked the doors of the chapel. He turned around in time to face the last glittering rays of the setting sun and stood triumphantly on the steps once more.

The last time he'd felt this way was when he had been successful in ridding the body of Matt McLaughlin of the demonic spirit that had been possessing it. He didn't realize then how badly he and his colleagues had failed to ensure the safety of everyone else who had been involved in any way, no matter how seemingly insignificant. This time, however, he was certain that everyone who had the misfortune of interacting with the demons had been properly blessed. He had no doubt that everyone was now properly protected in Christ – thus sealed off from any and all forms of demoniacal retribution.

He looked up into the sky and smiled as the first stray snowflakes started to fall all around him and on the gazebo that was decorated for Christmas and brightly lit on the green before him. The clouds that were now spreading out like dark fingers were thickening overhead, the first signs that the slowly approaching snowstorm was nearby.

Confident now that everything was in order, Bishop Phelan made his way around the chapel and walked down the long driveway toward the parking lot in the back of the building.

Snow started to collect on the wrought-iron fence lining the perimeter of the cemetery beside him. He turned his head as he walked and studied the spaces between the memorials that were stretching away as far as he could see. He thought of the faithful souls whose bodies were interred there who had passed from the sunlit majesty of the material world into the realm of spirit. He stopped and turned to face the cemetery. He withdrew his right hand from the pocket of his long black coat, traced the sign of the cross before him and at the wide cemetery beyond.

He opened the gate and drew out his aspergillum. He walked down the first row of graves and cast it upon the graves, first to his right and then to his left, as he recited the prayers from memory.

"I am the resurrection and the life, saith the Lord: he that believeth in Me, though he were dead, yet shall he live: and whosoever liveth and believeth in Me shall never die."

His powerful voice echoed throughout the cemetery as the snowflakes grew larger. He shouted out before him, "I know that my Redeemer liveth, and that He shall stand at the latter day upon the earth. And though after worms destroy this body, yet in my flesh shall I see God: Whom I shall see for myself, and mine eyes shall behold, and not another."

He entered the next row, casting holy water upon the graves beside him, and continued reciting the prayer. "We brought nothing into this world, and it is certain we can carry nothing out. The Lord gave, and the Lord hath taken away; blessed be the name of the Lord. Man that is born of a woman hath but a short time to live, and is full of misery. He cometh up, and is cut down, like a flower; he fleeth as it were a shadow, and never continueth in one stay."

His shoes were becoming wet. His fingers were going numb, but it did not matter.

"In the midst of life we are in death: of whom may we seek for succor, but of Thee, O Lord, Who for our sins art justly displeased? Yet, O Lord God most holy, O Lord most mighty, O holy and most merciful Savior, deliver us not into the bitter pains of eternal death. Thou knowest, Lord, the secrets of our hearts; shut not Thy merciful ears to our prayer; but spare us, Lord most holy, O God most mighty, O holy and merciful Savior, Thou most worthy judge eternal, suffer us not, at our last hour, for any pains of death, to fall from Thee."

He finally walked along the last length of the cemetery and approached the same gate he used to enter. He raised his head toward the sky and felt the cool embrace of the snowflakes as they landed on his face. He smiled and boomed, "I heard a voice from heaven, saying unto me, Write, From henceforth blessed are the dead which die in the Lord: even so saith the Spirit: for they rest from their labors."

Bishop Phelan stepped onto the blacktop driveway and looked up at the beautiful stained glass windows of the chapel. He turned on his heel and pulled the metal gate shut. It clanged and resonated all around him. He made the sign of the cross before him and said, "*Requiem aeternam dona eis, Domine,*" which in English meant: "Grant them eternal rest, O Lord."

He walked down the remainder of the driveway toward the back of the chapel and made his way to his car. He made the sign of the cross before it. He spoke with the authority of his station, with his conviction and as a demonstration of his faith that he had the power to call upon the power of God.

"Lord our God, You make the clouds your conveyance; You travel on the wings of the wind; You sent to your servant Elijah a fiery chariot as a means of conveyance; You guided man to invent this car which is as fast as the wind: Therefore, O Lord, pour now upon it Your heavenly blessings. Grant unto it a guardian angel that it may be guided upon the rightful road and be preserved against all harm. Enable those who ride in this car to arrive safely at their destination. For in Your ineffable Providence, You are the Provider of all things, and to You we give glory, to the Father and the Son and the Holy Spirit, now and always and for ever and ever. Amen."

He climbed in and closed the door. His mission in Connecticut had finally come to a close. He started the car and turned on the windshield wipers. He knew the drive back to the Archdiocese in Boston would take longer than he had expected, but he was fondly looking forward to several hours of quiet self-reflection.

But there was just one thing yet to do.

Chapter 28 – Surrender

UNBEKNOWNST TO VINCENT, a black shadow loomed over the back of the building. Seconds later, a tall figure stepped up to the office door and rapped on the glass with his knuckles. Vincent whirled around, approached the door with trepidation and opened it.

"Bishop!"

"Are you ready, Dr. Decker?"

Vincent gulped, "Ready for what?" He didn't like surprises.

The bishop didn't move, but his voice boomed. "You know of what it is I speak." The bishop hinted at that which Vincent truly wanted to find: a way to be rid of the demons and confusion haunting his mind.

"I...I haven't decided..."

"Vincent Decker," the bishop roared.

Vincent stepped back, startled. He had never been on the receiving end of his powerful, authoritative voice. He looked back around him and at his candle-lit collection. He wasn't ready...or willing to part with any of it – not yet.

The bishop eyed him suspiciously. He sniffed the air and his eyes darted back and forth at the many objects in the room. "We can start with the jewelry box!"

"The teeth?"

"They're cursed!" he shouted. "You must be free of their influence, my friend!"

Vincent heard his breath coming in gasps, and the shock of that, the shock that he was actually stalling for precious time to maintain possession of the teeth, both fascinated and appalled him at the same time.

Bishop Phelan reached into his pocket and pulled out a perfect square of purple silk cloth. Vincent felt mesmerized as he spread it open and centered it in his palm. Vincent flinched as his friend and colleague held his arm out before him.

"It must be done," he commanded.

Vincent backed away into the darkness of the room, but the bishop stood there unmoving and unflinching in his solid determination to help and deliver his friend from the terror that had been haunting him.

Vincent walked around a large round table and approached the shelf where he had left the small hexagonal jewelry box. He studied the shelf and the wind-up toy, the music box, and the unopened Silly Putty egg that were sitting on it. He studied the faint, dust-littered cobweb that stretched from the pair of authentic African death masks made of coconut husks and human hair to the blood-stained hat box that once belonged to a questionable fellow involved in a traveling circus. When he saw the empty space beside the statue of the medieval knight, he was hardly surprised. He knew, however, exactly where he would find it to be.

He turned around slowly and saw the candlelight reflecting in the glass of the jewelry box as it sat on the outside corner of his desk. He bent over the desk and pointed at the lid, proceeding to count every last one of the teeth inside, to make absolutely certain every one of them was accounted for. He heard the bishop clear his throat.

Vincent said, "Yes, yes...I'm coming!"

He picked up the jewelry box and jiggled it so he could recount them. After a moment, he wrapped his hand over the box and walked around the shelves toward the door and the bishop, who, Vincent was surprised to see, hadn't moved an inch. He held his arm out in exactly the same position it had been in when he went to retrieve the box. Vincent narrowed his eyes, raised his arm and gently set the jewelry box down on the purple silk cloth in the center of the bishop's palm.

"Good," the bishop said. Bishop Phelan pulled his silver aspergillum out of his shirt pocket and splattered the jewelry box with holy water. He gently placed a St. Benedict medal in the center of the glass and cast holy water on it again. Then he held the rod in his hand and folded the first corner of the cloth over the lid of the box and said, "In the name of and in the power of Archangel Michael." He splashed the cloth now resting over the lid of the box. The water seeped away into the silk. He folded the opposite corner over and continued, "In the name of and in the power of Archangel Raphael." He sprinkled holy water on it again. Additionally, he pulled the third corner over and chanted, "In the name of and in the power of Archangel Gabriel." Again he applied the holy water to the cloth and finally, he drew the last corner of the cloth over all the others while reciting, "In the name of and in the power of Archangel Uriel." The bishop blotted the final piece of cloth and all the others beneath it with the holy water. Bishop Phelan held his arm up toward the ceiling. "And in the name of and in the power of our Lord and Savior, Jesus Christ, we seal this vessel and the instruments of the Devil within it forever. We sever any and all connections between it and God's servant, Vincent Albert Decker."

Bishop Phelan pulled from his pockets two long white ribbons embroidered with gold edges and twelve evenly-spaced gold crosses in the center all along their length. He draped one in his palm from the center of his forearm, all the way up to his fingers and draped through them. He draped the other ribbon vertically across his open palm, the edges hanging off his palm, perpendicular toward the floor. He set the jewelry box, now held securely inside the blessed purple silk cloth, back in the center of his palm and proceeded to wrap the white ribbons around it, one by one, until they were all in place.

Only when the box was wrapped in the ribbons would he set it down on any other physical object – in this case, the empty white-painted window ledge. He tied the ribbons together and then reached into his pocket and withdrew a silver crucifix. He set it down on the box and secured it with the ribbons. Finally, Bishop Phelan splattered the box with holy water.

"In the name of the Father...In the name of the Son..." he thrust his aspergillum upon it a second time.

"In the name of the Holy Ghost!" he doused it a third time.

"O sweet Jesus, forgive us our sins and save us from the fires of Hell. Lead all souls to Heaven, and help especially those who are most in need of Thy Mercy. Holy Michael the Archangel, defend us in battle. Be our protection against the wickedness and snares of the devil. May God rebuke him; we humbly pray; and do thou, o prince of the heavenly hosts, we humbly pray, by the power of God, thrust into hell Satan and all other evil spirits who prowl through the world seeking the ruin of souls. Amen!"

"Amen," Vincent added.

"It is done, my friend."

"What now?" Vincent queried.

"It will be kept safe until the ground thaws, at which point it will be buried in consecrated ground and there it will remain – forever." Bishop Phelan leaned in the doorway and studied the remainder of the objects in the room. He waved his arm across the room and said, "Come spring, we will destroy all of these cursed objects you have assembled here, and you and the world will be better for it!"

Vincent looked around him. He knew the bishop was right. Hanging on to the cursed and negatively-charged artifacts never did anyone any good. "Come spring, then," he said with confidence. "I'll start making arrangements now, finding boxes and so forth, and finding a good place to burn and bury them in."

"That will be a good thing, Vincent." The bishop shifted his weight. "You're certain you've accounted for all of the teeth?"

Vincent reached up and touched his head and the small holes the teeth had made in his skull when the demon bit him. Somehow, but purposefully, the teeth had been ripped from the demon's jaws and were left embedded in his head in two even arches. "I am certain. I counted all forty-four of them. They're all in there. I kept all of them in my possession – all forty-four of them. "

"That was forty-four too many!" Bishop Phelan said.

Vincent nodded and exhaled heavily.

The bishop raised his fedora ever so slightly, a signal meant to thank him for his cooperation. Then he set it back down on his head. "Well...I'd best be going."

Vincent extended his arm as did the bishop, and the two men shook hands firmly. Vincent held the edge of the door and said, "I expect I'll be seeing you soon for some reason or another..."

"Not too soon, I hope," the bishop chuckled.

"After the new year, then," he said with confidence.

Bishop Phelan grumbled. He raised the blessed package in his hand and said, "Merry Christmas, my friend."

Vincent closed his eyes briefly, nodded and smiled. "Merry Christmas, Marcus."

Vincent closed the door and walked through the room, scrutinizing all the relics he had displayed there. He walked up to the center table and lit the many charcoal discs beneath the frankincense and myrrh in the censer. Once they started to burn, he stepped back as the plumes of sweet smoke began to spread through the room. He walked past a shelf on the room's side wall and saw a skull-shaped crystal gem sitting there. He picked it up and held it in one hand aloft before his eyes. It danced with the reflections of the many candles burning in the room, and those sparkles, in turn, set Vincent's eyes glowing.

Chapter 29 – Peace at Last

LATER THAT SUNDAY EVENING, Tyler walked down-stairs and peered down the foyer. He saw that Sarah was busily wrapping presents at the kitchen table. He crept down the hallway quietly, grinning from ear to ear. When Sarah looked up and saw him, she draped herself over the present she was wrapping and scolded him, "Tyler, this is for you, don't look at it!" Tyler grimaced at her. He turned his head so he couldn't see and walked down into the living room wielding his white plastic bag that contained the presents he had purchased at the mall. He called out to her. "Let me know when you're done because I have gifts to wrap for Mom and for Kelly."

"What did you get them?"

He scoffed and sat down on the sofa. "I'm not telling!"

"Good grief, like it's any big deal," she replied.

"Hey, I get almost as much satisfaction watching the rest of the family open their gifts as I do my own. It's more fun not knowing what everybody else got for each other, to me at least. It's like that much more intrigue and suspense come Christmas Day."

Sarah rolled her eyes and affixed some Scotch tape to the package. She moaned, "Simple pleasures for simple minds."

He whipped his head toward her. "I'm not simple-minded!" He knew it was just a joke, but it definitely struck a nerve. "Anyway, I completely forgot to tell you. The day I went to the mall and bought these presents, I went up to the

Toy and Hobby Store and had it out with the manager after he got mad at me for dissuading two young kids from buying Ouija boards and from unleashing the same demonic horror that we've experienced in their own houses."

Sarah stared at him blankly for several seconds. He studied her. Then she nodded and said, "Good idea! That was nice of you, looking out for strangers."

"That's because," Tyler continued, pressing his hand over his heart, "I'm a nice guy!"

Sarah filled out the gift tag. "Yes, Tyler...you're a good boy." She looked up at him and laughed aloud. "You're my special brother!" She laughed hard again. "You're a special boy."

Tyler beamed. "Do you think after a few years, we'll have a good laugh about all of this?"

Sarah stopped and pondered the situation and replied, "Tyler, I don't think our lives will ever be the same, and I don't think we'll ever laugh about any of it. I don't think being mauled in the living room and watching Dad projectile vomit all over the place will ever make me chuckle."

"Yeah," Tyler said. "That was so nasty."

Sarah groaned. "You didn't have to clean that nasty mess up!"

Tyler nodded and called out to her, "Hurry up and finish." He noticed a box of Christmas cookies on the coffee table, so he reached over and snatched one and took a bite. As he sat there chewing, he looked at the Christmas tree by the fireplace. He leaned over to check out the display of wrapped presents to see if there was anything new there he hadn't seen before. How he loved mystery gifts – especially when they were for him.

"All right, I'm done," Sarah called out.

"Finally," Tyler replied, excitedly. He got up, returned to the table and sat across from her. He opened the plastic bag and took out the calendars he had purchased.

Sarah leaned forward and examined them. "Nice, a

coloring book calendar. Kelly will really like that. Good find."

Tyler gave her a coy smile. "It's for you, actually." He chuckled.

"Great. Just what I wanted," she smirked. "Really, thank you, Tyler. You're too kind."

Tyler chuckled. "That's what you get for peeking." He looked up at her with wide eyes and said, "Hey!"

Sarah froze. Maybe she didn't really believe that they were all protected now and safe from harm after all.

"How about you make us some hot chocolate?"

Sarah narrowed her eyes and pursed her lips. She turned and looked into the kitchen. "You know..." she replied. "Normally, I'd tell you to go make it yourself, you know that, but it actually sounds really good right about now."

"Sweet!" Tyler exclaimed, as he reached for the wrapping paper. "Sometimes I actually like having an older sister."

Sarah got up and slid across the linoleum in her purple socks. She caught herself on the cabinet handles. She opened one door and then the other and looked back at him and asked, "Wouldst thou likest marshmallows or wouldst thou liketh thy cocoa plain, my Lord?"

Tyler belly laughed. He pursed his lips and did his best to emulate a British Royal, "Our supreme majesty wouldst most heartily enjoy it immensely should'st it come complete with delicious, gooey, melted marshmallows floating on top."

Sarah laughed.

He guffawed and flicked his hand at her and said, "Make haste, wench!"

"Oh," Sarah moaned. "That was just a bit over the top, buddy!" She grinned.

Sarah went to the sink to fill the teakettle and Tyler went to work measuring and cutting the gift wrap.

Tyler and Sarah sat together for the next half hour. They didn't really discuss anything of substance, other than comment about how good the hot cocoa tasted. It was a welcome and much needed period of peace and quiet tranquility. With the songs of the season playing softly in the background, Tyler finished wrapping both presents he had purchased. He affixed the name tags and bows and stepped down into the living room. Then he knelt on the floor and placed them gently under the Christmas tree. There, he sniffed the needles and admired the ornaments. He looked over at his sister and smiled as she took another sip of her cocoa and admired the gift she'd just finished wrapping. He truly felt that the horror he and his family and friends had experienced was finally over. He smiled at his sister. Everything felt peaceful and just about as perfect as it could be.

The McLaughlin family and their friends had finally and permanently been granted a reprieve from the terrible onslaught that was unleashed upon them. All they could do was hope and pray that it would last.

Epilogue

YVONNE SAXON SAT CROSS-LEGGED on a large orange pillow on the bare wooden floor of her study. Pumpkin, her orange Angora cat, lay curled up in her lap, purring gently. A single white candle flickered as Yvonne closed her eyes. She rested her open palms on her legs and focused on her deep inhalations and exhalations, and used those rising and falling movements of her belly to clear her swirling thoughts.

She found at last a place of deep peace and emptiness. She was contented, an empty vessel, accessing her innate clairvoyant abilities to seek the answers to her questions. The outside world didn't register to her. She fought hard to remain open to the subtle energies all around her, while doing everything in her power to maintain the detachment from the physical world.

Then she saw a flash of violet light in her mind's eye. The images slowly came into focus. As she discerned what came to be, she shook her head vigorously against the growing fear she felt in her core. The last slanted rays of daylight shone on Yvonne's face, perfectly framing her look of terror.

ANALYSIS

Prologue – Analysis

One of the most disturbing things that paranormal investigators, spirit helpers, demonologists, and exorcists can experience is the sudden, unexpected return of the demonic spirits they believed they had been successful at driving away. For psychics, this return often becomes apparent to them first through visions, messages, and their innate senses and feelings that allow them to discern the subtle vibrations that are emanating all around us from the spirit world. Psychics are almost always the early warning system for all the other people who were caught up in cases where inhuman spirits were involved.

This is possible through quantum entanglement or specifically through Sympathetic Vibratory Physics, because we are always connected to The Creator, to each other, and to all other beings in the universe – both in physical bodies and in their natural energetic spirit state.

After a few intense moments of discerning the nature of the spirit communing with her, Yvonne knew that she was dealing with a denizen of the darkness. Her cat, Pumpkin, did too, because cats are very sensitive and they can clearly hear and see into the non-physical dimensions to which most humans are oblivious.

When Yvonne detected the demonic spirit in her kitchen, she reached out with her psychic sight to try to determine what exactly she was dealing with. Because she was using clairvoyance, her innate ability to see into the spirit world, she was able to see its true form, the same form that it preferred to take when it manifested into the physical plane. Her cat could sense it, too, so he fled under the couch because he knew of the very real danger that threatened them both.

When inhuman diabolical spirits manifest into a physical form, they almost always appear as a mass of negative blackness. First, they appear as a small sphere in most cases, or if they have accumulated enough energy, they instantly appear as a large spheroid or even some variation of a humanoid, complete with arms, legs, a head, and a face – sometimes even with glowing, pulsating eyes, and a tail. Sometimes, they will complete their manifestation right before terrified spectators. A powerful sulfur smell almost always accompanies the manifestation.

Perhaps it goes back to the first accounts of diabolical manifestation where fire, brimstone, and sulfur were used to describe the encounters between people and demons. There certainly is validity to the ancient stories, if identical activity takes place in the twenty-first century. In rare cases, fallen archangels or devils have been reported to have materialized complete with horns, cloven hooves, and all the classical attributes of Satan or the Devil. Again, this image has been in the psyche of mankind since the beginning of recorded history, so there must be some reason why they continue to manifest like that to this day.

When Yvonne drew out her crucifix, she did so only to afford her a form of added protection, because the crucifix is imbued with potent levels of positive, high-frequency Unity Consciousness/Christ Consciousness energy. Its function was to repel negative energies and negative entities through the Universal Law of Attraction. The demon knew exactly who Yvonne was, and it also knew of her level of spiritual evolution and awareness and her ability to discern the nature of the other-worldly visitation. The purpose of the visitation was to issue her a dire warning that it and the other demons had returned. It was there to make their intentions known – to make the intended victims aware that they planned to exact their revenge on everyone involved in the McLaughlin case who had dared stand against them previously.

The visions the demons impart prior to such a campaign are some of the most frightening and disturbing you could imagine. If you have seen the movie, *The Conjuring*, you might recall the vision the demon gave to my friend and mentor, Lorraine Warren, when she was interacting with it, and the horrific scream she emitted shortly afterward. Yvonne received just such a vision, a series of visions, in fact, of what the demons planned to do. Yvonne knew the serious danger she and her friends and the McLaughlin family were in, and she acted to warn Vincent and Bishop Phelan as quickly as possible.

Chapter 1: Retribution – Analysis

Demoniacal retribution comes in many forms. It is often perpetrated on people who were in any way involved in a case, and especially on those people who were instrumental in helping the victims fight back against the demons that were oppressing them.

Some forms of demoniacal retribution are subtle, such as a string of bad luck; unforeseen random accidents that could have and should have easily been avoided; the onset of sudden unexplained health issues that cause a great deal of fear and anxiety; sudden signs of aging, such as withering skin; graying hair coming on suddenly, rather than gradually; difficulty sleeping due to continual nightmares; black circles under the eyes; vision problems; persistent cough or unexplained allergies where there had been none before; feelings of dread and isolation, hopelessness and depression; minor injuries that cause a sudden and complete loss of energy; minor mishaps; difficulties with relationships; fights; family feuds; fierce arguments; financial stresses, such as losing a job for no reason whatsoever; and many other events that could and would disrupt the daily lives of the oppressed. In more severe cases, people can be and usually are violently attacked in ways that would best serve to debilitate them totally.

When Vincent's hair started standing on end, he knew that he was in the presence of a spirit. What was really going on is that his body hair was acting as an antenna array, because our hair is actually an extension of our nervous system. This was discovered by accident when the Native American Indians serving in the Pacific Theater during World War II lost their innate ability to track enemy movements once their long hair was shaved per military protocols. Once they realized the connection and were allowed to regrow their hair, their abilities quickly returned.

Bad smells, such as rotting flesh, excrement, urine, and sulfur, are quite commonly associated with the presence of evil spirits. They sometimes go away as quickly as they come, but never without succeeding in their purpose, which is to frighten, disgust, and weaken those who are within their range. They are not real smells originating from physical sources, but merely the thought of the smells projected onto the recipients. We all know how we recoil when we smell a dead skunk on the side of the road, or the smell of a rotting animal. It's repulsive, and we can't wait to travel outside the range of the smell that is repelling us. Pools of urine, excrement, blood, bodily fluids, insects, worms, and black flies tend to repel most people – and for good reason. The demons know this, so they project the images or smells associated with these things, to cause us pain, to induce fear, and to make us physically sick. All these things cause us to broadcast fear and a host of other negative emotions.

Prayers or expressions of faith, and earnestly asking for the aid of Jesus, God, or any of the angels or archangels, is harmful to truly negative spirits, and is especially painful to demonic and diabolical spirits. Vincent knew he had to call upon that aid, but he also knew that he was risking demonic attacks upon himself for using such blatant forms of religious provocation. Challenging demonic spirits is always a foolish thing to do, because they are all too eager to accept those challenges and show the challenger what's what.

I have plenty of examples where the powerful name of Jesus Christ wreaks havoc in homes where demonic infestation is taking place. It's very strong and very real. When you think of, pray to, call out to, or beg for assistance from angels, archangels, or from Jesus or God – you are instantly drawing those beings to you and they are with you immediately. There is no time and space where things of this nature occur.

The negative entities absolutely do not want anyone to invite or summon the forces of love and light into homes that they are infesting, because they are mortal enemies, or polar opposites. They will try and interrupt the prayers or calls for assistance as soon as anyone attempts them. They will try to do this by intensifying their attacks, forcing people into a state of dread and panic, or by making them fear a vicious, relentless retaliation from the spirits.

Psychic paralysis is a terrifying thing to experience. It always begins with an intense pressure on the body, then it escalates until the victim is unable to speak, so they can't call out for help. If there are people nearby, it is also used to immobilize people near the victim to prevent them from interfering. When the victims realize that the people they had been counting on for help are being prevented from doing so, they reach a state of hopelessness, helplessness, and a panic. The more they panic, the stronger the paralysis becomes. At that time, the target is in extreme danger, because their defenses are worn down enough that the attacking spirits could actually enter them and seize control of their body.

A demonic attack is bad enough when you can move your body and attempt to defend yourself or flee the location in which it is happening. It's absolutely devastating when you can't move a muscle, yet you can feel every ounce of pain and every second of the terror being unleashed upon you. Paralyzing someone so they can't defend themself is the most underhanded thing that could happen during a fight, but these beings don't fight fair. Imagine if you will, becoming paralyzed and being forced to watch a demonic spirit phase into this dimension. Then watch, spellbound, as the face that it projects to you becomes clearer and clearer, causing an ever increasing level of terror – and then imagine hearing its sinister voice boring deeper and deeper into your mind to inform you finally of its intention to make you and your cohorts suffer for your interference. I can't imagine anything more terrifying.

Chapter 2: Sounding the Alarm – Analysis

As most priests, exorcists, and demonologists are aware, even though it may appear that evil spirits have been vanquished and that the cases have truly been resolved or have come to a close, there is always the very real danger and possibility that something was missed, or was done improperly or incorrectly, any of which would allow the spirits to return.

When Bishop Phelan received the urgent message from Yvonne requesting his personal intervention back in Monroe, Connecticut, he knew exactly what was transpiring. When the bishop learned that all the calls that Sister Margaret had placed to Vincent Decker had gone unanswered, despite the fact that she left messages on his message machine, he knew that the calls were being blocked and that the situation was rapidly deteriorating.

People who have the capability to help those who are undergoing severe demonic oppression often have considerable difficulty connecting with them over the telephone. Compare it to a burglar snipping the phone lines on a house he intends to rob, to prevent the owner from establishing communication with someone who could come and help. The very last thing evil spirits want for the people they're trying to ruin, and for those who have committed their lives to helping them, is to establish any kind of contact with each other. The demonic spirits know in advance the identities of the investigators, mediums, psychics, empaths, clair-voyants, priests, and exorcists that their victims are trying to connect with. They know that those special people have the ability to identify what is going on in the locations they have infested; they know how to find them and force them out of hiding, and ultimately, how to expel them from the location.

I have studied many cases of blocked phone lines, busy signals, garbled messages, and strange voices on the other end of the line. There are even cases where one party may hear the phone or the doorbell ringing, but it never actually rings on the other end. Things of this nature occur all the time when people are rushing to the aid of someone who is undergoing diabolical attack.

Bishop Phelan knew, because his attempts to call his friend were being blocked, that he had to go there person-ally. He also knew that time was of the essence, so he made the snap decision to brave the dark, wintry roads that very same evening in an effort to get to his friend as quickly as possible. Unfortunately for him, the demons had a plan of their own.

It was no coincidence that the windshield wiper blade separated from the support arm when the bishop was attempting to move it, nor was it a coincidence that the piece of metal bent up precisely in such a way to slice his finger open as badly as it did. It was an orchestrated event by the demons, because they knew it would lead to a rapid loss of blood and thus a loss of vital life force energy that the bishop would need to endure such a long journey in the dead of night. The demons successfully prevented him from leaving when he had planned to, so that the attacks upon Vincent could continue unabated for several more hours.

Negative spirits always have the same primary goal in mind and that is to cause as much fear and panic as possible, whenever and wherever they can. Whenever there are demonic spirits at work, one must be ever vigilant and understand that even the most minute disturbance or hindrance could very well be orchestrated by those evil spirits who will do everything they can to cause the target of their oppression to experience as much fear, anger, frustration, and rage as possible. For example, you could be reaching for a piece of paper or an envelope on a shelf, and all of a sudden an avalanche occurs where a whole pile of things comes down suddenly. You might think that it was you who had caused it to happen, so you curse your own clumsiness or lack of caution and scream and complain and cast off all kinds of negative emotions. That is exactly the kind of reaction the demonic spirits are trying to get out of you. You could inadvertently knock a glass over that splinters into a hundred pieces all over the floor while you're standing there in your bare feet. They know this will cause you anguish, because you know that not only is it a dangerous situation, but also that it will take a great deal of effort to clean it up properly, and you may have no time to spare to do so. You may not be able to find your keys, or your wallet, or something has gone missing that you know should not be missing at all.

Once these negative emotions are cast out of the electromagnetic field of the people being oppressed, the demons siphon off that energy, feed on it, recharge themselves with it and then use it to perpetrate even more diabolical attacks. It's a never-ending cycle until the people being oppressed stop, clear their minds, focus on love, and surround themselves with that emotion rather than broadcasting the whole slew of negative emotions that the demons crave. Unfortunately, most people don't think of this when they are undergoing attacks of their own.

Chapter 3: The Devil in the Dark – Analysis

It was in Vincent Decker's version of Ed Warren's Occult Museum that the horrific attacks upon him began to take place on a scale he could scarcely have foreseen. He had always believed that he was protected and that his knowledge of parapsychology and demonology would give him the upper hand when dealing with cases involving demonic spirits. The demonic spirits knew this, of course, so at the end of the previous volume, in their last desperate bid to maintain a connection with him in the physical plane as they were about to be ousted from the McLaughlin house, one of the demons bit him on the head and left behind in his skull the physical manifestation of the teeth of an ancient boar from a genetic strain never before seen, according to the Yale scientist who analyzed them. What Vincent didn't realize or understand – was why.

I can confidently say that after working for and with one of the most famous and respected demonologists in the world, the late Ed Warren, I know a great deal about demonic spirits, their powers, and their methods of exerting that power in the physical plane. In the case of the teeth, I alone surmised that they acted as inter-dimensional doorways or portals or conduits between the demonic realm and the third dimension. That is precisely the reason the demonic spirit left them embedded in Vincent's skull. The teeth were the reason that the spirits were gaining entry into his house. If one tooth had become dislodged from Vincent's skull inside the McLaughlin house and rolled out of view, under the stairs for instance, that single tooth could have acted as a conduit that would have allowed the demonic spirits entry when the family was least expecting it, just as the Ouija board allowed them entry the first time. In the case of the Ouija board, a doorway was opened through the exercise of free will and The Universal Law of Intention, originating on the physical plane and allowing access from the spiritual dimension. In the case of the teeth, a doorway was opened via the same Universal Law of Intention by way of the demon's will alone, originating from the realm of spirit into the physical plane. Fortunately for the McLaughlin family, not one of the teeth was left in their basement during the time the last suffumigation was being performed, when Vincent was bitten.

Therefore, it was the teeth that Vincent was drawn to, because they formed a lasting connection or transit point between the spiritual dimensions and the third dimension, using Vincent's life force energy to help power the vortex. Think of them as homing beacons, if you will. The demons strategically maneuvered the jewelry box off the shelf where he habitually left it and teleported it onto his desk, so the teeth would be closer to his energy field, and so he would focus his intention upon them, and thus empower them through his recognition, more than if they were left elsewhere in the room, out of sight and therefore out of mind.

Not only was Vincent caught up in a war within his own home and office due to the vast assortment of negatively charged or cursed artifacts on display there, but also his energy was being siphoned off and depleted so he could be viciously attacked and then paralyzed when he tried to fight back. I liken this to the opposite end of the spectrum when exorcists douse a possessed human body with holy water while it is being animated by a demonic spirit. The administration of holy water causes a great deal of pain at a minimum and at best, completely debilitates the demon if it is incapable of resisting it. The same thing was going on against Vincent Decker. He was being doused with waves of negative energy and he was being paralyzed and caused a great deal of mental anguish. Being near such negatively charged objects is just as bad as being inside a demonically infested house, because your electromagnetic field is constantly under bombardment.

Demonic spirits seem to get great pleasure by using things that human beings find repulsive, either by manifesting them in physical form or by projecting those images and smells into the minds of the oppressed. These things include noisome stenches, such as rotting flesh and feces, and revolting images, such as worms, maggots, flies, and decaying bodies.

Vincent Decker was a hardened spiritual warrior, but even he needed help when the attacks started occurring inside his own home. Sometimes – often – the best hope paranormal investigators have is the assistance of the brave, learned men of the cloth who are the pillars of their spiritual communities, with a far deeper level of commitment to their faith than the average layperson or demonologist.

Chapter 4: Divine Intervention – Analysis

Approaching, passing, or driving by a property that is infested by demonic spirits is one of the most disturbing feelings that a sensitive person could ever experience. It is like staring at something that you know deep in your core just doesn't belong there, as though it has been displaced out of time and space. When approaching a "haunted house," if your gut feeling tells you to turn around the other way and get out of there, rather than proceed any further, by all means follow that advice by always trusting that instinct. It will never lead you astray. Those tingling sensations and those gut feelings are coming from the deepest recesses of Who You Are and they should always be heeded without question, because they could also be gentle nudgings of your spirit guides or guardian angels who are trying to protect you and save you from going down a dangerous road. Most people associate the odd feeling with the house itself, but in reality, it's the negative electro-magnetic fields of the demonic entities present inside the house that cause those dark feelings of dread and despair. Sometimes, the feeling is so intense that the hairs will stand up on the back of your neck. You may even feel tingles on the top of your head accompanied by a distinct uneasy feeling that something is wrong and that for whatever reason, you should run away from the place as quickly as your legs can carry you.

When we recite the Twenty-third Psalm, our aura expands and becomes very powerful. I recently had confirmation of this from a remarkable man I know personally named Master Stephen Co, a pranic healing master who has the ability to see the electromagnetic fields surrounding the body. He knows from first-hand observation that when someone recites this psalm, their aura explodes and expands into a brilliant sphere – a potent defensive shield against the demonic. This is because when it is recited, you are using The Universal Law of Intention to "defend yourself against evil."

It always amazes me that certain animals are associated with negative spirits and the demonic. One such creature, of course, is the black crow. This is not to say that these black birds are negative, demonic, or anything out of the ordinary at all, but it seems that where evil spirits are present, crows tend to appear more menacing than they seem to be at other times. Perhaps it has to do with their menacing caw or the fact that they eat the corpses of small animals. Perhaps it has to do with their color. Color is a function of vibrational frequency. Black is the lowest frequency, which means it is negatively charged. Negative spirits and demonic spirits are attracted to black colors. I believe it is because they find it a simpler task to manipulate and/or control them better than lighter, higher frequency colors. We never hear of a threatening demonic blue jay, or cardinal, or yellow parakeet. They certainly wouldn't appear very threatening at all.

Vincent had been plagued by headaches just prior to learning about the McLaughlin Case and then those headaches evolved into piercing, debilitating migraines. This was a systematic escalation in the attacks upon him. When he mentioned hearing the strange tones in his ears, Bishop Phelan knew that they were attempting to disable his five physical senses, first with his eyes and then with his ears.

A friend of mine, Bishop James Long, has been experiencing headaches and migraines for quite some time now. He, too, stands boldly against the dark, evil spirits who seek the ruination of mankind, and I believe the headaches that my friends, Vincent and James, suffer are due to the presence of and the pressures created by demonic spirits. Bishop Long told me that whenever he becomes aware of a case involving true demonic spirits, he will begin to suffer horrific migraines. He says that he is never without three migraine pills in his pocket when he enters an infested house, nor is he without two large bottles of the pills in his car just in case. He knows that the demonic spirits prey on our weaknesses or our vulnerabilities. When he is working on a case and begins to suffer migraines, he will pray to his patron saints, Saint Christopher, Saint Francis of Assisi, and Saint Benedict, for relief and protection. Often, despite his prayers, the migraines become so debilitating that he has to leave and allow another priest to finish a house blessing or an exorcism.

Chapter 5: Defying the Darkness – Analysis

Willfully entering a building known to be infested by demonic spirits can be one of the most dangerous things anyone could do, because there is a very real danger that although you may make it inside, the spirits there could decide to do everything in their power to prevent you from leaving, so they can attack you at their leisure. It takes a profound level of faith and immense courage to stand in your own light and in the power of God the Creator and set foot into a location where multidimensional, diabolical, evil spirits have established a foothold. Multiply that uncertainty and dread by a factor of ten when that location is your own home or place of business that you absolutely must access.

I remember the first time Ed Warren took me to a demonically infested house. I was apprehensive as we drove up together in his car. It felt strange to gaze at it from the car. Something was just "off." When we parked, we walked up to the front of the house. It was a white colonial with a white screen door. I gazed up at the second story as Ed inserted the key, turned the door knob, and walked in. The door made a crashing sound in the metal frame and then the door creaked open. The interior was dark with wood paneling and dark green carpeting, an old sofa and recliner and several non-distinctive wall decorations. He led me into the kitchen and it was there that I had a very uneasy feeling. He asked me what I felt and I told him that I felt a weighted presence there, as though the air was making it harder to walk through the room. Then he opened the door to the basement and stood there staring at me. He asked me if I wanted to go down there. I hesitated and finally acquiesced. The stairs creaked and groaned. Then Ed slammed the door behind me and switched off the light. I was more amused than frightened. I waited for him to make the next move and then I heard him chuckle on the other side of the door. The light came on and I heard him tell me to go downstairs to see if everything was okay. I did as he asked and I reached out with my senses. It was cold and damp down there, but I didn't feel anything out of the ordinary. When I started up the stairs, he opened the door and waited for me to come into the kitchen. I knew he was just testing me and I really wasn't at all frightened. When we were leaving, he asked me if I'd like to spend the night in the house alone. I told him that while I wasn't afraid to, I really didn't think it would be in my best interest to do so. He told me always to trust my feelings and never to feel ashamed for not putting on a brave face. I think I earned a good deal of Ed's respect that day.

When Vincent was walking through the house with the bowls of smoking incense, he was performing a Roman Catholic ritual known as suffumigation, which is essentially the process of fumigating a place with high-frequency, holy incense traditionally comprising frankincense and myrrh, coupled with prayer to dispel negative energy and make the location inhospitable to evil spirits. It is very effective if done properly by people who know what they're doing and who have the faith and conviction to see it through. The smoke must billow through every square inch of the house in question. This is precisely what Vincent was doing in his own home and office. Sage and sandalwood are also very potent where things of this nature are concerned. This allowed him to fumigate and seal the house, forcing the demonic spirits away.

Chapter 6: Devastation – Analysis

When Linda and Kelly were driving by Union Cemetery, it was a good thing Kelly was preoccupied, because through her very recognition, she could have recalled the tragic events that began the McLaughlin family's haunting experience just a few months earlier. Recognition is a very dangerous thing because our awareness and our focused thoughts are extremely powerful. If Kelly had seen the cemetery and recalled the terror she had experienced, she could have initiated contact with yet another spirit lurking in the cemetery through the emanation of her fear. Luckily for her, and for her family, that was not the case.

The reason this is so important is because by simply thinking of spirits, they are drawn into our awareness, and because we are immensely powerful creators in our own right, those beings or entities sense those subtle connective energies and become aware of the thoughts of the people who are giving them recognition.

The most dangerous consequence of this is that the connection can be re-established. That is the very worst thing that could happen, because it invites the same activity into one's life to begin all over again. Sadly, and unfortunately for many families, this recurrence is quite common.

This is precisely why we all warned the McLaughlin family to do their best to put the entire situation out of their minds. Unlike a number of other families who have been attacked and then seem to love the attention that being on the receiving end of demonic oppression brings them, most families, like the McLaughlins, desire no recognition at all – and with good reason. It's bad enough to go through that awful experience by yourself. It's another thing entirely to make your neighbors or your community aware of it, because often the poor people's lives become a media circus with strangers driving by at all hours taking photographs, poking fun at them, making unfounded accusations, and worse. All these things do nothing but aggravate the problem, because more and more people become aware of what has been going on, and then feed it through their own recognition. All one needs to do is read about the Smurl family in the book, *The Haunted*, or about the Lutz family in *The Amityville Horror* to understand how badly things turned out for them when they went public. Very rarely did anyone go out of their way to be kind to either family or to lend them support. Rather, the affected families invited ridicule, scorn, and a host of other negative reactions which only perpetuated the problems they were facing rather than help them in any way.

You see, giving a spirit any recognition at all empowers it. This is because our focused awareness is immensely powerful whether we know it or not. When you recognize something, you focus all your faculties upon it and you then draw the experience of interacting with that thing into your reality. This happens through the Law of Attraction. What you focus your awareness on is what is made manifest in your reality. This is much like receiving a medical diagnosis that reveals you have contracted some dread disease to which you were otherwise oblivious. When people get sick, they often recover simply by feeding their body the right nutritious foods or medicines and, most important, by believing they will overcome the sickness as surely as the sun will rise the next morning. But when you think about that thing and therefore bring it into your awareness, again using the example of that unexpected call from your doctor, you strengthen or weaken whatever condition he tells you that you have, simply by your reaction to it. Your thoughts decide whether it is something you will overcome or something that will overcome you. When you give something recognition, you're essentially saying to it, "I see you! You're real and I give you power! You are now made manifest in my reality." Then it becomes so. Therefore, we must be very careful what we pay attention to, and what we expose ourselves to on television and in the movie theaters.

When you open your awareness by sitting in a dark theater watching a movie about demonic spirits and the horror they unleash upon the people in the story, you are giving the subject and scenario a great deal of energy. You are recognizing that demonic spirits exist, and that they have powers beyond your imagining. You are then placing yourself in the same situation that the characters are experiencing in the movie. By doing so, you are telling the Creator that you consent to these situations and you therefore invite the possibility of the same thing happening to you – simply by thinking about what you would do in just such a situation. When sitting in a dark movie theater, trembling in fear or screaming at the top of your lungs as you watch the horrific scenes in the movie unfold, you are casting off huge amounts of fear energy. Guess what kind of entities are present with you in that theater, gobbling up all those delicious fear energies!

When I was re-creating the terrible true events that transpired in the McLaughlin case while writing my debut novel, *Dark Siege: A Connecticut Family's Nightmare*, the prequel to the book you are reading now, I had to be extremely careful not to attract the same demonic spirits that were involved in that case right into my own home, even though it was a case that occurred twenty years earlier. I am a powerful creator. I also know that I am powerfully protected from within and by sources and forces outside of me. To ensure that my writing and living space was "off limits" to these demons while I recollected those terrifying events, I continually burned frankincense and myrrh at my desk because it was my intention to actively fumigate against all negativity and negative spirits. I often took breaks to meditate and focus on being a field of pure, unconditional love, and radiated that love outward until it surrounded my body and my dwelling to push away negativity and negative entities through the Universal Law of Attraction.

I believe that the McLaughlin house was successfully sealed off from the demonic spirits through the ritual known as suffumigation mentioned in the previous portion of the Chapter Analyses.

Because the house was sealed off, I believe that the demonic spirits lurked outside the house, and specifically around the property line and on the road. Because Julie Marsh was so instrumental in helping the McLaughlins connect with Yvonne and myself, and because she was driving toward the house after the demons had found a way to return, I believe their intention was to maim her, both to make an example of her and to make her suffer. Rarely do they ever succeed in actually killing someone.

Since Kelly was a sensitive, and the demons had already established a connection with her through prolonged interaction, they found it easy to implant the images involving Julie's forthcoming accident. Of course, she felt badly about her Auntie Julie getting hurt, but the way in which she told her mother confirmed to me that she was already used to the methods with which the demonic spirits communicated with her. It was a very matter-of-fact statement, as though it was sure to happen, and there was nothing anyone could do about it.

Remember, these demons are inter-dimensional beings originating from outside our third dimension where we can see and hear and touch. When Kelly forewarned her mother about the accident, it caused Linda a great deal of fear and panic. The demonic spirits were using that breach in her electromagnetic field to influence her thoughts, and were sucking her into an extraplanar vortex where everything seemed to be distorted and spinning, strange, and disorienting. She was in reality stuck between dimensions and she was experiencing both simultaneously. The demons kept her inside a swirling invisible prison so she could do nothing but watch the horror unfolding before her panic-stricken eyes – in slow motion.

Can you imagine the mental anguish going through her mind during these bizarre events? Guess who or what was feasting on that fear buffet!

When she was finally released, it was because the demons desired it. They could have held her there for as long as they wanted, but they wanted her to experience the full force and shock of the terrible collision when the delivery truck smashed her friend's van from behind.

The delivery driver claimed he saw the van turn into the driveway and as he was just about to pass the driveway, the van was mysteriously positioned right in front of his truck. There was no time to react and nothing he could do but slam his foot on the brakes. How is this possible?

There are only two possibilities. Either the delivery driver was tricked into seeing and believing that Julie's van turned into the driveway when the demonic spirits implanted those images directly into his mind, or they teleported the van right back into the road at the last second.

The first explanation is a simple task for the demons to accomplish. The second task, teleportation, was also a simple task for them, even though the ramifications are much more interesting. To cause an object the size of a delivery truck to dematerialize or break up into atoms and then reassemble or re-materialize elsewhere is a feat of epic proportions, and a power that true demonic spirits possess. Interestingly enough, the delivery driver himself would have to have undergone the same process. Because it all happened in the blink of an eye, his rational mind could not deduce what had really happened. He, too, was in shock.

The entire accident scenario could not have come at a worse time. The McLaughlins had remained free of any form of haunting activity since the successful exorcism of Matthew at the end of October. They were in the festive, holiday spirit, and were planning on a peaceful Christmas Season full of joy and peace and happiness. Linda knew deep in her core when she first heard her daughter warn her of the impending accident that their brief respite was precisely that. When she was caught up in a demonic mind trap, forced to witness her best friend's brush with death, she knew that they were all in serious trouble.

Chapter 7: Caught in the Web – Analysis

The demonic spirits definitely had a hold on Kelly. Not only were they capable of using her as a mouthpiece, but they were able to breach her electromagnetic field by causing her a great deal of fear and anxiety by implanting the images of the accident in her mind. Linda just left her there by herself in the front yard, which caused her additional fear, as did her uncertainty about the extent of her Auntie Julie's injuries. Once Linda was preoccupied, Kelly was especially vulnerable because she was left alone. The demons taunted her with indecipherable voices and sounds that caused her eventually to black out and fall down into the snow when no one was paying any attention. This allowed the demonic spirits to breach her defenses and to weave dark tendrils inside her. If the process hadn't been interrupted by her father and then by the timely arrival of Vincent Decker and Bishop Phelan, they could very well have succeeded in seizing her body and possessing her fully.

The demon knew it had precious moments left to complete the possession, so it maneuvered itself away from Vincent and attacked him when he drew within range. The incredible strength that Kelly displayed by blasting the two-hundred-pound man away as though he were a toddler, told them that they were dealing with a very serious situation. She was not fully possessed, but she was definitely being influenced and controlled. This happens when an outside intelligence vies for control of the body currently being used or animated by the spirit of a human being.

By rushing in when he did, and by producing his blessed holy symbol and casting holy water onto the body that the demonic spirit was attempting to control, Bishop Phelan could very well have saved Kelly from full possession just in the nick of time. The reason why holy relics and holy water are so effective is because of their polarity.

Holy water is water that has been purified, prayed over, and blessed by a priest or holy man. The strength of the blessing is based on the strength of the faith of the one who has blessed it, and – most important – his intention while he is interacting with it. Bishop Phelan is a man of unshakable faith so the water was immensely powerful. But how can water be powerful?

Japanese scientist Dr. Masaru Emoto, has discovered that thoughts, emotions, and intentions introduced into water can change and rearrange the water's molecular structure. After he held a glass of water and focused his intention on a particular emotion, he froze the water, and upon examining the frozen crystals, he noticed that they were different depending on which emotion was projected onto the water. This is explained as Sympathetic Vibratory Physics. The work is fascinating. I encourage everyone to read more about Dr. Emoto's profound work.

I believe that holy water is blessed and infused with the ultimate power in the universe – the power of God. Think about how powerful water becomes when the intention is to supercharge it with the power and positive energy of the Creator of All That Is. What do you think that holy water would do when cast upon a negative or demonic spirit? It would be the equivalent of pouring sulfuric acid onto our human flesh. When we use holy water on the demonic, we often hear and record blood-curdling wails of agony, because obviously it works.

Chapter 8: A Rainbow in the Dark – Analysis

Stress and fear, and the health of the physical, spiritual, emotional, and mental bodies all affect the strength of the aura – the energy defense shield that surrounds us all and protects us from negative entities and from evil. Fear causes our electromagnetic field to retract and pull closer to the body causing small holes to open up, which result in energy leaks and breaches in our defenses for other energies and entities to slip through.

When Yvonne Saxon arrived, she was panicked because as she was racing toward the house, she mentally saw the black spirits swooping in and surrounding Linda. She also saw flashes of the horrific accident in front of the house. She saw images of the ambulance and the fire truck and the police car. When she saw her friends standing there, her first response was to thank God that they were unharmed. Then she felt the outside edges of Kelly's auric field to make certain that it was intact with no breaches or energy leaks.

The aura is the electromagnetic field that surrounds the human body and every organism in the universe. The Human Energy Field is a collection of electromagnetic energies of varying densities that permeate through and emit or exit from the physical body of a living person. These particles of energy are suspended around the human body and encapsulate it in an oval field approximately two to three feet in diameter. It extends above the head and below the feet into the ground. Each one of the subtle bodies that exist around the physical body has its own unique frequency. They are interrelated, and affect one another and the person's feelings, emotions, thinking, behavior, and health. Therefore, a state of imbalance in one of the bodies leads to a state of imbalance in the others.

Every living thing has an electromagnetic field. Each field is similar in size and shape, but each had its own color variation. Color is a function of vibrational frequency. Each electromagnetic field had a distinct brightness or luminescence. Some are clearer than others. Each color has a specific meaning.

Our aura reflects our current level of spiritual evolution as well as our general level of health, our state of mind, and much more. Spirits can be attracted to us based solely on the brightness and the color of our aura. They are attracted to pretty colors through the Universal Law of Attraction just as those in the body are. Positive spirits are attracted to bright, vibrant colors, and negative spirits are generally attracted to darker colors.

Wearing crucifixes, medals, relics, and crystals are all powerful forms of protection. The level of protection gained from wearing such an item is based upon the intention that the creator had for the item when it was originally crafted, the intention of the wearer, the faith that the wearer has in the object being worn, and the abilities of the material from which it was crafted. Crystals are capable of absorbing, conserving, storing, focusing, and emitting energy. Each type of crystal is unique, as are its abilities. They are living first-dimensional beings, each with their own memory, personality and capabilities. Each crystal has a color. Color is a function of vibrational frequency. Everything is vibration.

If people want to protect themselves from negative energies, they should wear crystals that deflect or absorb those energies. One of the many crystals that have an especially powerful effect on negative energy is the amethyst.

Amethysts are violet in color, and violet frequencies found in lavender oil, meditating on a violet light, or wearing purple or violet clothing protect the wearer by deflecting negative energy. Roman Catholic priests hearing confession wear purple stoles around their necks to deflect the negative energy that is projected on them when sins are released to God. Catholic exorcists wear purple stoles around their necks to protect themselves against evil spirits. Wearing an amethyst crystal around the neck for protection is an excellent way to deflect negative energy. The size of the crystal does not matter as long as the color is on the deeper side rather than on the clearer side.

Wearing black or green tourmaline or carrying a chunk in your pocket is a great defense against negative energy, because it absorbs negative energy. It is very important to learn how to routinely cleanse and purify your crystals, however, so that they can release, clear, and transmute the negative energy that they have absorbed. For example, if a black tourmaline is full, because it has absorbed all the negative energy that it can, it could actually harm the wearer because it is so full of negative energy. Why? What does negative energy attract? It attracts more negative energy.

By smudging crystals with the smoke of sandalwood or sage, you are doing your crystals a great service by making them useful to you again. If that sounds fantastic, remember that many ancient cultures knew about, worked with, and adorned themselves with crystals of all shapes, colors and sizes.

Chapter 9: Picking Up the Pieces – Analysis

Vincent and Bishop Phelan knew the dangerous situation Julie was in following the demonic attack on her vehicle. Because she was injured and in shock, she was in an extremely vulnerable state, a state that the demonic spirits were sure to exploit. When Vincent and the bishop arrived, their primary goal was to ease Julie into a relaxed state, so the Bishop could bless her without alarming her or alerting her to the very serious danger she was in. They also needed Julie's permission to go in and bless her house, so they could be sure there would be no demonic intrusion. Once the bishop had personally blessed her, he was confident that she was sufficiently protected. They asked Linda to accompany them to the cafeteria to make sure that she was aware of what was going on, so she could keep her wits about her and her guard up.

Back at the McLaughlin house, Yvonne wanted to allow Kelly to rest where they could all keep an eye on her. And then she needed Matthew's permission to walk through and examine the house in its entirety to make sure everything was all right. The reason she needed Matthew's permission is because it was his house and he had to agree to giving Yvonne unrestricted access for her to be as effective as she could be. She sensed nothing out of the ordinary, because the two suffumigations performed there in the past had been successful.

When Yvonne noticed Kelly's drawing in her coloring book, she knew she had been drawing images that she had been seeing in her mind. They were not physical beings she was seeing, but something that was being projected into her psyche.

It was an alarming situation to be sure.

The one-eared stuffed bunny is Kelly's favorite toy. I focused on it, because I wanted to distinguish it as different from a "haunted item" like Vincent keeps in his office. The bunny was not negatively charged, as Yvonne determined by her "psychic" tour.

Chapter 10: Humiliation – Analysis

Diabolical spirits can bring about drastic sickness and pain in a split second, and their goal is always the same – to weaken their targets, to punish them for resisting and ultimately to possess them and seize control of their bodies. When Jimmy's sudden stomachache came on, neither Jimmy nor Tyler knew that the demons had come to call on them to begin their campaign of terror against them. Demons can totally debilitate someone with only a thought. The same type of thing happened in the previous volume when the demons in the McLaughlin house caused Matthew to keel over and vomit all over the fireplace in the living room. They can cause any number of emotions to erupt and consume the minds of the living, and they can cause any illness or disease symptom to manifest in the blink of an eye.

Because these are beings who are filled with hate and rage, it was easy for them to exert their control over the football players who already had a mutual distaste for both Jimmy and Tyler. The demons aggravated the situation and caused even more tension and animosity there in the classroom and out in the hallway. While the football player who attacked Tyler might have had the reasonable self-control not to physically attack Tyler, it could very well have been the demons who influenced him to attack Tyler the way that he did.

The demons love to divide and conquer, which is precisely why they caused Jimmy to become sick and not

Tyler. Once they were separated, they were easier targets to manipulate and harm.

Chapter 11: Into the Fray – Analysis

Animosity and conflict fuel demonic spirits like gasoline to an open flame. They love to cause strife and tension and fear and foreboding, and then they bask in and soak up the negative emotions that come about as a result. I believe that the same is true with the epic battles that took place in the Colosseum in Rome, which were fueled by the negative energies cast off by the massive numbers of people who gathered there to witness the brutal and bloody contests. Demonic spirits thrive and feast on such energies, so they do all that they can to instigate and initiate conflict.

It is highly probable that the demons influenced the football players through the power of suggestion to go ahead and gang up on and fight Tyler when he was alone and most vulnerable. The freshman boy who was sent to Tyler with a false message could have very well been influenced by the demonic spirits as well. Or it could have been simple peer pressure or raucous teenage antics. In all probability, it was a combination of all three.

Chapter 12: Confrontation with Chaos – Analysis

A Ouija board is old, maybe even timeless. It is an instrument with which to open a channel of communication to the spirit world and, if we are not extremely careful, a key that can unlock a doorway into our own. A Ouija board is the single most dangerous piece of occult paraphernalia in history and its sole purpose is to enable contact with and to invite negative, inhuman, diabolical spirits of all kinds into this world. Nothing good ever comes through them to communicate with us, and immeasurable harm often comes about as a consequence of their use.

The Ouija board is sold as a game. It's manufactured commercially and sold by the thousands, but it is most certainly *not* a game. Do you know where the company that produces it is located? Are you ready for this? Salem, Massachusetts. Are you familiar with Salem? If you're reading this book, I'd bet that you are at least somewhat familiar with it. Salem, Massachusetts, is where the witch trials were held in 1692. They were a series of hearings and prosecutions of people *accused* of witchcraft. The amount of suffering, misery, injustice, and death that occurred there is staggering. As a result, the entire area around that province, including Salem Village (now Danvers), Ipswich, Andover, and Salem town, is a supernatural and preternatural epicenter.

The most dangerous aspect of using a Ouija board is the

gradual, unquenchable desire to use it more frequently and for longer periods of time, until the point when the user can't seem to put it away. This is called obsession, and as with any addiction, it is extremely destructive and dangerous.

Obsessed users generally feel more and more unsatisfied with the answers that they might be receiving or with the quality of the communication in general, even though they spend more and more time using the board. They might make a connection with a particular spirit and never really know whom they are communicating with. If they seem to have lost contact with their special spirit friend, they can't seem to rest until they are able to talk with him or her again. The user becomes a recluse in most cases, ignoring friends, family, and even forgoing food and sustenance.

This is all by design to wear the user down, lower their defenses, and quickly gain the upper hand, then offer – or in reality, *demand* – something of the user in exchange for more time and more information. Despite the alluring nature of the special offer, this always comes at great cost in the long run, despite how attractive the offer seems to be at first.

Above all else, the spirits are attempting to gain the user's trust. They will imitate or claim to associate with or be connected to a pleasant personality that the user knew – or especially, and most effectively – a recently deceased relative, loved one or friend.

The spirit will claim to be your grandfather, for instance. It will tell you what your real grandfather bought you for your birthday, it will tell you about names, dates, and places that are absolutely accurate, and therefore earn your complete trust.

If the spirit knew what present your grandfather bought you for your birthday, and it knows your actual birth date, and knows the unique term of endearment that your grandfather called your grandmother – that only *he* would know – then the spirit you are communicating with must be the spirit of your grandfather, right?

Wrong!

The spirits that you are communicating with are not bound by the human body and are no longer shut off from their psychic abilities like the majority of the living. They're energy, and they can read and influence your energy without your even knowing it. When the user asks a question that he or she already knows the answer to, or when the user has a specific answer in mind when asking the question, all the spirit has to do is read the user's mind, get the answer he or she is looking for, and use it to satisfy and fool the user.

Then what? When the spirit has succeeded in gaining the user's trust, it's in. What wouldn't you do for your dear, departed grandfather who was trying to make contact with you from the great beyond?

One of the most infamous cases involving a Ouija board was the case of Annabelle, in which an inhuman spirit fooled two women into believing that it was the spirit of a little girl. The women became so obsessed with the board and so concerned with the spirit of the girl with whom they were communicating that they quickly agreed to help her. The only trouble was, it was definitely not the spirit of a little girl.

When the spirit asked for permission to live inside one of the women, the woman knew that something was wrong, so she refused. Good choice. But she did give it permission to live inside the life-sized Raggedy Ann doll that they had in their apartment. The second that they gave the alleged spirit of the girl permission to live inside the doll, all the contact on the Ouija board suddenly stopped. The chaos that broke loose in the following days produced some of the most frightening activity on record.

If you'd like to read the entire story about Annabelle,

you can find it in the book, *The Demonologist*, by Gerald Brittle. It is full of some of the most horrifyingly real cases of preternatural, diabolical infestation and oppression I have ever studied.

When it comes to Ouija boards, you can't be sure who or what you are communicating with, nor can you ever trust the messages being conveyed. Broken sentences or one-word messages are not very clear forms of communication.

When a Ouija board is used with focused intention to open up a channel of communication between the third dimension and others – that is exactly what happens. The strength of the portal, doorway, vortex, star gate, wormhole – or *whatever* name you wish to use – depends on the strength and conviction of the users, and again, as with all things, the intention used to open it in the first place. It is one thing to be a curious teenager who uses a Ouija board with the intention to "test the waters" and see if contact with a spirit is even possible. It is another thing entirely to use the Ouija board with the intention of opening a permanent gateway into dimensions inhabited by diabolical entities so that those denizens of the dark can use it to invade our dimension.

Just as the old woman who had appeared to save Tyler and his friends from going down the road of no return by dissuading them from buying the Ouija board in the previous volume, Tyler felt the need to warn those two poor boys about the horrific chain of events that happened to him and his friends and family. He didn't know what came over him when he lashed out as he did, he stated that it was just his gut feeling that they were after a Ouija board and that he should intervene. When he yelled at the manager, he was filled with rage that the man would allow the Ouija boards in his store without knowing the real danger that they posed to unsuspecting kids. It took all his self-control not to lash out and strike the man with his fist – this was without question the influence of the demonic spirits that were following him, since they first attacked Jimmy while the two were in school.

The sudden, mysterious reappearance of the old woman who had warned Tyler and his friends not to buy the Ouija board could have been one of two things. It could have really been the spirit of the old woman who could very well have been one of Tyler's spirit guides. The spirit could have lured him out of the car, because she knew that the demons intended to destroy the engine and she wanted Tyler out of harm's way in case something happened that could cause him injury, or the demons could have recreated her image to lure him out of the car, so they could better affect the engine as they did. He himself was protected and his electromagnetic field could have thwarted their attack, because it was a blessed, positive field.

The demonic spirits didn't like it when Tyler denied them fresh young Ouija board victims, so they performed what we call a "negative miracle" by stripping every wire in the engine of his mother's car and causing the battery acid to eat though the battery case to demonstrate that fact. This was a warning to all of them that they had returned with a vengeance. Damage of this nature is rare, because it's physical proof that demonic spirits exist, and they never like to leave evidence. They prefer to remain hidden in the shadows.

One circumstance in which demonic spirits affected my vehicle happened to me when I had offered to drive Ed and Lorraine Warren and my fellow investigators up to Bittersweet Farm in Vermont to conduct an investigation. Early in the morning on November 30, 1990, I climbed into my mother's brand new Dodge Caravan to prepare for my drive. I closed my eyes and said, "I wash this van in the blood of Jesus Christ so that it and all the passengers within will be protected on our long journey to and from Vermont." After I started on my way, as I was traveling northbound on the Merritt Parkway on my way to pick up the others at the Warrens' house, a black BMW came up beside me on the right. I didn't think anything was amiss until I noticed the other car begin to shake and wobble. Then before my astonished eyes, the other car started swerving and fishtailing to the point where the driver appeared to be losing control of the car. Seconds later, it accelerated past me, and veered into my lane, ten yards ahead of me, at a perfect ninety-degree angle, and came to a screeching halt in the center of the road. I hit my brakes, but too late. I smashed right into the side of the BMW, shattering the glass in his driver's side window. I turned on my emergency flashers and got out to check on the other driver and find out what had happened. Neither of us was harmed, but upon conversing with the driver, he said that it was as though his car had hit a solid patch of ice and that the car was just stripped right out of his control. There was definitely no ice on that roadway. The temperatures were in the high fifties. When the police arrived, they had a great deal of difficulty believing what the driver said he had experienced, simply because it was impossible for there to be any ice on the highway and upon further examination, there was definitely none on the road as the driver had suggested.

When I got to a payphone to call the Warrens so I could tell them what had happened and thus explain the reason for my tardiness, after a period of silence, Lorraine almost called the entire trip off because she knew that the diabolical spirits were the real culprits. They didn't want us to make the trip to Vermont to help the family so they did everything in their power to sufficiently damage the vehicle we were planning to use. They could not affect the vehicle I was driving, because I had personally blessed it and bathed it in the blood of Jesus Christ. They did, however, affect the other car because it had not been blessed that morning, if ever. This is a shining example of how powerful prayer and blessing and intention really are. If I had not had the fore-sight to bless the vehicle before I started on my way, perhaps things would have gone quite differently. Perhaps I would have been injured or even killed in a seemingly unremarkable "accident."

A similar circumstance happened to Bishop Phelan when he was rushing to help another family that was under diabolical siege. When he rushed to his car that he'd planned on using to go to their aid, his driver's door would not open, no matter how hard he tried. Neither would any other door, despite the fact that they were all unlocked and the handle should have disengaged from the locking mecha-nism allowing easy entry. Once he'd broken out his window and climbed inside, his key would not fit into the ignition, as if there were a solid piece of metal preventing him from inserting his key. Frustration mounted and it wasn't until Bishop Phelan cleared his thoughts and prayed that the demonic activity eased up enough to allow him to start the car and go on his way.

When Vincent examined the station wagon, he knew full well who the culprits were. He knew then, as they all did, the danger that Tyler and his friends were in.

Chapter 13: Seduction – Analysis

A spirit has no physical body, and therefore it has no gender. A human spirit incarnates innumerable times in innumerable shapes, sizes, and of course, in both sexes. An angel, an archangel, or a fallen archangel or devil has never had a gender, because it has never animated a physical third-dimensional body. But when it manifests itself and attacks a living human being, it takes on or assumes one of the only two genders that it has available to it.

Diabolical spirits can bring on serious sickness and pain in a split second, and their goal is always the same – to weaken their targets, to punish them for resisting, and ultimately to possess them and seize control of their bodies.

We all have lustful thoughts. But when demonic spirits are involved, they will use that lust to their own advantage and often it results in sexual attacks upon an unsuspecting human being. But how is that possible? How can an immaterial being have sex with a physical being?

A *succubus* is demonic spirit that seduces and initiates oral and vaginal intercourse with heterosexual men and also with bisexual and homosexual women. The sexual preference of the victims, of course, always determines what gender the demonic spirit manifests itself in and therefore determines what types of sexual interaction will occur during the encounter. A succubus most often appears as a beautiful woman with breasts and female genitalia, that most closely matches or precisely imitates the object of the target's most intimate, secret desires. They will use this guise to approach the target and use it to gain the target's consent to come closer and thereby work their way into their electromagnetic field. It will initiate the vital exchange of energy by stoking the victim's flames of desire. Then once it has achieved the intimate connection, the embrace, or the acts themselves, as we saw with the succubus that attacked Jimmy, it will reveal its true form, paralyze the victim, and have its way with him or her. The goal is to siphon off the sexual energy of the victim for its own diabolical use.

Sexual energy is very powerful. When two people engage in a loving embrace and desire one another, they cast off enormous amounts of positive sexual energy into the world. Sadly, when someone is being sexually assaulted, the amount of negative sexual energy that is cast off is horrendous and it unleashes negative energy into the world.

The fear of being violated is strong enough. Multiply that by a factor of ten when you can't see the invisible attacker that originates from another dimension or plane of existence entirely. Multiply that by another factor of ten when you know that the thing attacking you is a demon or a devil who hates you with all its being. The intention of the demon was to cause Jimmy to experience as much fear and panic as possible to siphon off more of that precious energy.

When a virgin experiences his or her first orgasm with another sentient being, the sexual energy travels up the spine and the energy cast off from that first orgasmic experience literally explodes through the crown chakra. It is extremely potent. The demonic spirit resonates at the lowest vibration. It cannot feel or understand love. It can, however, cheat the system and coerce a living human being into granting access to its vital life force essence. If the succubus had succeeded in bringing Jimmy to orgasm, it would have feasted on the most precious, private, intimate energetic waveforms that a human being can cast off. Fortunately for Jimmy, he called upon divine protection just in the nick of time. The demon wanted no part of that and vanished instantly, though not without leaving behind the vile residue.

My friend, Bishop James Long, has intervened in many cases where unsuspecting men were sexually seduced and attacked by demonic entities. The attacks almost always begin subtly, but they gradually escalate into something far more sinister. In one case, a man who had dabbled in Satanism and black witchcraft as a young man paid the price much later as an adult – specifically, during a period when the sexual relationship with his wife was waning. When the encounters first began, he would have dreams of the perfect woman coming to him and seducing him. His body's movements while engaged in the dream-state encounters would disturb his sleeping wife and they would have heated arguments about it when she woke up. It got to the point where his wife refused to sleep in the same bed with him.

As soon as they were separated, and he was in his bed alone, the encounters became more vivid and much more intense. He even began to look forward to and welcome them. It was only after he and his wife had a horrible argument that he realized the seriousness of the situation and it was then that he declared his intention to make the encounters stop in any way that he could.

The next evening, when the dreams came to him again, he tried to resist the beautiful, alluring woman and he tried to block out the lust he had felt for her on previous encounters. Then the demon revealed its true form by projecting a series of ghastly images into his mind. Up until that point, it had been consensual. Now she...*it*...was forcing his compliance. He knew it intended to go right on seducing him, whether he wanted it to happen or not.

When he was finally able to shout out and verbally protest the interaction, he found himself paralyzed and unable to resist. This time, the demon displayed herself in all her vile, sickening wickedness. He felt powerful, painful, vicious tugs on his testicles. Then the attacks started to happen when he was awake. The pain in his scrotum was so intense that it felt like someone was holding a lit match under his testicles.

The excruciating pain forced him to go to the doctor, who, of course, found nothing wrong with him at all. The attacks became more pronounced and more violent the more he protested and resisted to the point where he felt his anal cavity being stretched as if someone were using a plunger on him. When Bishop Long got involved, the severity of the attacks diminished significantly and ceased altogether over time.

Chapter 14: Coming Clean – Analysis

When Tyler felt dread coming over him, he quickly identified the similarity between that experience and the times he'd felt it in the house and in his bedroom when his house was infested. When he looked out the window and saw the black wolf stepping down from the boulders and leaping into his yard, he knew he was in serious trouble. It was one thing for the demon to be present, but it intended to announce its arrival for the sole purpose of terrifying him. It worked.

It took a great deal of courage for Jimmy Reading to come over to the McLaughlin house alone at night on his bike to reveal the intimate details of his sexual attack. The demons knew all those facts. They are masters at causing people to feel dread, fear, shame, guilt, and any negative emotion you can think of, because they know that most spirits in human form are good-natured. They relish the fact that they can play off the guilt and shame and humiliation of their targets. Even though sexuality is the most basic, primal human function and necessary for the survival of the species, it is also the most misunderstood aspect of our lives and the most fraught with that slew of negative emotions. We have been taught to feel ashamed of our bodies and of our desires whether they be masturbation or procreation, so when forced to reveal the most intimate details of the attack, the revelation both helped and hindered Jimmy.

We are energetic beings. When we experience an orgasm, our auric fields explode into higher dimensions and we tap into frequencies that nourish and heal our bodies and connect us to our Creator. That's why we say, "Oh my God!" when we are involved in a passionate embrace or when we orgasm. It's a state of pure bliss. When two human beings share their bodies with each other in reverence of the other and to experience joy and love, the energetic connection is incredibly powerful. We exchange our innermost essence with our partner. The orgasm is a massive blast of psychic energy cast off from the body, exploding outward.

I believe that to the demonic, the pure, virginal life force orgasm is enormously potent. For the demon to siphon off that energy for its own uses is the ultimate sacrilege. I believe it creates a lasting connection between the two beings that absolutely must be severed if it is ever established.

Yvonne knew the seriousness of the situation and the implications of the succubus' attempt to steal Jimmy's virginal life-force essence for its own use. He was extremely fortunate.

Chapter 15: A Call to Arms – Analysis

Kyle Foster had no idea what had been happening to the others. He had put the entire haunting situation that occurred two months earlier out of his mind and felt confident that because he had been going to church and because he had intensified his religious studies, he was protected and invulnerable to demonic attack.

When Tyler and Yvonne arrived to inform him about what had happened to the others and especially to Jimmy, Kyle opened his awareness to the possibility that he could be next. He gave that probability recognition and therefore power, and he strengthened it through his subconscious fear, even though he put on a brave face.

Yvonne could detect the strong bond between Tyler and Kyle. She sensed a yet deeper connection than Tyler realized was there, but Tyler was ignorant of it. The demons, however, were watching and they used that information later for their own devices.

Chapter 16: Skinned Alive – Analysis

Sadly, the animal companions of humans who are interacting with demonic spirits often face the most horrendous
attacks, because they aren't as well protected as human
beings are. Cinnamon was no exception, especially because
he went after the demons outside the McLaughlin house at
one point earlier as described in the previous volume. The
demons remembered this. They never forget. They never
forgive. They knew how negatively it would affect Tyler
and Kelly if they slaughtered the dog in a most inhumane
and violent way. So that is precisely what they did. Everything they do is to cause their human victims as much
anguish and pain as possible.

The loss of Cinnamon, the anguish the cruel display
inflicted upon both his owners and the McLaughlin family,
was a tremendous blow to their hearts and their resolve.
Nothing is quite so traumatic as losing a pet that you feel
you were responsible for protecting and safeguarding. Tyler
was absolutely devastated. Of course, it was designed this
way to wear him down and to break his morale.

Luckily, Yvonne was present. She could discern that
Cinnamon's spirit was right there beside his doghouse.
Soon after, it was discovered that Kelly was far more sensitive than anyone had believed. Knowing that the spirit of
the dog was still there with them in their time of anguish
helped Tyler greatly. The loss of the dog in physical form

helped Tyler gain a further understanding of the spirit world when he felt the dog's light body in the living room.

All living beings with intelligence survive the death of the physical body. It's just the natural way of things. All that they are doing is shifting from the third dimension into the next, which is just outside the narrow range of frequencies visible to our physical eyes.

I know this from experience, because I had a beautiful pure white Persian cat named Frost who recently died in my home in Austin, Texas. Guests in my home who had never seen my cat and who never knew that I ever had one, asked me if I had a white cat, because they saw him here and there out of the corners of their eyes. The consciousness that was Frost remained in the place where he felt at home during his most recent incarnation. Because we had a close, lasting, special, loving bond, he was still with me, even though my conscious mind could not detect him. Frost was and is very much alive in his spirit. I talk to him all the time as if he is still around me, because he is. I don't hear him talking back to me, but I do often feel and sense his presence.

Children are often very sensitive, meaning they can see and hear what most adults cannot. Sadly, they lose that sensitivity as they grow older, because they are told that what they are able to see is only fantasy, or child's play. They are told that it is time to "grow up," and so in what is sometimes called "pulling down the veil," the subconscious mind closes off those special innate abilities that connect them to a vastly greater range of frequencies and vibrations that exist all around us. Whether or not we have full waking conscious access to them, these vibrations, dimensions, and densities are very real and they interpenetrate us and connect us all to each other, to the rest of the universe, and ultimately, to all of creation. Sensitive children view their psychic abilities as if they are completely normal because, of course, they are.

Children who use their psychic awareness have a very special, close, and lasting bond with animals, especially their feline, equine, and canine companions. Some lucky children are raised by parents who nurture their beautiful abilities and encourage their growth, expansion, and development. Other children simply refuse to shut them off or find it impossible to shut them off, and those people are called "mediums" or "clairvoyants."

Everyone has the potential to be a medium or clairvoyant. Everyone is psychic. Some are beginners, intermediates, and others masters, just as is the case with any other ability or skill that we use. It all depends on how much time and energy we spend on developing them. Unfortunately, rather than honor our psychic abilities, we are taught to shun them, or to shut them off, because they are not considered normal.

It is this sensitivity that allows people who are psychically attuned to connect to a series of vast dimensions just outside of the range of frequencies that our limited five senses can properly decode. Some people spend their entire lives accessing these frequencies; others only dabble in them; and sadly, for the majority of the population, most never even utilize them at all, nor do they even believe that they exist.

No one really ever dies. The earthly, physical, three-dimensional body is simply the vehicle we use to interact with the third dimension. When we are done using it and when we are ready to move on to other adventures, lessons, or experiences for our soul's evolution, we simply leave the body behind. If the body takes a fall, or grows old, malfunctions, becomes ill, or is damaged beyond repair, we simply discard it.

Our soul is never harmed in any way, because it is eternal. It has no form. Nor does it have a gender. We experience many lifetimes in both sexes. We also have both masculine and feminine energy. Some people have more of one than the other. Other people are balanced equally. That is why we have such remarkable diversity among the population. When we leave our physical bodies, we retain all our experiences and memories. Many people die a peaceful death and are glad to be free of their aging or failing bodies. Many who are killed suddenly in a car accident, in a tragic way, or in battle may find it traumatic or shocking, depending on their state of mind when they experience the sudden death of the body.

Souls coming in and souls going out are always interacting with their families and loved ones. Spirits are around us all the time, sometimes throughout our entire lives. They come and go, just as friends come and go. Often, people sense departed loved ones in their presence by smelling their perfume or scents that were associated with their body. Just because we don't see them doesn't mean they aren't there. Sometimes we hear them whispering, or think that we catch a glimpse of them out of the corner of our eyes, or pick up or sense their wisdom or counsel when we are perplexed and especially when we are thinking about them. It's nothing unnatural. We are all connected – always.

No living thing can be destroyed. The physical body or 'space suit' can be rendered inoperable so that the Conscious Awareness or Soul animating it vacates it and leaves the third-dimensional world, but no one in the history of the planet earth has ever "died" in the usual sense of the word.

No matter what happens to the body, whether the body perishes on the operating table, or mangled in a car wreck, or succumbs to old age, or even if it is blown to bits in an explosion, our infinite field of conscious awareness remains intact. We maintain full conscious awareness. We can see, hear, think, and reason just we could while in the body. In fact, we can see and hear much more clearly than we could when using the limited body. Our aches and pains, our disease conditions that the body was experiencing no longer affect us, because we are free from its constraints. It is at this time that many of our natural abilities spontaneously activate, when we remember that we were never the body at all – and when we remember that the body was simply the vehicle or space suit with which we explored the physical, third-dimensional world.

When the human spirit realizes that it is completely unscathed, no matter the condition of the body upon its death, it quickly discovers that the spirit form cannot interact with the physical world in the same way that it could when animating the physical body. So instead, it learns to manipulate physical matter by directing its focus and intention on a small object and "willing" it to move. Because the spirit body is resonating just outside the limited range of the five human senses to decode, they find it impossible to communicate with the beings who are still animating physical bodies. They quickly learn that because they are no longer limited by their own body, they can read the subtle vibrations or thoughts of those people and they can imprint messages in their minds at times when the recipient is relaxed and in a receptive state.

The ability to block out messages from spirits is a natural defense in my opinion, because if we could hear them all, we would find it very distracting and difficult to focus on the material world which we are meant to interact with while in the body.

I have heard first-hand testimony from many psychics that they wish they could turn off their sensitivity for that very reason. It's hard to focus on your own life when you are constantly being confronted by discarnate human spirits requesting help. But these people know their abilities are a gift from the Creator. It is their life purpose to be of service to these spirits and to help them bring resolution to their plight and help them cross over correctly.

With regard to seeing spirits, I can give you one such

example that has happened to me. One evening back in 1992, while in Spokane, Washington, I stopped by Crystal Clear, owned and operated by my dear friend, psychic Barbara Doede. I had been telling her about how badly I wanted to see spirits and to see the electromagnetic energy fields surrounding all life forms. She asked me to stand before her, close my eyes, and center myself by taking three deep breaths and exhaling slowly. Once I had done that, I felt her press something cold and flat against the center of my forehead. I knew it had to be a gemstone because her store was full of them. She asked me what I saw. I told her that I saw a violet light in the center of my forehead. She told me that my answer was a good one and after a minute she asked me to describe what I was seeing at that time. I told her that I was seeing a white light. She patted me gently on the cheek and said, "You're a good boy." I had no idea what she had done to me or what would occur later that evening because of it.

Shortly afterward, I went to an evening Medieval English Literature class at Eastern Washington University's Spokane Campus. As I was calmly sitting in the back of the class waiting for it to begin, I suddenly saw brilliant single-color auras around the professor and around every one of the students in the class. There were different shades of blues and greens mostly, some oranges and variations of all three. The professor, however, was the only one who had a yellow aura. It was astounding. My jaw literally hung wide open. I finally had confirmation that this was all real. I was seeing what spirits see around living bodies. I was seeing what clairvoyants were able to see.

Chapter 17: A Clash of Titans – Analysis

Bill Miller was punished for his involvement in the McLaughlin case before thousands of spectators due to his pride and arrogance. The demonic spirits desire nothing more than to bring a proud man to his knees as swiftly and powerfully as possible. This is why humility is considered such a virtue. It is the polar opposite of arrogance.

It was a simple task for the demonic spirits to co-habitate and control Bill's opponent. Bill sensed the hatred spewing from the other man and he quickly became aware that he was not dealing with a mere man, but something far more evil, far more sinister and diabolical. When a human being is controlled by a demonic spirit, he has the strength of ten men. Therefore, his opponent was able to overwhelm him and crush him beneath his incredible strength, shattering several of his bones and deflating his pride in one fell swoop.

It took Bill under its spell and devastated him before his girlfriend, his teammates, and an entire stadium of aston-ished spectators. If you could imagine the energy boost the demonic spirits received from all the opposing team's cheering fans and could imagine the black spectral forms of the demons themselves strutting down the field soaking it all in, you would see quite a remarkable scene indeed.

Chapter 18: Reunion – Analysis

Julie Marsh hadn't had an alcoholic beverage in close to a decade. What on earth do you suppose would cause her to want to partake in one when she was just leaving the hospital following her traumatic accident? If you guessed that it was the demonic spirits using their power of suggestion, you are well on your way to understanding the deeper, darker mysteries of the world.

Drugs and alcohol weaken the electromagnetic field surrounding the body by creating small holes in it. Those holes can be breached, and both discarnate human spirits and demonic spirits can then manipulate the thoughts and actions of their targets who are affected by alcohol.

Julie had been blessed and protected by Bishop Phelan, so her energy field was bright and powerful. The demons, of course, knew this and the only way that they could hope to ensnare her in their clutches would be to break that natural protective barrier down by influencing her to ingest enough alcohol, or to wear it down by interacting with her personally and causing her immense fear.

The idea of drinking alcohol was never Julie's idea at all. When dealing with demonic spirits, it is absolutely vital to remain vigilant, go over each thought that races through your mind, and always second guess your actions when they don't seem like they are in your own character.

Chapter 19: Annihilation – Analysis

Kyle Reading suffered the worst form of inhuman, diabolical attack known. It is one thing to experience the tender embrace of a lover, even when a demonic spirit is masquerading as that perfect lover. A great deal of pleasure and joy is still involved, as long as the demon remains disguised. It is another thing entirely to be physically battered, flung onto a bed, stripped of your clothing, and violated in a vicious way. This is always the end result of demonic sexual assault. It almost always begins in a sublime dream state. Rarely does it begin with such blatant disregard for an individual's boundaries.

The demonic spirits first sensed Kyle's lust when he and Jimmy barged into the chapel during Matthew McLaughlin's exorcism. The demon even called him by his full name and told him that it knew his sins. Kyle's secret desires for Tyler were used against him. First, the demon smashed Kyle's head down on the desk to stun him and cause him to be more vulnerable. Then, it used the likeness of Tyler to approach him, penetrate his auric field and seduce him through his tender touch. It tempted Kyle to reach out with his tongue and lick his friend's navel, something that Kyle probably would have refrained from doing, so as not to cross the line between a friendship and something more, but he felt powerless to resist the temptation.

Demons excel at temptation. The sexual encounter would have continued and would have occurred in a non-violent manner if Kyle hadn't suddenly dismissed his lust and instead told Tyler that he loved him. At the time, the demon was siphoning off the energy of lust and reacted violently when Kyle transmuted that lust into love.

These are wicked, vile, negative beings. This becomes blatantly obvious when one witnesses their reaction to the emotion of love. It was the opposite reaction Kyle or anyone would ever expect, because the demon masquerading as Tyler reacted violently instead of compassionately. Then, once its act was over, the demon displayed its preternatural power and proceeded with the most despicable attack.

Chapter 20: Revelations – Analysis

For Kyle to convey to Tyler what had happened to him and why, Kyle knew he'd first be forced to reveal his secret feelings for him. Tyler knew, of course, but neither of them had ever acted on those feelings. The revelation of those feelings was not the reason Tyler fell into a laughing fit; the concept and images of the nature of the attack were the reason. They'd all have laughed themselves silly if they had heard of the attack happening to a stranger, or if they had seen it in a movie. It's the same reason we all laugh when we see someone fall down on the ice, even if we are good-natured people. For some reason, it's human nature to find it amusing to see someone lose their balance. For some reason, it's comical.

Kyle knew this, of course, but he couldn't help but get angry and feel hurt. The demon who had perpetrated the attack was still nearby and it used the energy cast off from Kyle's anger, guilt, shame, and horror against the two boys minutes later.

When an inhuman spirit envelops someone in an invisible sphere of horrid-smelling, rotting flesh, it sickens the human and forces him to flee out of its range. The exact opposite is true when a human burns ecclesiastical incense or sage or sandalwood where an inhuman spirit is present. It is awful and debilitating for the negative or inhuman spirit.

Inhuman, diabolical spirits find great pleasure in harming human beings in any way they can. They do this because they are furious at God for casting them out and for transfiguring them into vile creatures.

Chapter 21: Unwelcome Guests – Analysis

The McLaughlin home was properly sealed off and the demons were doing everything in their power to sneak their way inside, first by hijacking Kelly's body after they caused Julie's "accident," and then by posing as children in need of assistance in the dark, cold evening hours. They never fight fair. They don't need to. They will do anything and everything they can to invade our world, steal our energy, sap our strength and our willpower and our faith, and punish us in any way imaginable for resisting them.

Although capable of astounding feats, demonic spirits can never quite materialize as a perfect human being. There is always something off about them. I believe it is God's will, and we can count our blessings if that is truly the case.

In this case, the demonic spirits materialized as children, but even Sarah knew something was terribly wrong when she saw them. Perhaps, it was the negative energy that she sensed. While the demons hoped that Sarah would follow her normal impulse to automatically allow the children inside first and ask questions later, when Sarah hesitated, they quickly mesmerized her to force her to bypass her hesitation and coerce her to open the door for them and invite them inside.

The demonic spirits need human beings to exercise their God-given free will to allow them entry into their lives and into their homes. Without it, they are restricted and prevented from unleashing their full fury upon their victims. Once they gain entry, however, as was told in the first volume, all hell breaks loose – literally.

When Linda reacted the same way that Sarah did, the demonic spirits tried to seize control over her mind and body to force her to open the door. If Yvonne hadn't been there to intervene, the infestation of the McLaughlin house would have begun all over again in earnest and it would have been a nightmare beyond nightmares, because no one would have been prepared for the vengeance the demons would have unleashed upon them and the vicious onslaught that would have ensued.

The demonic spirits had planned to use Kelly as their trump card in case all the other methods that they used to gain entry into the house had failed. They had already been influencing Kelly in the previous days to draw the likeness of the children in her coloring book to help her generate a sense of familiarity with them, as if they were her spectral family coming to visit. So when Kelly ran down the steps, she immediately identified the children as friends and rushed right up to the window. When the little boy went right up to her and pressed his hand against hers, it made a successful transference of his energy into hers, because she was using her free will to allow that interaction to take place.

No one understood this while it was happening, not even Yvonne, and I was not inside to witness it. This is how sinister and underhanded these beings are in their operations. They failed to coerce Sarah to let them inside by taking advantage of her blind impulse to help children in need. Then they failed to hypnotize her.

They failed to coerce Linda to let them inside by using her motherly protective instinct to cause her to open the door and invite them in. They could have succeeded in causing Linda to open the door while she was in a hypnotic state, but Yvonne intervened.

They failed to coerce Kelly to rush in below the reach of the others and open the door for them as well. But they succeeded in making contact with her through the glass. So in the end, they won by weaving their way into Kelly's energy field when she exercised her free will to connect with the boy. I can tell you, as you are well aware by now, that the entity Kelly was interacting with through the glass was most definitely not a little boy.

Thankfully, Yvonne's psychic abilities allowed her to remain free of the hypnotic suggestion the demonic spirits had used against both Linda and Sarah.

When I arrived and pulled into the driveway, I became aware of the seriousness of the situation as soon as I saw the children on the front porch and in the yard. I knew that the only way to counter the demonic spirits was to be present in God's infinite love and to expand that love to repel the negative spirits. They had not gained access to the house. They had not been able to co-habitate Sarah or Linda, and Yvonne was keeping them at bay while they tried to force their way into the house, which would have only been a temporary incursion for them, if they had actually succeeded.

Yvonne saw them for what they really were. I knew what they really were, and Sarah and Linda discovered what they were, once they were free of the demonic influence.

This case occurred in 1993. I was unaware then of the phenomenon paranormal researchers and cryptozoologists now call "Black-Eyed Children." The similarities between these bizarre creatures and the descriptions of demonic spirits and the race of extraterrestrials seen all over the planet called "The Greys" is fascinating.

Chapter 22: Discerning the Truth – Analysis

When we had gathered inside to discuss the insidious attempt to gain entrance into the house, I tried to explain to the family that despite the fact that Julie, Bill, and Jimmy had all been attacked, the McLaughlin house was itself sealed off, because I had twice performed the Roman Catholic ritual called suffumigation there.

One other interesting situation involving my practice of this ritual happened while I was attending Eastern Washington University in Cheney, Washington. I received a phone call from Lorraine Warren informing me of a case she became aware of in Rathdrum, Idaho. She asked if I would investigate the case on their behalf, because I was a seasoned investigator and I was so much closer – geographically. When we deemed it necessary, I performed suffumigation there one evening with one of my students. Every time I crossed the threshold into another room, the kitchen telephone would ring – three times. It rang three times to mock the Holy Trinity and it was intended as a distraction to break my concentration.

Fortunately, I was very familiar with the activity and distractions that can go on at times like these, and I continued on undaunted. To be successful with suffumigation, there must be nowhere for spirits to flee while remaining inside the house. The smoke must completely billow through every square inch of the house in question. Sage and sandalwood are also very potent where things of this nature are concerned.

To practice the ritual for yourself, purchase a censer, or a flame- and heat-resistant bowl or dish, a roll of charcoal discs and a bag or canister of frankincense and myrrh. Light the charcoal discs with a match or a lighter and apply the incense on top until it generates smoke. Carry this bowl throughout your room or your space and allow it to billow everywhere. Do this whenever you wish to add a pleasant, safe, high-frequency aroma to your area and to fumigate against negativity and negative spirits. You can purchase these supplies from any Catholic Supply Store.

Chapter 23: A Plan of Action – Analysis

When Yvonne, Vincent, Bishop Phelan, and I were all gathered together, we had the chance to discuss the situation with the beleaguered McLaughlin family in the safety and solitude of their own home. The house was indeed secure, as we suspected all along, and that suspicion was verified through Yvonne's psychic sensitivities. We all had our theories as to why the demons were back in full force, both attacking anyone who was involved in the case previously and attempting to coerce their way back into the house.

Bishop Phelan had come all the way from Boston to help rid the McLaughlins and their friends of the demonic attacks and to bring permanent resolution to their case. For him to feel confident that the people and their houses and cars were sealed off and protected, he knew he had to do everything in his power through the Church and its methods.

My method is to help people realize their intimate and permanent connection to God, the Creator of the universe, and to be able to call upon that protection to surround themselves in a field of God's pure, unconditional love – the highest frequency of all and the most powerful force in the universe. This method works, but when someone like Bishop Phelan is involved, who is generous with both his time and his expertise, and especially when he has access to and the full support of the Roman Catholic Church, I always defer to him.

So many people suffer the wrath of demonic attack without any support from the clergy or the Church at all. What a sad state of affairs that is. I feel blessed beyond measure to have been able to work with and study under such a pious, dedicated, and devout man.

Chapter 24: Unleashing the Beast – Analysis

During the evening, Kelly tossed and turned and was prevented from getting any deep sleep. She was also tormented by visions that the demons implanted into her mind to cause her duress. When she awoke in the morning, she was so disoriented, it took her many minutes to come to her senses. This was because she was fighting for control of her own mind and body, which were being heavily influenced by the demonic spirit who took the form of the little boy who had made a connection with her the previous evening.

The demons knew Kelly would want to rush outside to help build the snowman that her brother and his friends were making. They also knew that if they let her run downstairs and act completely normal by releasing their hold on her, she would disarm any defenses the rest of the family would have raised and cause them to let their guard down enough to allow her to go outside to help.

Once outside, after she had helped the boys set the second section of the snowman in place, the demons sapped Kelly's energy and strength to the point that she collapsed and couldn't move. It was then that they finally seized control of her and shortly thereafter did everything in their power to coerce Tyler to let her inside again. When they realized that no one was going to play along, and when they saw the demonologist and the bishop turn in to the driveway, they knew the fight was on and the gloves came off.

Once Vincent and Bishop Phelan exited their car, they knew that their suspicions were right. They needed to work very well together to subdue the demons and take Kelly to the Chapel where they could exorcise them.

Chapter 25: A Perilous Journey – Analysis

The last day or the last few hours before an exorcism or a deliverance is scheduled to take place is often the most critical time when it comes to the safety, health, well-being, and even the life of the possessed or the co-habitated. The demons know that they are out of time and they will either intensify their attacks on everyone else around them to break down their will in hopes of possessing them also, or they will cause as much damage as possible to the possessed before they are ultimately forced to vacate their bodies – including killing their victims while the victims are still under their influence and control.

That is why Vincent and Bishop Phelan sat with Kelly in the back of the car to subdue the demons whenever they began to stir during the transit from the house to the Chapel. Driving a possessed individual to a church or a chapel is a very frightening experience to behold. The demons know they are being taken into a building filled with the smoke of frankincense and myrrh, of healing, holy, positive energy, of crucifixes, religious symbols, artifacts, and priests who have dedicated their lives to God and to good works.

The black wolf that Vincent encountered was the same that Yvonne and Tyler had encountered and the same that Linda and Julie encountered in the previous volume. It was, of course, a demonic spirit. It appeared before Vincent to frighten him. Although it fled when Vincent commanded it to leave, it was really just waiting for the opportune moment to strike and strike it did, by causing the gear shift lever to switch into the *Drive* position and engage the accelerator to crush Vincent against the tree and/or kill him in the process for standing in their way. Luckily, the inability of the car to gain any traction in the snow saved him from what could have been a catastrophic injury.

Even though the demon was subdued on the ride to the chapel, when they arrived in the parking lot, the demon had one last chance to kill anyone it could before being moved inside to face expulsion. The rapid opening and closing of the car doors were meant to frighten and injure as many people as possible should they approach the car to help the bishop. Of course, Vincent was prepared for this, and even though it was frightening for a few minutes, it did not sway his determination to hold the door open long enough to pull the bishop out.

Exorcism is one of the fifteen sections of rites and blessings described in the Rituale Romanum, or Roman Ritual, as it is popularly titled. It is a very old and very serious ceremony used by trained Roman Catholic exorcists, who possess intimate knowledge about the diabolical world, and knowledge is power. Neither I nor any of my fellow investigators are exorcists, nor would we profess to possess the willpower, commitment, and piety that these few special people do.

The spirits involved are either fallen angels or arch-angels. No mortal man has any power over them, nor could man contest that incredible power. Only as long as the exorcist is under divine protection – for he is doing the work of God – does he have any chance of success and to ward off possession of his own body. Because of this, before an exorcism takes place, an exorcist must obtain a state of grace with God. He does this by going into seclusion, by praying day and night for divine protection and assistance and by fasting for three days.

The exorcist will never warn the demon that he will personally cause it great harm or that he will personally force it out. That would be preposterous. It would be an open and direct challenge to the spirits possessing the possessed, and invite an attack on himself. Instead, he uses the powerful names of God, Jesus Christ, and Michael, or words that the demon despises to make it vacate a human host.

Some of the most violent activity ever recorded occurs during an exorcism. The distorted and screeching voices and screams and the foul language that comes forth can be most disturbing indeed.

Because the demonic spirits can read the minds of anyone they choose to, they know and use people's sins against them, especially at critical moments during an exorcism when their concentration and focus is needed most. Interestingly, once a person confesses a sin to a priest, or to God, the demon has no access to that personal information, as if it had never existed at all. It certainly lends credibility to the claim that sins confessed before God are indeed forgiven.

Names are very powerful. When an exorcist succeeds in forcing the demon to reveal its name, the demon has given away a huge portion of its power. From that moment on, the exorcist can direct his prayers and rites against the demon specifically by name. It is much more effective than a general prayer toward a nameless spirit or a group of them. Kelly was never fully possessed, so the exorcism drove the spirits away relatively easily after the demon revealed its name.

If the demons truly have omniscience, or precognition, and they can know who the investigators involved in the case will be before the investigators themselves do, one would think that they would have the foresight to know that many powerful, committed, pious religious men like Bishop Phelan would intervene and expel them from the house and ultimately free the possessed. So why would they even bother continuing the struggle when they are sure to be on the losing side? Perhaps it's blind ignorance or delusions of grandeur on their part. They did, obviously, rebel against God, which was sure to be a losing battle from the very beginning, so maybe they are so badly corrupted by their lust for power and their desire to dominate others that they simply don't know any better or don't care about the consequences. Fortunately, there are many brave people in the world who are eager to do their part to help unfortunate people who are plagued by supernatural and preternatural infestation, oppression, and possession.

Although this particular case used the profound and powerful exorcism from the Roman Ritual to expel the demons and suffumigation to cleanse the house, it is not just Roman Catholic exorcists using Catholic rites who are successful at driving away demons, and it is not just Catholic suffumigation that is successful at cleansing or purifying houses. I know of holy men, shamans, rabbis, Japanese Shinto priests, and powerful spiritualists and light workers who have been equally successful at driving negative spirits and demons out of the possessed, and cleansing and purifying houses. Regardless of the modality or the particular religious faith, the primary, essential force that they all call upon is the power of our Divine Creator, Source, Father/Mother God. Whichever name you give to this consciousness, it is the same consciousness. Calling upon God is the one fail-safe that all of creation can count on in our most desperate time of need.

We are all part of God. We can never be separate from God, because we are individualized aspects of the totality of God. A metaphor I love to use is: "We are all individual sparks that were cast off from the Sun, but we are all still part of that glorious, radiant Sun." God created all of

Creation. He also created the universal laws that govern His Creation, so that all of Creation functions in perfect, flawless harmony. Calling upon God for assistance in driving out rebellious, aggressive, evil-natured, diabolical spirits is all that needs to be done, as long as we have absolute faith that we have the right to call upon that aid, and that it is for the highest good of the possessed.

We must also realize that God is the only real power behind expelling the demons. We could never expel them on our own. God is more powerful than any demon or devil, because God is the creator of all that is. God is life itself. How then, can anyone or any individualized aspect of God rebel against the total sum of all of God's perfection?

Having absolute faith that it is God who is the ultimate power in all of Creation is the single most important thing for anyone to realize and remember when they embark upon the path of a paranormal investigator. One must have absolute faith and conviction that, because they are acting as a divine instrument of God, they are fully empowered and fully protected as long as they call upon God's power to expel negative entities, especially the demonic. This is especially essential when it comes to witnessing or performing an exorcism.

Witnessing an exorcism is undoubtedly one of the most horrific things one could ever imagine. It is one thing to go see a movie or read a book that does a very good job at making you feel isolated, alone, and vulnerable, or scaring you out of your mind. It's another thing entirely to witness the real thing in person.

What are demons exactly? What are these dreadful, powerful beings full of hate and rage? Why are their powers so great and how can they bypass the laws of physics so easily and create what many demonologists call "negative miracles" when the rest of the creatures of the world are bound by those laws?

Recently, mainstream scientists have concluded that the

world in which we live, and the entire visible universe as a whole, is one gigantic holographic illusion or simulation that a vast assortment of infinite fields of conscious awareness has chosen to experience simultaneously. Furthermore, the bodies that we animate and therefore use as "space suits" to interact with this illusory world are severely limited to the point of being almost totally handicapped and incapable of interfacing with all our innate abilities. Additionally, the only beings that seem to be capable of interfacing with this universe in their full capacity are the beings known as angels and demons.

Divine souls that animate human bodies here operate at less than ten percent of their capacity due to the limited nature of the body. It has been suggested through biblical references and numerous other sources, such as the Sumerian cylinder seals, that the human body once operated at a much higher capacity with a much longer lifespan, but that body system was hijacked and governed through genetic manipulation to become much less powerful than what it could truly be. Therefore, the human body was once capable of much more than we have known it to be capable of in our current lifetimes.

Human spirits are now coming into bodies that have evolved and have been activated and therefore have three- and four-helix DNA systems. These children have what would appear to the average human to be miraculous powers because they are using up to twenty percent of their brains. Imagine what these children will become as they continue to evolve.

Imagine what powers these beings would be capable of should they function at one hundred percent of their brain capacity. This is the reason why the angels and demons have powers beyond imagining and it is why ordinary humans feel so powerless against them.

My mentor, friend, and demonologist, the late Ed

Warren, was fond of saying, "God is more powerful than the Devil, but no man is!"

God the Creator is indeed more powerful than anything in His creation. This is absolutely true. How could it be otherwise? How could the created ever believe that they could become more powerful than the Creator? It's ludicrous. The created may eventually evolve to become "like" the Creator, but could never become something the Creator is not, because though the created contains the same DNA as the Creator, some of that DNA might never be activated until the Creator decides to activate it.

I believe now, as I have gained a more thorough understanding, that I can confidently say that God the Creator is more powerful than the Devil but no man is – based upon man's current understanding of who and what he is. As an infinite field of conscious awareness animating a limited body, man is stunted and handicapped compared to a demonic spirit operating at one hundred percent capacity. An infinite field of conscious awareness who is aware of who and what it is, as the great I AM presence rather than just the body, is much more powerful a force against the demonic simply through that awareness and understanding. I believe that it is precisely this knowing and understanding that allows the normal human being to become enlightened – an exponential increase in power and protection when engaging darkness and demons through the authority of the great I AM presence within, which is God the Creator – the most powerful force in the universe.

An infinite field of conscious awareness animating a twelve-helix body that is using one hundred percent of its capacity is a force unlike anything ever seen on this planet in the annals of history. This is truly the I AM angelic presence fully activated and empowered. In this form, it can be said with certainty that man is as powerful as any demon or the Devil himself. I believe we are all going there and sooner than we think. Many of us are well on our way and

we are noticing the activations in ordinary people all
around us – simultaneously.

Chapter 26: Absolution – Analysis

It is always so interesting that demonic entities seem to know every last detail about the lives of the people interacting with them, especially their most intimate secrets and especially their sins—unless they are confessed before God prior to the exorcism. Once sins are confessed before a priest, the demons have no ammunition to use against us. It's as if they never knew of the sins at all. The Devil, however, never forgets.

If someone does not confess their sins before an exorcism, the demons will always use those sins to embarrass that individual by bringing those sins to the awareness of everyone else, often causing great shame and guilt. The intention is to sow distrust between those present during the exorcism to disrupt the flow, break the concentration of the exorcists and priests, and ultimately to bring the entire ritual to a screeching halt.

The devout holy men know this full well, so they will always make sure that everyone present confesses, whether they believe in confession or not. Remember the Law of Intention. Regardless of your faith in any particular doctrine or religion, if your intention is to purge your sins and purify the body, mind, and soul, and to prevent the diabolical from using your life experiences as a weapon against you and the mission at hand, then that is exactly what will happen.

Catholic confession, however, is not the only method with which one can purge oneself of one's sins, mistakes, or bad choices. Everyone has the right and the innate capability to talk to God. God doesn't need an intermediary or priest to hear you. You are just as special as every other person on this planet. God created you and therefore God will hear you. If you quiet or still your mind, He will converse with you via telepathy. Remember, the spirit world has no space and time. There is no distance between you and God. You don't need to look up into the clouds or imagine God to be in some unreachable place where you are not permitted an audience with Him. Merely think on God and God will be with you, and you will be at peace.

I have always said that there is no difference between an American Indian climbing a mountain and meditating on the Great Spirit in his own way and someone who goes into a Catholic church and prays. It is the same God. The two methods are of equal importance and equally effective based solely on their intention. Intention is everything in every circumstance, always. Earnest seeking will always be rewarded.

Chapter 27: Requiem – Analysis

The world is replete with brave, pious, learned men of the cloth who have ascended the ranks in their churches and organized religions, who bask in the spotlight like glowing stars declaring their great works from the tallest parapets. And then there are those humble servants of God who prefer to remain anonymous, scouring the shadow-filled streets as the unknown spiritual warriors and defenders of mankind that they are. The man portrayed as Bishop Phelan was just such a man. He gave tirelessly of himself toward the service of others.

It was not enough to save the McLaughlin family from demoniacal attack. After staying late, even while knowing the approaching snowstorm would hinder his journey home, he took his time to walk through the adjacent cemetery to acknowledge and bless the physical remains of the fallen faithful.

His mission was completed that fateful December evening, and meandering on the wintry roads as snow fell from above, he calmly and peacefully made his way back home.

Chapter 28: Surrender –Analysis

The life of a demonologist can be a long and lonely road, fraught with danger around every turn. Most demonologists I have known in the past and those whom I know today who have been asked why they ever got involved in the field have said that they felt it was "a calling" that led them to delve into the dark secrets of the world and to learn of the denizens of the other realms to which most people were oblivious.

Two of the most famous and well-respected paranormal researchers in the modern era are the late Ed Warren and his wife, Lorraine Warren. They are the pioneers of the modern ghost-hunting craze that thrives to this day and they deserve all the credit for bringing their profound knowledge and understanding to the general public, first through their astounding lectures and presentations, then through their books, such as *The Demonologist*, *The Devil in Connecticut*, *Deliver Us from Evil*, and *The Haunted*, through their news stories, documentaries, and their full-length blockbuster movies, such as *A Haunting in Connecticut*, *The Conjuring*, and their forthcoming release, *Annabelle*.

The Warrens earned celebrity status throughout Connecticut, New England, the United Kingdom, Australia, and the world through their tireless efforts to help people in need of their unique skill sets. They were as likable as any kind couple you could hope to meet, and they were genuinely interested in helping people deal with unseen spirits.

I first learned of Ed and Lorraine Warren when I was

attending high school in Stratford, Connecticut, a small state where people like the Warrens, who were well known as "The Real Ghostbusters," had little chance at a normal life outside the limelight. It wasn't until I was a senior in high school, after my mother and sister and I had moved to Westport, that I first found one of the Warrens' books, *The Demonologist* by Gerard Brittle, on the shelf in the Staples High School library. It was a book that completely changed my life, because I was immediately and most seriously thrust into the dark and dangerous world of the paranormal.

After I finished the book, I was terrified, not for myself, but for the poor families who had endured such terror at the hands of demonic spirits who had infested their lives and their homes.

Infestation is the first stage of demonic interaction. A demonic spirit infests a home the way a flea infests a dog, because neither the flea nor the spirit belongs there. The second phase is called Oppression, where the demonic spirits actively seek out and attack specific people in an effort to wear them down, fill them with dread, break their will, and make them vulnerable to the third and final stage – Possession, where the demonic spirit attempts to push aside the spirit of the person animating the physical body and seize control of it for their own use.

I had no religious artifacts around the house. I hadn't ever needed any, because I had a deep and thorough understanding of my intimate connection to the Creator and I relied on that connection for protection. Even so, the book made me want to find some form of religious protection, so I fashioned a crucifix out of popsicle sticks and Scotch tape – just to be sure. As funny and strange as that might sound, it is exactly what happened.

I returned the book to the library, and it wasn't until 1990 that the seed that had been planted when I read that book had grown sufficiently to effect the profound change in my life that was to come next.

Sitting in my friend's car, he and I were listening to the radio. The discussion was about the buzz that was going on about the house that the movie *Three Men and a Baby* was filmed in, and more specifically, the spectral form of the teenage boy holding a high-powered hunting rifle that was seen during the editing phase of the production. As my friend and I listened to the story, I told my friend that I had read one of the Warrens' books a few years earlier and that it was interesting to listen to this new information about a case that was occurring at the present time. Eventually, we learned that the Warrens were called in to investigate and that Lorraine Warren, who is a light trance medium, discerned that a teenage boy had committed suicide with a high-powered hunting rifle in the house where the movie was being filmed.

I turned to my friend and said, "That'd be so cool to work with them." His reply was, "Yeah, no kidding!" We went about our day and parted ways later that evening.

The very next day, my friend called me and said, "You're not gonna believe who just called me!" I asked who it was that he was so surprised to hear from, and he told me that the person was none other than Ed Warren himself. My reply was "C'mon!" He told me that Ed Warren had called him because he had been having heart issues as a result of dealing with all the terrifying cases he'd been involved with through the years and he wanted a medic on his team. My friend was a former Combat Medic with the rank of Captain in the U.S. Army and was ideally suited for the job. He was at the time employed with one of the major Emergency Medical Services in Connecticut and he had been recommended to Ed when he had sent out the general inquiry.

He told me that he had been invited to Ed and Lorraine Warren's weekly Monday night meeting at their School of Paranormalology in the Warren Occult Museum adjacent their house. I told my friend that it was time for me to get involved and that he had to get me in there.

The next evening, he called me and said that he had told Lorraine about me and that she had invited me to come to the class on the following Monday. I felt that this was a crossroads in my life and that everything was falling into place exactly as it was supposed to be.

My friend and I arrived that next Monday evening at 7:30 p.m. on the dot. We knocked on the door to the Occult Museum and one of the Warrens' investigators, Andy Thompson, opened the door and welcomed us inside.

The moment I saw Lorraine, I felt tingles throughout my body, as though I had just met someone I was destined to meet. Her bright, wide smile and calm demeanor were quite pleasant to experience and she came right up and greeted me with a "Hello, my dear. I'm Lorraine Warren." She immediately asked me two very pointed questions, one right after the other. I knew they were of paramount importance. She asked me, "How strong is your faith, honey?" I told her that I had an immensely strong faith and that I had an innate understanding that I and the Father are One. She smiled brightly. Her second question was, "Why do you want to get involved in work of this nature?" I told her that I had read *The Demonologist* and of the synchronicity that coupled our intention to work with them and the sudden phone call that enabled that to happen the very next day. I told her that I wanted to help the poor people who were suffering at the hands of the demonic spirits. She said, "It's a calling, then!" I agreed with that statement wholeheartedly. She gave me a hug and said, "Welcome aboard, Jason." We smiled at each other. Everything was transpiring exactly as it was supposed to be.

That evening, I began my exciting journey into the unseen realm of the paranormal with two of the most special people ever to come into my life. It is with great pride that I can now say that Ed and Lorraine Warren were my mentors, my friends, and in my later years, my colleagues. Ed Warren left the physical world back in 2006, but Lorraine carries on his legacy. She is still the pillar of the paranormal investigation community and she continues her profound work to this day. I love her dearly.

There are many people around the globe who have emulated the late Ed Warren's Occult Museum, and Dr. Vincent Decker was no exception. Though this seems a fascinating, esoteric hobby, it is rife with the possibility and probability of dangerous consequences. I know and understand the danger involved with leaving "negatively charged haunted items" in the care of people who don't know how to properly deal with them, but why anyone with that knowledge would want to hoard those items in a museum in their own home or home office or even in an outbuilding attached to their dwelling, and why they would want to lure people into such a place and allow them to interact with those objects both physically and energetically is beyond my understanding.

Why would any seasoned demonologist want to lure an unsuspecting public into such a place where their electromagnetic fields are interacting with both the cursed objects themselves and the negative electromagnetic fields of demonic spirits attached to them? Allowing people to give the cursed objects recognition through their focused awareness and observation and therefore allowing them to form a permanent connection with the objects and the essences of the spirits associated with them, just boggles my mind.

People like this, who play on people's curiosities or fears and then stand with their hands out waiting for their palm to be greased with cold hard cash for the opportunity to do so, are doing nothing but a disservice to people and to humanity as a whole.

In my opinion, the connection that these spirits have with the objects needs to be permanently severed and these objects need to be blessed, destroyed, and properly disposed of. Their energy needs to be transmuted by being buried in the earth, not revered, preserved, and displayed on shelves like precious treasures. They are nothing of the sort. Hanging onto a collection of truly cursed or negatively charged objects that come from locations where demoniacal infestation has occurred is a disaster of epic proportions just waiting to happen.

As a student of Ed Warren, while in his Occult Museum going over evidence I'd collected on a case I'd investigated on their behalf, I accidentally bumped into one such object. Ed said it was the most dangerous item I could have interacted with. He said he had to bless me to protect me from any unfortunate ramifications of that interaction. Why he would keep such objects around in the first place upset me. The fact that I could come into direct contact with them, with the resultant interaction potentially causing me misfortune, pain, or lasting psychic or spiritual harm, didn't frighten me, it angered me.

The question I would pose to people with regard to this bizarre hobby or activity is: Are you of service to self or of service to others? People who keep these items say that they are keeping them safe and out of the hands of the public who are clueless about how to safeguard them. That is, of course, a valid point. But by keeping these items around and then charging the public money for access to them, thus exposing these unsuspecting thrill-seekers to potential harm, are you under the impression that you are not directly responsible for what might happen to them?

To me, this is like keeping an assortment of dangerous chemicals or a collection of razor-sharp medieval weapons on display in a small room, claiming to be keeping them out of the hands of people who don't know how to handle them safely, while allowing groups of people to tour the museum filled with these extremely dangerous items, any number of which could cause them injury or death.

Chapter 29: Peace at Last – Analysis

The McLaughlin family was advised never to speak of the horrific experiences they had endured and were told never to give the supernatural and preternatural activity any recognition whatsoever. As far as I know, through these many years, they have remained free from any form of demoniacal retribution because I have not heard from them since.

This case came about due to the casual act of passing by a cemetery in which an earthbound human spirit made a connection with a bright, beautiful young girl. It spiraled out of control once a teenage boy and his two best friends made the tragic mistake of buying and using a Ouija board with which to initiate contact with the spirit lurking inside the house.

I decided it was imperative to recreate the McLaughlins' tale to warn people about the dangers associated with the negative occult – and *specifically* the use of a Ouija board – but more important, to explain how these things come about, through my understanding of quantum physics and the Universal Laws and through my many years of experience as a seasoned investigator who has the privilege of working with the pioneers of the modern paranormal investigation movement, the late Ed Warren and his wife, Lorraine.

I pray that I have done a good service to all the good people involved in this case by preserving their anonymity and telling their story as accurately as possible. I know they will find solace if the retelling of their story will dissuade others from walking the same dark, dangerous, and crooked path that they started down, that fateful October afternoon.

END

About the Author

Jason McLeod is a paranormal investigator, spiritualist and empath. He has spent the last 28 years helping individual families deal with both the human spirits who linger in their lives and the inhuman spirits who seek to ruin them. His training and experience began by following in the footsteps of his close personal friends and mentors—the late Ed Warren and his wife Lorraine, bestselling authors, movie consultants, and the original ghost busters who started the modern ghost hunting craze that thrives today. He conducts engaging presentations on the subjects of Spirituality, Consciousness, Quantum Physics, Meditation, Metaphysics, Paranormal Investigation and Demonology on Radio Broadcasts, and at Paranormal Conventions, Spirituality Expositions, in Churches and at New Age Events throughout the world.

If you've found this book interesting, the Author would sincerely appreciate it if you would please kindly take the time to write an honest review about it and post it on amazon.com.

Please visit the author's website: www.darksiege.com for information on his investigations, classes, upcoming releases, personal appearances at paranormal conventions, photographs, audio and video presentations, and more.

If you wish to contact the author directly, you are encouraged to do so by email at: darksiegebook@gmail.com